D1570071

Bernard Schweizer is Associate
Professor of English at Long Island
University. He is the author of *Rebecca West:
Heroism, Rebellion, and the Female Epic* and
*Radicals on the Road: The Politics of English
Travel Writing in the 1930s.*

Hating God

BERNARD SCHWEIZER

Hating God

The Untold Story
of Misotheism

OXFORD
UNIVERSITY PRESS
2011

OXFORD

UNIVERSITY PRESS

Oxford University Press, Inc., publishes works that further
Oxford University's objective of excellence
in research, scholarship, and education.

Oxford   New York
Auckland   Cape Town   Dar es Salaam   Hong Kong   Karachi
Kuala Lumpur   Madrid   Melbourne   Mexico City   Nairobi
New Delhi   Shanghai   Taipei   Toronto

With offices in
Argentina   Austria   Brazil   Chile   Czech Republic   France   Greece
Guatemala   Hungary   Italy   Japan   Poland   Portugal   Singapore
South Korea   Switzerland   Thailand   Turkey   Ukraine   Vietnam

Published by Oxford University Press, Inc.
198 Madison Avenue, New York, NY 10016

www.oup.com

Oxford is a registered trademark of Oxford University Press

Library of Congress Cataloging-in-Publication Data
Schweizer, Bernard, 1962–
Hating god : the untold story of misotheism / Bernard Schweizer.
p. cm.
Includes bibliographical references.
ISBN 978-0-19-975138-9
1. Misotheism. I. Title.
BT168.S49   2010
231.7—dc22   2010006016

9 8 7 6 5 4 3 2
Printed in the United States of America
on acid-free paper

To my wife, Liang,
and my friend, Roland,
life-long travel companions
to new ways of seeing

Contents

Hating God

Introduction

C'est tout un monde d'idées qu'il faut retrouver derrière "The supreme evil, God." Que Messieurs les Critiques commencent. (A whole world of ideas needs to be discovered behind "The supreme evil, God." May the critics begin.)

—Denis Saurat (1938)

THIS STUDY ORIGINATED IN A PROFOUND SENSE OF BAFFLEMENT AND mystery. I was researching the work of the British journalist and novelist Rebecca West while reading Philip Pullman's trilogy *His Dark Materials* on the side. Although these writers have little in common, besides both being British and based in greater London, I repeatedly bumped up against a similar religious stance in their work: an aversion to divinity verging on God-hatred. I couldn't place that affect on the spectrum of religious dissent ranging from atheism to Satanism: it was not atheism, since the hostility to God obviously presumes the existence of God; and it wasn't Satanism either, since opposition to God doesn't automatically lead to reverence for God's adversary. I was surprised that even academics who normally had answers for everything were nonplussed when queried about this feeling of personal animosity against God. The mystery deepened when I began to realize that the existence of anti-God sentiments often fails to register even when people directly look at it, as if the statement "I hate God" (or any of its variations) dissolves into thin air the moment it is uttered.

Here is an example of what I mean: Zora Neale Hurston's acclaimed novel *Their Eyes Were Watching God* (1937) contains clues to the narrator's, and possibly the author's, outspoken rebellion against God. These clues—beginning with the title and continuing with allusions to the Book of Job throughout the novel—find their explicit summation in the following passage: "All gods who receive homage are cruel. All gods dispense suffering without reason. Otherwise they would not be worshipped. Through indiscriminate suffering men know fear and fear is the most divine emotion. It is the stones for altars and the beginning of wisdom. Half gods are worshipped in wine and flowers. Real gods require blood" (145). I have chosen this example because Hurston's novel is not an obscure object of academic specialists. Being taught at high schools and colleges across the nation, it has achieved cult status and is read every year by more than one hundred thousand impressionable young minds.[1] To my surprise, however, a review of relevant critical literature on this novel revealed that not one scholar had considered this statement as a potential sign of the author's contempt for God. Similarly, when I taught *Their Eyes Were Watching God*, my college students never chose this anti-God statement for commentary and, when directed to it, they couldn't quite make sense of it. So, I asked myself, why are so many people unaware of this antagonistic faith? And why do they fail recognize it even when confronted with it?

The long answer to these questions is contained in the rest of this book. As for a short answer—this negative religious attitude has escaped detection partly because those practicing it tend to be secretive about it, fearing the consequences of owning up to their anti-God stance too openly. I claim that Hurston's rhetorical maneuver of shifting the object of her blame into the plural ("all gods") is only one of many techniques used by writers and intellectuals to conceal, even as they hint at, a view that they know would be considered grossly irreverent and blasphemous by many. My study will remove the camouflage and peel away the layers of disguise to reveal the true nature of anti-God rhetoric in the works of numerous writers and thinkers over the course of time. Certainly, opponents of God have had good reason to be circumspect. To say openly "I hate God" in some nineteenth-century societies could have caused trouble comparable to publishing cartoons ridiculing the Prophet Mohammed today.

One of the people who experienced retribution for publishing attacks against God was the Romantic poet Percy Bysshe Shelley. He had already tasted the wrath of the establishment after publicly proclaiming his unbelief in a pamphlet titled "The Necessity of Atheism." This got Shelley expelled from Oxford University in 1811. But what he did next could have had more serious consequences. In 1812–13, he wrote a work of social and intellectual revolt titled *Queen Mab: A Philosophical Poem*, in which Moses is depicted as a murderer, Yahweh[2] is portrayed as a sadistic projection of the collective human imagination, and Christ is termed a "malignant soul" (Canto VII, 172). This poem pioneered a top-down approach of religious subversion: instead of denying religious belief or undermining the tenets of Christian teachings in general, it aimed its arrows directly at the Almighty and his son. This was blasphemy of the highest order and therefore subject to prosecution by law in the United Kingdom at that time.[3] Knowing the risks of his endeavor, Shelley privately printed only 250 copies of the poem, and then went to the trouble of removing the printer's name (his own!) by cutting out the title page and clipping the printer's information from the final leaf of most of the booklets. He further limited his exposure by distributing no more than 70 copies among personal acquaintances whom he deemed sufficiently sympathetic to his project. But the poem was still disseminated widely enough to cause him serious trouble. In 1817, Shelley lost his Chancery trial for custody of his two children by his first wife, Harriet, on the grounds of his anti-Christian stance. *Queen Mab* was used as evidence to demonstrate his corrupting influence (Wheatley 83–85). But the notoriety of *Queen Mab* only stoked demand for the text among radical circles, and in 1821 a London bookseller by the name of William Clark printed a pirated edition of the poem. Shelley, from his self-imposed exile in Italy, immediately distanced himself from the work, condemning it in a letter sent to *The Examiner* as a "crude and immature" (20) product of his youth. Fearing serious repercussions, he promptly sought to block further sales of the work. His concern was justified: the Society for the Suppression of Vice stepped in, prosecuted Clark, and had him sentenced to four months' imprisonment for blasphemous libel (Wheatley 85).

Knowing firsthand the consequences of openly defying the religious and political orders, Shelley preemptively shifted his tactics to conceal further attacks against God: while Canto VII of *Queen Mab* contains quite straightforward assaults against biblical teachings, Shelley's next attack against God, *Prometheus Unbound* (1820), succeeds in deflecting accusations of blasphemy by purporting to be about classical mythology. Yet anyone looking for evidence of Shelley's enmity toward God will easily detect it in that poem as well. For one thing, Shelley tellingly manipulates the "original" myth that informs his plot. In Aeschylus's version, Prometheus is reconciled with Zeus because Prometheus had some knowledge that Zeus needed to neutralize a threatening prophecy against him. By contrast, Shelley stated in the preface to the poem that "I was averse from a catastrophe so feeble as that of reconciling the Champion with the Oppressor of mankind. The moral interest of the fable, which is so powerfully sustained by the sufferings and endurance of Prometheus, would be annihilated if we could conceive of him as unsaying his high language and quailing before his successful and perfidious adversary" (*Poetry and Prose* 133). There is nothing here that the Society for the Suppression of Vice could reasonably define as anti-Christian. However, from what we know about Shelley's beliefs, we can confidently say that the real subject of his aversion was not Zeus or Jupiter; rather, "the Oppressor of mankind" and "perfidious adversary" of humanity was a thinly veiled version of Yahweh. Consider this passage:

> But thou who art the God and Lord—O thou
> Who fillest with thy soul this world of woe,
> To whom all things of Earth and Heaven do bow
> In fear and worship—all-prevailing foe!
> I curse thee! Let a sufferer's curse
> Clasp thee, his torturer, like remorse!
> Till thine Infinity shall be
> A robe of envenomed agony;
> And thine Omnipotence a crown of pain,
> To cling like burning gold round thy dissolving brain! (Act I, 282–291)

Clearly the language of this passage is not polytheistic or "pagan." Besides talk of Heaven and Earth and addressing God as "Lord," references to God's infinity and omnipotence are essentially concessions to theism. And when Shelley uses the conspicuous terms "Almighty God" and "Merciful God" (Act II, Scene IV) to refer to Jupiter, he is evidently asking his readers to take the cue and redirect his attacks from Jupiter to Yahweh. In a particularly provocative departure from the original, he twists the plot of the Prometheus story to have the supreme god killed off in the middle of the play. Despite thus presenting a scenario of full-fledged deicide, Shelley escaped further entanglements with the official guardians of public virtue and religious piety. The disguise of his God-hatred had succeeded, since lashing out at Jupiter was not considered to be an act of blasphemy.

These examples demonstrate some of the different approaches used by writers to publish their attacks against God. Not surprisingly, different degrees of concealment were used to mask the real nature of the God-hater's project. On a scale from the most severely closeted to the most openly unapologetic presentation of God-hatred, Mark Twain falls into the former category. Indeed, Twain kept his fiercest condemnations of God entirely to himself, confiding them only to his private journals.[4] Similarly, the anti-God rhetoric of Emily Brontë is not easy to detect, but relentless probing can bring it to the surface, as demonstrated in Jill Dix Ghnassia's study *Metaphysical Rebellion in the Works of Emily Brontë* (1994). Zora Neale Hurston is somewhat less secretive about her rejection of God than Brontë, and Rebecca West even less so than Hurston. At the opposite end of this progression stand writers like Algernon Swinburne and Philip Pullman, who make no bones about their hatred of God, thought they typically reserve their blasphemy for literary treatments.

In fact, literature is *the* principal conduit for expressions of animosity against the Almighty. God-hatred's affinity for literature is partly due to the make-believe potential, the *as if* factor of literature, which has served as a defense against public prosecution of authors from Flaubert to Joyce and Nabokov. But literature has another incomparable advantage over straightforward nonfictional discourse when it comes to the hostility against God: the imaginative scope of literature allows one to toy creatively with an idea that is both troubling and difficult to act upon. Indeed, only in fiction is it really possible to wrestle with God with any degree of realism, since God cannot be compelled to face off with his opponents in the real world. Until today, therefore, elaborations on the theme of God-hatred have typically taken the form of literary explorations, whether it be Elie Wiesel's play *The Trial of God* (1979), Philip Pullman's fantasy trilogy *His Dark Materials* (1995–2000), or James Morrow's *Blameless in Abaddon* (1996).[5] All three stories provide shelter for the rather shocking hypothesis that God is guilty of gross negligence, dishonorable conduct, and criminal behavior. In fact, this hypothesis is the basis of God-hatred.

At this point it becomes desirable to abandon descriptive expressions like "God-hater" or "opponent of God" in favor of a term that lends itself more easily for the purpose of classification, a word that is comparable to other labels for religious dissent such as atheist, or agnostic, or Unitarian. Several possible terms suggest themselves as a name for the God-hater, and I will briefly outline them one by one:

THEOSTUGES: This term appears in the Bible, specifically in the Greek original of St. Paul's Letter to the Romans. There, a word transliterated as "theostuges" (roughly "hateful to god") is used to convey St. Paul's harangue against "gossips, slanderers, God-haters, insolent, arrogant and boastful [people]" (1:30). But the term theostuges has never caught on. In fact, the word is sufficiently ambivalent to cause some biblical translators to believe that it refers to God's hatred for sinful men rather than to man's hatred of God (Anidjar 7–8). That reading has not found general support, though, and the consensus still holds that St. Paul is using the term in an active sense, meaning that a theostuges person is someone who hates God rather than one being hated by God. Any adoption of the term is further hampered by the fact that, technically, it is an adjective, and yet what we need is a noun. Finally, the meaning of the word "theostuges" cannot easily be inferred from its Greek components, as the word stugeo ("to hate") is far less well known than the Greek root of misos for hatred. For these reasons, we can bypass the term as a potential candidate to identify haters of God.

PASSIONATE ATHEIST: Physicist Freeman J. Dyson suggested the term "passionate atheism" to refer to enemies of God. But Dyson's term falsely categorizes the hatred of God as a subcategory of nonbelief: "There are two kinds of atheists, ordinary atheists who do not believe in God and passionate atheists who consider God to be their personal enemy" (4). While the phenomenon Dyson invokes is surely that of God-hatred, his chosen term is ill advised. For one thing, it can easily be mistaken for just a more emotional profession of atheism than is usual. Thus, when Beneatha in Lorraine Hansberry's play *A Raisin in the Sun* (1958) shouts that "There simply is no blasted God—there is only man and it is *he* who makes miracles!" (51), she surely expresses a more passionate atheism than somebody who would calmly state, "You know, I don't think God exists." But this is obviously not what Dyson has in mind. No atheist, however, no matter how passionate, can really hate a divinity he considers to be nonexistent in the first place. Thus, we can safely discard the term "passionate atheism" to denote the phenomenon this book is concerned with.

METAPHYSICAL REBEL: This term is Albert Camus's coinage. He used the label throughout Part Two of his long meditation on the history and philosophy of revolt, *The Rebel* (1951). This book, in turn, came out more than a decade after fellow Frenchman Denis Saurat's invitation to write an extended study of man's hostility to God. In a volume of literary criticism titled *Perspectives* (1938), Saurat had briefly discussed *Atalanta in Calydon*, Swinburne's verse drama in which the Chorus protests against "the supreme evil, God." Saurat then wrote àpropos of this expression: "C'est tout un monde d'idées qu'il faut retrouver derrière 'The supreme evil, God.' Que Messieurs les Critiques commencent."[6] Whether or not Albert Camus knew about Saurat's book and "invitation," it is fair to say that *The Rebel* contains the first sustained critical study of the history and philosophy of God-hatred.[7]

But Camus's pioneering effort to chronicle the phenomenon of "metaphysical rebellion" has neither spawned a following nor initiated a trend in religious studies or religious approaches to literature. His ideas were duly noted and then put aside, to be only rarely revived, as in Jill Dix Ghnassia's study mentioned above, *Metaphysical Rebellion in the Works of Emily Brontë*, which argues that Brontë's texts are replete with disguised signs of the author's deeply held religious skepticism bordering on enmity against God. In general, however, the idea of "metaphysical rebellion" is now about as dated as the term "theostuges." This may have to do, in part, with the fact that metaphysical rebellion is too abstract and Kantian a term to do justice to the visceral antidevotional feelings expressed by God-haters. Camus apparently chose the term because he linked the emergence of God-hatred to the Enlightenment. In any case, the formula did not stick.

MISOTHEIST: My own preferred term for the enemy of God is miso*theist*. Built on the same model as the word "misogyny," the term consists of the prefix "misos," Greek for hatred, and "theos," the Greek word for God. In contrast to words such as "misogyny" or "misanthropy," however, which carry negative connotations of bigotry and even immorality, to call somebody a misotheist should cast no aspersion on that person. A misotheist does not hate a whole segment of humanity in summary fashion, as the misogynist or misanthrope does; a misotheist is not necessarily constitutionally disposed to crankiness, intolerance, or violence. Also, one can argue with Elie Wiesel that "you can hate only a human being" ("Talking" 272), implying that hatred per se is relevant only to interpersonal relationships. Similarly, in *The Nature of Hate* (2008), we read that "you can hate a person or you can hate a group: The feelings you experience are largely the same, although the target is different" (Sternberg 51). Robert Sternberg's own "duplex theory of hatred," which is based on the close proximity of love and hatred, is equally premised on the existence of a human target for hatred. This view largely disqualifies the hatred of God as belonging to the same category as the hatred of people. In other words, misotheism is not on the same level as, say, hatred of Jews, hatred of women, or Ann Coulter's hatred of liberals. These latter forms of hatred are consistent with the view "that love represents human maturity and fulfillment, whereas hate represents a perversion of the positive possibilities for mankind" (Sternberg 52). The misotheist, by hating a virtual enemy—that is, one that is neither mortal nor physically present—places himself outside the dichotomy outlined by Sternberg above.

Since God is not a person or an interlocutor, to be hostile to God means really to marshal the negative emotions of hatred toward an entity that is absolutely outside the human sphere, something intangible, not in a direct relationship with the hating person. In extension of this view, hatred of God is not performative, not acted out. One doesn't know if the hatred ever "arrives," and even if it does, it should not really have an impact on the hated, given the supernatural quality of the deity. Thus, the most immediate effect of God-hatred is on the misotheist himself, for whom it serves a therapeutic function. Although seemingly directed at the figure of God, misotheism reflects a passionate concern for the affairs of man. And that goes a long way toward explaining why a humanist of Wiesel's caliber is capable of being at the same time a misotheist.

Simply put, misotheism is a response to suffering, injustice, and disorder in a troubled world. Misotheists feel that humanity is the subject of divine carelessness or sadism, and they question God's love for humanity: "Why did the God of Israel manifest such hostility towards the descendants of Israel?" asks Elie Wiesel in *A Jew Today*

(1979, 10). People in different situations may ask: why did God manifest such hostility against the Tutsis of Rwanda? Why did God manifest such hostility against the people of Europe and America during
the great Spanish influenza pandemic in 1918–19? Why did God
show such hostility against the people of Indonesia, Thailand, India,
and Sri Lanka during the tsunami of late 2004? Of course, the charge
of hostility is hypothetical, since it is attributed to God, and God's
motives are not known. But it is conceivable or even likely that once
a man or a woman sees these kinds of calamities as expressions of
divine hostility, he or she will feel hostility in reply. A feeling of
injustice only exacerbates the matter. As Sternberg has noted: "It
seems reasonable . . . that someone feels hate just because he or she
has suffered what is perceived to be an injustice" (38). Similarly, a
sense of divine injustice is a major factor contributing to the development of a misotheistic outlook. The feeling of injustice can stem from
personal misfortune such as thwarted ambition or a frustrated love
relationship, but it more often stems from undeserved suffering on a
grand scale such as an epidemic or a genocide. Some people with an
otherwise intact belief in the supreme deity will lay the blame for
such calamities at the foot of their god. And so a misotheist is born.

Having clarified the matter of nomenclature and given a rationale
for the term "misotheist," I now want to differentiate misotheism as
a stance apart from other forms of religious heterodoxy or unbelief,
notably atheism, agnosticism, antitheism, Gnosticism, and deicide.

TRADITIONAL ATHEISM: Two basic forms of atheism are com-
monly distinguished, and neither of them accommodates enemies of
God. First there is strong atheism, which asserts that God does not
exist; weak atheism, by comparison, only expresses a lack of belief in
God. Yet neither stance would care to investigate the moral character
of God. To illustrate the fundamental incompatibility between nonbelief and god-hatred, I refer to Annie Besant's classic atheist manifesto
"Why I Do Not Believe in God" (1887), which she coauthored with
Charles Bradlaugh. Interestingly, Besant briefly contemplates the possibility of a bad god as the object of human loathing, but then dis-
misses such an option as incompatible with the position of atheism:

> To believe that all the slow stages of blood-stained evolution, that the
> struggle for existence . . . were designed, foreseen, deliberately
> selected as the method of creation, by an almighty power—to believe

> this is to believe that "God" is the supreme malignity, a creator who voluntarily devises and executes a plan of the most ghastly malice. . . . But, again, the condition and the history of the world are not consistent with its being the creation of an almighty and perfect cruelty. While the tragedy of life negates the possibility of an omnipotent goodness as its author, the beauty and happiness of life negate equally the possibility of an almighty fiend as its creator. (n.p.)

This line of thinking, which represents the true atheistic approach, renders it impossible to conceive of God as either a supreme evil or as the source of goodness. To the atheist, both the loving and the cruel god are irrelevant since to her neither exists.

NEW ATHEISM: Writers like Christopher Hitchens, Richard Dawins, and Sam Harris have been characterized by religious scholar Karen Armstrong, among others, as "new atheists" (xvi) because of the militant, public nature of their unbelief. They, too, speak contemptuously about the Judeo-Christian god, but what their anti-God rhetoric really amounts to is a protest against a God others believe in. When Richard Dawkins offers his catalogue of Yahweh's shortcomings, he is not voicing criticism of a supernatural being but rather arguing against *a system of belief* that is centered on a contemptuous fictional figure: "The God of the Old Testament is arguably the most unpleasant character in all fiction: jealous and proud of it; a petty, unjust, unforgiving control-freak; a vindictive, bloodthirsty ethnic cleanser; a misogynistic, homophobic, racist, infanticidal, genocidal, filicidal, pestilential, megalomaniacal, sadomasochistic, capriciously malevolent bully" (31). Dawkins does not address God directly, nor does he feel any real anguish with regard to these alleged shortcomings of God. Since God is a nonentity for him, his attack is only part of a more general critique of the religion founded on belief in that God.

Similarly, Sam Harris is not concerned with any god in the real sense of the word when he writes that "the God of Abraham is a ridiculous fellow—capricious, petulant, and cruel—and one with whom a covenant is little guarantee of health or happiness" (*End* 173). It is no different with Christopher Hitchens, who in *God Is Not Great* (2007) says actually very little about God, although what little comment there is on the subject of Yahweh is far from flattering, too: "The cobbled-together ancient Jewish books had an ill-tempered and implacable and bloody and provincial god, who was probably more frightening when he was in a good mood (the classic attribute of the dictator)" (175). None of these three most prominent "new atheists" is primarily concerned with disproving the existence of God or even of a good god. Hitchens himself has stressed that "I am not even an atheist so much as I am an antitheist; I not only maintain that all religions are versions of the same untruth, but I hold that the influence of churches, and the effect of religious belief, is positively harmful" (*Letter* 55). In this sense, the "new atheists" of today should really be called the "new antitheists" since all three writers take aim at theistic religion in general, rather than at the existence of God alone.

AGNOSTICISM: Agnostics admit that God may or may not exist and that they simply don't have enough evidence to decide either way. Against strong atheism ("God does not exist"), agnostics will maintain that it is impossible to prove a negative proposition. Likewise, how can one prove that there is no monster in Loch Ness? With regard to Nessie, most people are probably agnostics, saying that the monster's nonexistence is likely, though it has not been definitely proven, thus maintaining a narrow margin for its possible existence. The same goes, by and large, for the agnostic's attitude toward God.

Agnosticism had a large following in Britain and America during the second half of the nineteenth century, partly because it appealed as a convenient middle path between traditional faith and outright atheism. Nobody could really fault you for being an agnostic; it was the default position for many Darwinians and positivists who were not ready to embrace complete unbelief. At the same time, as James Turner demonstrated in *Without God, Without Creed* (1985), agnostics such as Robert Ingersoll, Charles Eliot Norton, and Thomas Huxley (who coined the term "agnostic") felt compelled to substitute a rationalist belief in nature, in science, or in humanity for their suspended belief in a transcendent God. But while agnostics such as Ingersoll may have delivered thundering speeches against biblical Christianity and church dogma, they are not on record as having argued that God is evil or the enemy of man. Thus, misotheism is not compatible with agnosticism either.

ANTITHEISM: The antitheist rejects theistic religion. Theism is a doctrine defining the nature of God. Specifically, theism dictates that God is the creator of the universe while being himself uncreated, that he is eternal and infinite, and that he is all-powerful (omnipotent), all-knowing (omniscient), all-present (omnipresent), and all-good (omnibenevolent). If the antitheist rejects this conception as representative of religion per se, then he is really indistinguishable from the antireligious person. Alternatively, the antitheist can specifically reject the monotheistic aspect of theism in favor of a variety of other religious positions. The nineteenth-century theologian Robert Flint put it succinctly: "Short of atheism there are anti-theistic theories. Polytheism is not atheism, for it does not deny that there is a Deity; but it is anti-theistic, since it denies that there is only one. Pantheism is not atheism, for it admits that there is a God; but it is anti-theism, for it denies that God is a Being distinct from creation and possessed of such attributes as wisdom, and holiness, and love. Every theory which refuses to ascribe to God an attribute which is essential to a worthy conception of His character is anti-theistic" (Flint 2–3). In this light, misotheism both is and is not antitheistic. It selectively rejects some of the theistic attributes, notably divine benevolence and in some cases also the omnipotence of God. But misotheism is not antitheistic in the sense of being antireligious.

GNOSTICISM: The Gnostics were members of an early Christian school claiming to receive direct esoteric knowledge beyond the doctrines of church and scripture. These claims rendered them heretics in the view of fellow Christians. One of the main reasons why the Catholic Church so vigorously stamped out Gnosticism in all its different manifestations, including Manichaeanism, Sethian Gnosticism, and Catharism, was that Gnosticism is essentially an antitheistic faith. Specifically, Gnostics believed the world to be created by a demonic power, the demiurge. In this faith, it was Ialdabaoth, the serpent with a lion's head, who called forth the world and its inhabitants. The whole creation myth is extremely complicated and differs from one Gnostic branch to another. But the general outline of it is that Ialdabaoth is a botched spawn of the deity of wisdom, Sophia. After escaping her vigilance, he surrounds himself with other demonic powers, the archons, to create the world in order to outdo the supreme god. Adam and Eve are merely pawns in the hands of Ialdabaoth to gain a competitive advantage over the highest god. Inadvertently, though, Ialdabaoth breathed some of his mother's wisdom into the first human beings, with the result that they were not easily manipulable puppets, but had some integrity. In a fit of rage, he throws them out of Paradise, then personally impregnates Eve to conceive Cain and

Abel on her, making them sinful to increase human misery (Williams 11–12). Compared to the fully fleshed concreteness of the demiurge, the supreme deity of the Gnostics, sometimes called "Invisible Spirit" (Williams 9), remains an unknown, hidden, and disinterested power, more closely aligned with the hidden god of Epicurus or deism than with the fatherly authority of the Bible. Although the notion of a demonic and tyrannical creator, that is, the demiurge, may resonate with some of the misotheists' ideas of a sadistic God, it is safe to say that misotheists are not likely to be bound by the dogmas of any particular heresy, be it Gnosticism, Manichaeanism, or Deism. As will emerge in this study, opponents of God are far more directly influenced by contemporary sociopolitical conditions and by personal circumstances than by obscure cosmological myths and arcane doctrines.

DEICIDE: This variety of religious dissent is in fact relevant to misotheism. As A. N. Wilson has demonstrated in *God's Funeral* (1999), deicide came into its own during the nineteenth century, and it manifested itself in two major ways: on the one hand there were the explicit deicides, notably philosopher Friedrich Nietzsche and his forerunner, Max Stirner, as well as Thomas Hardy, whose poem "God's Funeral" provides Wilson's title. On the other hand, there were a number of "indirect" deicides, including the father of evolutionary science, Charles Darwin, the pioneering geologist Charles Lyell, the sociologists Marx and Engels, and the psychologist William James, all of whom demonstrated that the physical, the animal, the social, and the psychic worlds had no need for God and that it was therefore opportune to get rid of any vestiges of him.

Among the various nineteenth-century deicides, the one that most easily comes to mind is, of course, the radical German philosopher Friedrich Nietzsche, who may well be the first to put the assertion that "God is dead" into print. But Nietzsche was hardly the first one to have conceived of such a radical idea. According to Lewis Lapham, Nietzsche's statement was only the culmination of a long, slow development in Western thought: "God [was] disemboweled by Machiavelli in sixteenth-century Florence, assassinated in eighteenth-century Paris by agents of the French Enlightenment, lost at sea on a voyage to the Galápagos Islands, blown to pieces by German artillery at Verdun, garroted by Friedrich Nietzsche on a Swiss Alp, and the body laid to rest in the consulting room of Sigmund Freud" (Lapham 8). One could easily add a few more instances of deicide pre-dating Nietzsche: there is William Blake, who all but "kills" God (whom he renamed Urizen) in his early prophetic poem *America*. And, as indicated above, Shelley "killed" Jupiter, alias Yahweh, in *Prometheus Unbound* (1820). But although God may have been killed several times over, as Lapham remarks in his article, he has never been entirely deposed: "By the middle 1980s, I understood that God had worked another of his miracles, risen from the graves of skepticism and science, moving east from Oklahoma with a great host of gospel-singing Baptists" (Lapham 8). It emerges here that Lapham's bone of contention is not God per se but rather religion and in particular the influence of the religious right on American politics. His animosity against God is not a personal matter, nor does he appear to be particularly sincere in his jocular history of deicide. But insofar as the deicide works for the destruction of God within a genuinely religious framework, he is an enemy of God rather than an enemy of religion.

Clearly, assuming the existence of a cruel, tyrannical, or maddeningly indifferent deity, is not the same as opposing the idea of religion as such. Rebecca West is a case in point: though she fulminated against God in her private musings, her published works show a pronounced respect for certain aspects of religion, especially religion's role in fostering artistic traditions, and in offering a valid technique for grappling with the ultimate questions of existence. Then there are those, like the Victorian poets Algernon Charles Swinburne and James Thomson, who vilified both Yahweh and Christ but professed an enthusiasm for pagan religious thought that bordered on the fanatical. Even Nietzsche, a devotee of Zoroaster, was, according to Erich Heller, "by the very texture of his soul and mind, one of the most radically religious natures that the nineteenth century brought forth" (100). Thus, enemies of God do not so much target religion as they attack the moral character of a god whom they hold responsible for personal tragedies, collective calamities, and the general imperfection of the universe.

This brings me to the important questions of the morality of misotheism. If there is a common denominator among the various God-haters treated in this study, it is that practically all of them are beholden to ideas of liberation and justice. Of course, being mere mortals, these people have their foibles, they have their blind spots and their pet peeves; but, taken together, they are committed to speak truth, to engage in humanitarian work, to seek social justice, and to oppose bigotry. Percy Bysshe Shelley is representative of this disposition. He was no saint, as evidenced by his youthful dalliances with women and his desertion of his first wife, Harriet, for Mary Wollstonecraft Godwin. But, at the same time, he was a true visionary, a defender of liberty, and a strong advocate for social justice. His second wife, Mary Shelley, testified to his having had "the purest habits in morals, full of devoted generosity and universal kindness, glowing with ardour to attain wisdom, resolved at every personal sacrifice to do right, burning with a desire for affection and sympathy. . . . He was animated to greater zeal by compassion for his fellow-creatures. His sympathy was excited by the misery with which the world is burning" (284). Although Mary Shelley may not be an impartial commentator on the subject of her husband's moral values, others, including such humanistic luminaries as Mahatma Gandhi and Henry David Thoreau, corroborate her admiration for him (Weber 28). Shelley was a true philanthropist, a champion of all sentient beings, and an early social reformer working on behalf of the exploited working poor. Though raised in an aristocratic household, he early on recognized the immense human cost of England's rapid industrialization, and he did not hesitate to lend his name to the fight for the betterment of the working poor.

This emphasis on the essential decency of misotheists stands in direct contrast to Albert Camus's treatment of the metaphysical rebel, or hater of God. On the whole, Camus was deeply ambivalent about this stance. On the one hand, he was attracted to the nobility of the revolt, insisting that "rebellion is one of the essential dimensions of man" (21). To him, "rebellion, though apparently negative, since it creates nothing, is profoundly positive in that it reveals the part of man which must always be defended" (19). On the other hand, Camus consistently linked metaphysical rebellion to nihilism. He worried that when pursued to its logical conclusion, metaphysical rebellion leads to "metaphysical revolution. The master of the world, after his legitimacy has been contested, must be overthrown. Man must occupy his place" (58). The 1930s and 1940s had taught Camus what happens when a man, fired by totalitarian ideology, steps up to the pedestal and installs himself as the new deity. For Camus, "to become God is to accept crime" (59), and the result of metaphysical rebellion, when carried to its ultimate conclusion, leads to "absolute negation" (101). This negative assessment is heavily influenced by the excesses of fascism and communism during the preceding two decades, excesses that Camus sees as a result of what happens when "the spirit of metaphysical rebellion openly joins forces with revolutionary movements" (103). And the deplorable result of "this convulsive effort to control the world and to introduce a universal rule" (103) are the horrors perpetrated by the likes of Hitler and Stalin. To Camus, metaphysical rebellion "can turn to hatred of creation or to exclusive and defiant love of what exists. But in both cases it ends in murder" (101). It is here that my approach parts company with the thinking of Camus.

In my researches I have not found evidence that God-hatred usually, or even occasionally, runs the course from iconoclasm to deicide, to revolution, to nihilism, to murder, and to state tyranny. More frequently, it runs from perplexity about the state of the world or anger about undeserved suffering, to protest against God, to feminism (Rebecca West), to antiracism (Zora Neale Hurston), to republicanism (Algernon Charles Swinburne), to humanist activism (Elie Wiesel), and to secular liberalism (Philip Pullman). Even the politicized misotheists that I consider in this study, notably Pierre-Joseph Proudhon, Mikhail Bakunin, as well as Élisée and Elie Reclus, were anything but murderous revolutionaries red in tooth and claw. Their philosophical anarchism, ranging from mutual aid to syndicalism to cooperation, did not encourage terrorism or spawn violent revolutions. If anything, it is precisely the idealism and humanistic zeal of these rebels against God that prevented their ideas from enforcing the kind of "absolute negation," nihilism, and murderous absolutism that Camus worried about as a possible consequence of metaphysical rebellion. Whatever their individual shortcomings, misotheists of various stripes tend to come down resolutely on the side of humanism, justice, compassion, and progress.

But I am not only more optimistic than Camus with regard to the moral implications of misotheism, I also use a different procedure to investigate my subject. Indeed, Camus does not strictly distinguish between different types of God-haters and uses the term "metaphysical rebellion" rather sweepingly. In my view, the investigation into this phenomenon calls for a more nuanced terminology. While there are basic tenets that all enemies of God share, such as a passionate belief in the dignity of man and an instinctive recoil from the manifestations of a capricious and wrathful deity, it is necessary to distinguish between different manifestations of misotheism:

AGONISTIC MISOTHEISM: People like Zora Neale Hurston, Rebecca West, and Elie Wiesel represent this type of misotheism. They are struggling with the understanding that God is not entirely competent and good, while resenting the need to praise and worship him. These misotheists wish that they were wrong in their negative assessment of the deity and would prefer God to be benevolent and caring after all. At the same time, they are racked by grave doubts, and they keep up a constant quarrel with God. I call this attitude "agonistic misotheism" because this stance is characterized by an ongoing internal struggle and by the agony over one's negative relationship with God.[8] It doesn't seem that Camus's thinking about metaphysical rebellion had room for these troubled opponents of God.

Agonistic misotheists are torn between hope and despair, they suffer from their inability to believe in a good god, and they often seek refuge in the figure of Christ. As a rule, agonistic misotheists were initially pious in their youth, but they could not help being utterly disappointed with God's performance and with the overall course of the world as they grew older. Their case against God is based on personal experience, on their outlook on history, and their racial, gender, or ethnic identity, all of which have taught them that the universe is not well ordered and could therefore not reflect some divinely ideal plan. Something has gone wrong with the universe, they argue, if millions of pious believers can be slaughtered without the slightest trace of divine intervention, if prayers remain consistently unheard, and if personal indignity and suffering come down on good people without explanation or rationale.

These agonistic misotheists infallibly identify with the biblical figure of Job, although they do not follow the pattern of Job's wrestling with God, insofar as his temporary rebellion against God is followed by meek acceptance of divine supremacy. Writers such as Mark Twain, Zora Neale Hurston, Rebecca West, and Elie Wiesel are perennially quarreling with God and voicing their protest, sometimes vociferously and sometimes more quietly. But always they are seeking to enter into a dialogue with God; they are trying to tease God out of his reticence, and they will not give up until they have wrested some answer, some meaning, some explanation from God. This may explain why agonistic misotheists keep reiterating their complaints without cessation—for an answer is not forthcoming. Their persistent provocation could be seen as a form of prayer: they believe enough to keep trying.

Some of these artists may even experience phases of religious resurgence, as exemplified in Rebecca West's attempt to convert to Catholicism in the early 1950s, or in Elie Wiesel's gradual return to a more orthodox Jewish position of affirmative faith toward the end of the twentieth century. But always, at bottom there is this rankling doubt that God might not have man's best interest in mind.

Although Jewish protest theology is the most explicit and "institutionalized" version of agonistic misotheism, it is by no means the case that protests against an abusing god, a god of indifference, and a god of silence are limited to the Jewish tradition. Feminist Christian writers such as Rebecca West and Zora Neale Hurston are equally inspired to lodge their protest against God's disappointing (patriarchal) performance, although their protests tend to be more restrained than those of their Jewish counterparts. Indeed, Jewish writers such as Elie Wiesel and Paul Celan would routinely publish works registering sharp disappointment with God and making blasphemous accusations against the Almighty in print. By comparison, Christian agonistic misotheists like Rebecca West and Mark Twain tend to reserve their strongest attacks against God (as mentioned above) to their private diaries or to unpublished drafts of stories and essays, hinting rather indirectly at misotheism in their published works.

ABSOLUTE MISOTHEISM: It is a different story with those enemies of God, including Shelley, Thomson, Nietzsche, Swinburne, Shaffer, Hardy, and Pullman, who exult in the demise of the deity. I call this group of God-haters "absolute misotheists." Their expression of God-hatred can be dark and tormented, as in the case of James Thomson's "The City of Dreadful Night" and Peter Shaffer's *Amadeus*, but more frequently absolute misotheists are rather triumphant and cheerful, especially when the demise of God is seen as the dawn of a new day (Nietzsche and Pullman) or when God's fall is an occasion for creative experiments with alternative gods (Swinburne). As indicated above, absolute misotheists are not to be confused with atheists, since they still maintain a degree of religiosity and channel feelings of a religious nature into their attacks against God. At the same time, absolute enemies of God differ from agonistic misotheists because they are not doubting, they are not trying to enter into a dialogue with God, and they are not secretly hoping to be proven wrong in their condemnations of God. Absolute misotheists only want to trample God and eliminate him altogether from the world.

The best way to achieve this is by bringing him down to the human level and then by destroying God with the arsenals of literature, that is, through language and imagination.

POLITICAL MISOTHEISM: The third group of misotheists that I deal with are the political variety. Political misotheists are perhaps the most marginal members of the tribe of God-haters, insofar as they stand at the threshold of antitheism properly speaking. Indeed, their diatribes against the deity seem to be inspired by a general rejection of religion as a system of oppression, or at least as an ideology that provides exploitative institutions with an enabling rationale. But reading the blasphemous tracts of political God-haters, one cannot deny that they are inspired by a genuine, if inverted, kind of religiousness. Contrary to today's antitheists like Hitchens, Dawkins, and Harris, the erstwhile political misotheists such as Pierre-Joseph Proudhon, Mikhail Bakunin, and the Reclus brothers are so relentless, inventive, and passionate in their attacks against God that they indeed invoke Shelley, Swinburne, and Nietzsche, except that their rationale for attacking God is not primarily humanistic, cultural, or metaphysical but rather specifically political.

Despite their rationalist rhetoric, political misotheists tend to address God as a personalized figurehead rather than as a mere figment of the collective imagination. Their attacks against God are carried by a genuine sense of dread compared to the casual and more nonchalant blasphemies of today's antitheists. In a sense, political misotheists take God rather seriously. They storm against him because they recognize that the oppressive political structures that flow from the supreme godhead are having a real socioeconomic impact; they do not think that exploitative conditions will go away simply by declaring that "God is dead" in the fashion of absolute misotheists. However, because political misotheists are so closely associated with the philosophical anarchists of the nineteenth century, they have virtually disappeared with the demise of anarchism as a viable system of political economy or activism.

These three types of misotheism, agonistic, absolute, and political, are unified by their shared opposition to God; however, they are distinctly dissimilar in the way they approach their subject and in the way they conceive of their ultimate project. Obviously, the political misotheists do not generally engage in literary projects. Their expressions of God-hatred are limited to various forms of political rhetoric, from the rousing speech to the manifesto and the philosophical tract. The absolute misotheists are of a more artistic disposition. For instance, Philip Pullman is never quite as eloquent in defining his religious stance as he is in presenting his absolute misotheism in the form of fiction, notably in his trilogy *His Dark Materials*. And as we know, Nietzsche chose the form of a verse play, *Thus Spake Zarathustra*, to elaborate his ideas about the demise of God. Just as absolute misotheists are drawn toward literary treatments of the death-of-God motif, so agonistic misotheists also operate chiefly through the vehicle of literature. Hence, the six case studies contained in Part II of this study all deal with literary manifestations of misotheism: three chapters will be dedicated to absolute misotheists (Swinburne, Shaffer, and Pullman) and three to agonistic misotheists (Hurston, West, and Wiesel).

Having established these three separate traditions of misotheism, I should point out that any individual can conform to more than one type of misotheism. For instance, there is more than an ounce of political misotheism in Swinburne, a predominantly absolute misotheist. And as for the agonistic misotheism of Rebecca West, there is an element of deicidal misotheism in her work as well, such as expressed in her "belief in a wholly and finally defeated God."[9] But despite some overlap between the different directions of misotheism, a given writer usually belongs mostly to one of the three categories described above. Thus, while Camus applies the concept of metaphysical rebellion equally to Lautréamont, Dostoyevsky, and Bakunin, I consider the first an absolute misotheist, the second an agonistic misotheist, and the third a political misotheist. My own procedure further differs from Camus's method as I treat the philosophical history of misotheism separately from its literary manifestations. If the nonliterary expressions of misotheism are characterized by declamation, argument, and denotation, the artistic treatments of the theme are often carried out by speculation, imagination, and connotation. These two axes of misotheism are sufficiently different to warrant a separate treatment.

Part One of this study is designed to lay the groundwork of the discussion in historical-philosophical terms. Here I provide a chronological overview of the more straightforward manifestations of misotheism from Epicureanism to deism, to utilitarianism and anarchism, and to feminism and secular humanism. This history of ideas will flow as one continuous narrative, and it will inform the case studies that follow in profound ways. Often in the case studies I will refer to, say, Proudhon or Nietzsche without elaborating in detail on the connection; or I may assume some prior knowledge of anarchism or deism because these concepts and their relevance for misotheism have been thoroughly covered in this section of the book.

Part Two, which makes up the bulk of this study, is devoted to the creative, literary manifestations of misotheism. As indicated above, literature has been the principal forum for public expressions of God-hatred in the past two hundred years. In my six case studies of representative misotheistic authors, I will map out the considerable power of ideas behind their work. The sequence of these case studies is arranged chronologically and ordered as a series of contrasting pairs. The first case study, dealing with the absolute misotheist Algernon Charles Swinburne, is paired with the agonistic misotheism of Zora Neale Hurston. The rationale underlying this combination is to reveal the radically different approaches that these two artists took: while Swinburne exulted in the open declaration of his blasphemy against God, Hurston concealed her resentment against God in myriad ways, with the result that hardly anybody has heretofore noticed this radical tendency in her work. Rebecca West and Elie Wiesel constitute the next pairing. The basis of comparison here is the fact that both artists underwent a temporal change in their negative assessment of God: Rebecca West moved from an explicit God-hatred to a phase of relatively conventional piety in the middle of her life, before returning to intensive expressions of agonistic misotheism. Elie Wiesel, by contrast, was at first a very religious man; then he became a vocal opponent of God, before gradually finding his way back toward a more conventional Jewish piety. The third and final pairing, between Peter Shaffer and Philip Pullman, demonstrates two opposed affective poles of misotheism: Shaffer explores the tortured aspects of his mentally unbalanced misotheists, while Pullman shows the sanity and, indeed, the saving grace of absolute misotheism in his adolescent heroes.

In my readings of these six outstanding creative writers, I will tease out the meaning of their rebellion against God. Using their work as a touchstone, I shed some revealing light on the more troubled aspects of man's relationship to the divine. Indeed, one final question remains to be addressed, and that is: what causes a perfectly rational, decent, responsible human being to go on the warpath against God? A closer look at this question will reveal a variety of reasons, ranging from personal tragedy to psychological trauma, or from a historical crisis such as a social or political upheaval to a natural catastrophe. In general, however, all of these specific causes for God-hatred can be traced back to the problem of evil: looking around them, misotheists cannot believe that slavery, pogroms, genocide, world wars, tsunamis, plagues, and a host of other natural and man-made disasters are compatible with the existence of a wise, compassionate, and all-knowing god. Rebecca West illustrates the difficulty of squaring the existence of mass slaughter with the foresight of a beneficent god. With reference to the unprecedented horrors occurring on the battlefields of World War I, she concluded that "the hurt that God has done to the world is too great for any forgiveness. . . . One hates our fathers for having committed themselves to such a worship and wonders how they would have fancied God was kind" ("New God" 4–5). Obviously, for her the paternalistic god of Christianity has lost its credibility. But if World War I shattered many people's conception of a benevolent god, worse was to come. In the words of Elie Wiesel, the horrors of the Holocaust could not be reconciled with the idea of a just god: "Why, but why should I bless Him? In every fiber I rebelled. Because He had had thousands of children burned in His pits? . . . I was the accuser, God the accused" (*Night* 64, 65).

West and Wiesel are representative of all those who saw evil on such a scale that it exceeded any religious coping strategy or theological rationalization that they had learned. As the theologian John Roth has put it, "history itself is God's indictment" (7). Specifically the free will theodicy seemed to them discredited when millions were sent to their graves as a result of impersonal forces such as nationalism, totalitarianism, or imperialism and when personal agency seemed to be largely eclipsed by both subconscious impulses (as channeled by charismatic dictators) and supraterritorial chain reactions that culminated in two world wars. Faced with unprecedented historical crises, the idea of God's culpability was more persuasive than notions about original sin, divine grace, and Providence as devised by St. Augustine and other early church fathers.

Misotheists bump up against another one of St. Augustine's religious principles: *capax Dei*.[10] In its most basic meaning, *capax Dei* is "the capacity that constitutively links man to the transcendent" (Marion 88). According to St. Augustine, God has implanted in human beings the intelligence and receptivity to intuit God. In *De Trinitate*, Augustine wrote that this receptivity is the precondition for eligibility to be saved. An angry denunciation of God, such as Shelley's or West's, contradicts the teaching that God has provided human beings with the spiritual ability to perceive him in his glory. Surely, a diabolical apprehension of God as man's enemy cannot be God's gift, unless God were to incriminate himself. So, if the ability to perceive God is a gift from the Almighty, then rebels against God would say that it is a gift not worth having. One can argue that by spurning *capax Dei* they damn themselves, since acceptance of God (a gracious God) is precondition for salvation. Of course, from their own perspective, no blessing can issue from an evil or indifferent god, and thus the whole notion of *capax Dei* is voided.

Misotheists are dominated by a different receptivity, what one could term *capax homini*, or an ability to receive man, or things human. They are concerned with the conditions of human happiness and with the ultimate causes of suffering, and they cannot square their empirical knowledge about these matters with what they were taught to believe about God. They make a negative leap of faith, trusting their own judgment and placing their sense of moral outrage above the fear of God.

This book will demonstrate not only that misotheism exists and that it has an interesting history and a typology of its own, but also that misotheists are generally motivated by admirable humanistic impulses. The centrality of literature to this study further highlights the humanistic quality of this uncomfortable stance. But while literature in the past two hundred years has offered an enclave of freedom for opponents of God, the time may be ripe for a transition to a new phase in the history of misotheism and indeed the history of mankind. As we take our heads collectively out of the sand and face the phenomenon of misotheism with the curiosity and openness that it deserves, we may well find that the horizon of our ideas about the nature of belief has expanded. The hoped for result of such a new awareness would be an increased tolerance toward those believers who cannot bring themselves to worship God in the prescribed way. Of course, such an upbeat assessment of antidevotional practices will not be to everyone's liking. By taking misotheism out of the closet, and by bringing some misotheists' formerly unnoticed views into the light, I encourage an open-minded recognition that the spectrum of religious attitudes is more diverse and potentially disturbing than we might have previously assumed. This kind of knowledge deserves to be revealed, especially as it is conducive to a better understanding of the vicissitudes of human faith and likely to yield a fuller picture of the history and richness of religious ideas.

PART ONE

A Brief History of Misotheism

A Brief History of Misotheism

The true remedy for fanaticism, in our view, is not to identify humanity with God. . . . It is to prove to humanity that God, in case there is a God, is its enemy.

—Pierre-Joseph Proudhon (1848)

The Book of Job

BOOK OF JOB IS A SUITABLE TEXT WITH WHICH TO BEGIN THIS SHORT history of man's hostility to the Judeo-Christian god. Job's story is an early specimen of the trial-of-God theme, and it is usually understood as teaching the lesson that one must not accuse God for the existence of evil but rather should meekly accept even seemingly undeserved suffering and random evil without turning away from God. Surely, Job's cautionary tale offers strong arguments to the believer that the Almighty has his own reasons for doing what he does and that the pious must refrain from second-guessing his motives and actions. But the Book of Job also contains a minor character, Job's wife, who flies in the face of such piety; she resolves to become an implacable enemy of God because she feels that the sufferings she and her husband had to endure give proof that God is capricious and unkind.

Let us remember the course of events: Job is a virtuous, God-fearing, and popular man in the land of Uz. In fact, he is so pious that he "over-fulfills" his devotional duty just in case he or any of his seven sons had committed an unintentional sin. Yet God singled him out to be a test case for man's absolute submission to the divine will because Satan had claimed that only a man as happy and prosperous as Job would be so devoted to God. The Almighty accepts the challenge and bets that he can prove Satan wrong. In order to do so, God gives the devil leave to turn Job's life into a vale of tears by destroying his flocks, killing his staff, and butchering his children. To God's satisfaction, Job, although lamenting his unforeseen misfortune, refrains from holding God responsible for his downfall and does not curse him, concluding instead that "The Lord giveth, and the Lord taketh away; blessed be the name of the Lord" [1:21]). Then, Satan once again challenges God, saying that Job would lose his piety for sure if he were afflicted with suffering in his own person, and again God gives Satan permission to harass Job. This time he inflicts hideous itching and flaking skin diseases, reducing Job to a simpering wretch who scratches his sores with shards of pottery (2:8). At this point, several of Job's friends pay a visit and, after a long silence, begin a theological inquiry into the misfortune that has befallen their companion. After lengthy discussion with them, Job rejects their counsel that his misfortune must be the result of some unintentional sin or a divine warning against potential future sins. Job maintains that he did not and will not commit a sin, and he questions the Lord's fairness, but without cursing him. A key role in these theological debates is played by Job's friend Elihu, who argues that it is irrelevant to talk about the fairness or injustice of God because the Lord's actions and thoughts are outside the sphere of human comprehension. Therefore, the best path to take is one of unqualified faith in God's ultimate justice, despite temporary empirical evidence to the contrary. This, of course, is a canonical response to the problem of evil.

After more soul-searching and doubt on the part of Job, God makes an appearance in the form of a cloud or whirlwind and belittles Job for his doubts. Yahweh goes on to boast about his ultimate power in creating the world, in eclipsing the might of even the most majestic creatures, and in controlling the mighty forces of oceans and the winds that make a man like Job appear puny and insignificant. In this way, God demonstrates that he exists on a completely different plane compared to human beings and that he is not answerable to human reasoning and terrestrial complaints. This argument does not fail to impress Job, who finally acquiesces in the will of God. In return for abandoning his doubts about divine Providence and accepting the Lord's will, Job is rewarded with the complete restoration of his riches, with a return to good health, and with plentiful and charming offspring.[1]

But there is a flickering of dissent in this story: Job's wife is not willing to follow her husband down the road of complete submission to the divine will. She looks at the enormous accumulation of evil— her children's untimely death, the obliteration of her household staff, the destruction of their livestock—and grows incensed. In a fit of rage, she shouts that both she and her husband should "curse God and die" (2:9). Understandably, the Bible does not make a hero of Job's wife, and Job proceeds to scold her harshly for her blasphemy, and thereafter she is not mentioned again in the Book of Job. Despite the brevity of her biblical appearance, Job's unnamed wife really is the original misotheist, ready to curse God in open defiance and willing to be damned rather than acquiesce in divine caprice. Her blasphemy is not the result of pride or peevishness but the rational consequence of a moral outrage that incriminates God while making a virtue of the courage to rebel. In a sense, then, the indignant and fiercely independent misotheists treated in this book are the descendants of Job's wife.

That I trace one of misotheism's earliest expressions to the Bible rather than to, say, *The Odyssey* or *Antigone* is no coincidence. True misotheism is only imaginable in the context of a monotheistic religion. By comparison, the polytheist, who worships numerous gods, and the henotheist, who acknowledges one principal god among several divinities, is free to worship one god while expressing disdain for another one (or others). Even the gods themselves, according to classical mythology, feel animosity and hatred toward some among their number, as in the case of the famous quarrel between Poseidon and Athena in *The Odyssey*, or with the repeated clashes between Zeus and Hera. In such a polytheistic world, where gods are essentially men writ large, burdened with human weaknesses as well as endowed with superhuman prowess, it is as natural for deities to form alliances among each other as it is for them to attack other members of the pantheon. Even Yahweh was initially just one of several gods worshipped by peoples in the ancient Middle East. As Karen Armstrong has argued in *The Great Transformation* (2006), the rivalries between prophets of different gods, including Yahweh, Baal, and Anat—all vying for prominence around 800 BCE—were seen as a reflection of conflicts between these deities themselves. In the case of the Israelites, the conflict was settled when "Yahweh, who had won the leadership of the divine council, had sentenced them [the other gods] all to death" (Armstrong 67).

But hostility among the gods is not what I have in mind when I refer to misotheism, a stance that is based on man's antagonistic relationship with one all-encompassing God, notably Yahweh. In this sense, misotheism is total and categorical, entailing the subversion of an entire belief system that requires the pious worship of one God. Hence, the high frequency with which misotheists activate what could be termed a "heretical" kind of religiosity, reviving pagan gods or turning to a non-Trinitarian, historical Christ as the spiritual focus of their worship. The misotheist's devotional impulse is still there, but it is no longer aimed at an almighty singular deity.

Epicurus

Epicurus (341–270 BCE), one of the earliest outspoken critics of religious worship, lived mostly in Athens, where he maintained a philosophical school named "The Garden." Epicurus pioneered a rationalist view of the gods that undercut any reverential or fearful stance vis-à-vis deity. This paradigm shift caused Bertrand Russell to state that "the hatred of religion expressed by Epicurus . . . is not altogether easy to understand" (249). But Russell's word choice, hatred of *religion* rather than of gods, is revealing. Indeed, while Epicurus addressed the futility of religious worship, he was most eloquent in his disdain for the gods themselves. Russell's formulation "hatred of religion" might well be an attempt to circumvent a curious ambivalence in the reception of Epicurean thought. Indeed, if we look at discussions or fragments of Epicurus's teachings on religious matters, we are bound to encounter a persistent muddling of poly- and monotheistic references. On the one hand, Epicurus is credited with saying that "it is vain to ask the gods what a man is capable of supplying for himself" (*Remains* 117); on the other hand, the complement of this thought is put in monotheistic terms: "if God listened to the prayers of men, all men would quickly have perished: for they are forever praying for evil against each other" (*Remains* 135). Similarly, the famous "Epicurean Paradox," a series of propositions aimed at discrediting theism, refers to God in the singular: "God . . . either wants to eliminate bad things and cannot, or can but does not want to, or neither wishes to nor can, or both wants to and can. If he wants to and cannot, then he is weak. . . . If he can but does not want to, then he is spiteful. . . . If he neither wants to nor can, he is both weak and spiteful and so not a god. If he wants to and can, which is the only thing fitting for a god, where then do bad things come from? Or why does he not eliminate them?" (Lactantius 13.20–21). Lactantius, a third-century Christian apologist, attributed this formulation to Epicurus in order to attack the stance and to defend divine Providence against such skepticism. It should be noted that religious scholars like Mark Joseph Larrimore doubt whether Epicurus is indeed the source of this riddle (xix–xx). Regardless of whether or not the "Epicurean Paradox" is misattributed, Epicureanism does offer an answer to its unsettling logic.

The Epicurean solution consists in the idea of divine apathy. In *De Rerum Natura*, a first century BCE rendition of Epicurus's philosophy by Lucretius, we read that "it is essential to the very nature of deity that it should enjoy immortal existence in utter tranquility, aloof and detached from our affairs" (79). What he meant by this was that the gods, after having created the cosmos in the fashion of demiurges (that is, skilled workers), withdrew into a distant corner of the universe and left the world to its own devices. And because such absentee deities don't bother about human beings or the fate of the world, they need not be feared; neither, of course, need they be worshiped under these conditions, since there simply is no reciprocal relationship between divinity and humanity. Under this system, although the existence of the gods is not denied categorically, the moral claim that the gods are concerned about humanity and that they have a vested interest in dispensing justice and order on earth is undercut. In the last consequence, Epicurus's materialistic conception of the world rejected the moral significance of gods and denied that they had any influence over the afterlife; indeed, in his thinking there was no afterlife to begin with, since the body and spirit disintegrated into so many atoms at death. With these convictions, Epicurus comes across as an early crusader against the moral claims of religion, as a debunker of the notion of heaven and hell, and as a subverter of divine interventionism.

The secular thrust of Epicurus's views finds its counterpart in Roman literature in the disrespectful, teasing approach to the gods evidenced in works of Ovid and Lucian. People with an intact faith in the dignity and power of the gods would be unlikely to write, or enjoy, a book such as Ovid's *Metamorphoses*. It is difficult to see these tales of Ovid, composed around 2 CE, as anything other than manifestations of an advanced state of disillusionment with the Roman religion. In one story of the *Metamorphoses*, Apollo chases Daphne like a crazed sex maniac. Even though he is the god of medicine, he cannot heal his own fever, and although he is also the god of prophecy, he cannot foresee that his pursuit is doomed. The result is an elaborate joke at the cost of Apollo. Similarly, the cheating and philandering of the highest god in the Roman pantheon, Jove (or Jupiter), and his quarrels with his wife Hera are legion, and Ovid spares no opportunity to paint the gods in a ludicrous and all-too-human light.

The late Hellenic writer Lucian took the gods down one more peg. What is remarkable about his satirical *True History* (*Verae historiae*) is the fact that although the events are set in a mythical realm of supernatural characters who perform Herculean tasks and journey to the land of the dead, the events transpire basically in a religious vacuum. The gods make only cameo appearances or, worse, they become the butts of ribald jokes. Planting a spear in honor of Poseidon is an empty formality, and the battles between the god of the sun and the god of the moon are no more than carnivalesque comedies of error. That the gods are no longer safe from ridicule and slander in these works of antique literature is an indication that their hold over people's imagination had been steadily loosening and that their power to command awe and worship had probably dwindled beyond repair. At the same time, the gods of Homer, Ovid, and Lucian appear more likely to become the butt of jokes than objects of a deeply felt hatred. They are a bit too pathetic and fallible to elicit reactions other than the desire to outwit, scorn, or belittle them. The strongest irreligious sentiment they are capable of calling up is ridicule or simply indifference.

But things change once the religious system becomes monotheistic, with worship directed toward an all-encompassing deity who represents the *summum bonum*, who instills a sense of moral absolutes, metes out punishment for violations of this code, and requires absolute obedience. Surely, such a god is capable of instilling unqualified worship. But not only that. St. Augustine's religious sensibility prefigures the basic Christian relationship to God, namely, a mixture of awe, love, guilt, and humility. But while St. Augustine's love for God that suffuses the *Confessions* is impressive, the weight of sin that St. Augustine also conveys can be oppressive, with feelings of guilt at times reaching a fever pitch. This, however, poses a problem that might well constitute a motive for future animosity toward the divine object of worship. Since guilt is so central to St. Augustine's creed, and because his sense of shame and unworthiness before God is so overwhelming, this aspect of his Christian ethos may well harbor the seeds of discontent and eventual rebellion that can then lead to a complete rejection of the godhead. Indeed, one can argue that what inspires feelings of guilt in us is often also what we tend to resent. As Rebecca West said, "It is a characteristic of human nature that people feel hostile towards those they are conscious of having injured" (*Survivors* 45). Surely, St. Augustine almost obsessively enumerates his offenses against God prior to his conversion, as when he writes, "Meanwhile my sins were being multiplied" (*Confessions* 136); he considers his son, Adeodatus, as "born of me carnally, of my sin" (218); and he is grateful that his "most merciful Lord, pardoned and remitted this sin also, with my others, so horrible and deadly" (209). But some believers, after feeling constantly obliged to apologize to God, to repent for their sins, and to expiate their guilt, might be led to think that they had been insufficiently equipped by God to avoid those very sins, and thus might begin to conceive a hostility toward the very cause of their moral agony.

According to the self-declared agnostic Bertrand Russell, this resentment should indeed be a normal human reflex, and he wonders why God doesn't become the target of hostility more frequently than seems to be the case. In his essay "Why I Am Not a Christian" (1927), Russell bases his arguments on an essentially Epicurean basis: "Religion is based, I think, primarily and mainly upon fear" (22). He then concludes that "the whole conception of God is a conception derived from the ancient oriental despotism. It is a conception quite unworthy of free men. When you hear people in church debasing themselves and saying that they are miserable sinners, and all the rest of it, it seems contemptible and not worthy of self-respecting human beings" (23). Both Rebecca West and Russell voice legitimate concerns, West insisting that we tend to hate whoever makes us feel guilty, and Russell focusing on hatred inspired by those who cause our humiliation. And yet the will to believe, the power of God to command worship and love has never been seriously challenged by such arguments. And those who do experience feelings of rejection, resentment, anger, and even hatred for God—that is, misotheists— have always played only a minor role in the history of religious ideas, comparable to the ephemeral part played by Job's wife. But despite not being powerful in numbers, the ideas of misotheists have played a persistent countermelody to the hymns of faith across the centuries.

Thomas Paine

The French Revolution was the historical event that opened the floodgates of attacks against traditional Christianity and its god, with the burgeoning spirit of Romanticism deepening that mentality. The revolution made it clear to anyone that there seemed no power too great and no authority so absolute that it could not be challenged and overturned by revolt. Romanticism, in turn, fostered rebellious tendencies and glorified the individual while developing a panentheistic approach to religion that placed God as a transcendent essence of nature. Both impulses, the political and the spiritual revolutions, found their culmination in the archrebel Thomas Paine (1737–1809). In his capacity as public intellectual and revolutionary agitator, Paine penned both the revolutionary pamphlet *Common Sense* (1776), which stoked the fires of the American revolutionary spirit, and the treatise *The Age of Reason* (1794), which can serve as a manifesto of religious dissent. Interestingly, however, Thomas Paine kept the two modes of rebellion—one in favor of political liberty, and the other in favor of freedom from church doctrine—separate, as if they were discrete areas of human resistance and liberationist thinking. It would take Mikhail Bakunin to show the intimate interrelation of the religious and political orders (see later in this chapter). Paine is important to this stage of our story because he is among the first modern thinkers to come out in open defiance and direct denunciation of God. Witness his outrage against the biblical representation of God in *The Age of Reason*:

Whenever we read the obscene stories, the voluptuous debaucheries, the cruel and torturous executions, the unrelenting vindictiveness, with which more than half the Bible is filled, it would be more consistent that we called it the word of a demon, than the word of God. It is a history of wickedness, that has served to corrupt and brutalize mankind. (18)

It is presumably because of such statements that Paine has been branded an atheist, but this is not quite correct. Although his tract is an elaborate manifesto against Christian Trinitarian dogmas and against most of the biblical teachings, Paine still held religious beliefs: "I believe in one God, and no more; and I hope for happiness beyond this life" (5). Rather than being an atheist, then, Paine was actually a deist. He considered the Bible to be but a collection of fantastic myths (with the exception of the book of Job and the Psalms, the only parts of the Bible he acknowledged as genuinely religious). To him, the Old Testament was a horrendous concoction of falsehoods and lies, and he saw in the New Testament a ridiculous jumble of incongruent anecdotes, as well as a tendentious compilation of half-remembered legends about Christ: "the Bible and the Testament are impositions upon the world . . . the fall of man, the account of Jesus Christ being the Son of God, and of his dying to appease the wrath of God, and of salvation by that strange means, are all fabulous inventions, dishonorable to the wisdom and power of the Almighty" (156–57). The reductive tendency of such arguments can be inferred from the fact that the doctrine of atonement is actually not mentioned in the Bible. Equally emphatic is Paine's contention that "theology . . . is the study of human opinions and of human fancies *concerning* God" (34). Despite such oversimplifications, Paine's fearless denunciation of Yahweh proved heartening to future misotheists. And his contention about the socially constructed, collectively fantasized nature of God as conveyed through the Bible anticipated Ludwig Feuerbach's religious rationalism (as we'll examine below).

Although Paine hates the biblical god, he is not irreligious, and his abstract, distant, deist god has a passing similarity with Epicurus's deity. The traditional explanation for the god of deism, that is, the "watchmaker god," implies that although God created the world (not ex nihilo but rather like a skilled worker), he left it to its own devices once he was finished with creation, much like a watchmaker releases his mechanism into the world where it functions independent of his care. Thus, the deist god can be accused of the same kind of apathy toward the fate of humankind that characterized the absentee gods of Epicurus. It is quite inconceivable that one would entertain passionate feelings, either of love or of hate, for such a distant, detached deity. But while Epicurus appears to have rather scorned the whole concept of deity, possibly because of the anthropomorphic quality of his understanding of the gods, the deists' furor was specifically directed at Yahweh because they saw in him a repulsive human invention, a personal deity who clashed with their abstract, transcendent god.

James Mill

This deistic tendency to rationalize Yahweh as a hateful collective human construct can also be found in the thought of the British thinker James Mill (1773–1836), father of the utilitarian philosopher John Stuart Mill. In his *Autobiography* (1873), John Stuart Mill recalls his father's aversion against "doing the will of a being, on whom [Christianity] lavishes indeed all the phrases of adulation, but whom in sober truth it depicts as eminently hateful" (26). One notes the carefully chosen adjective of "hateful" as the attribute of God. John Stuart Mill goes on to outline his father's (and his own) attitude toward divinity as follows:

> I have a hundred times heard him say, that all ages and nations have represented their gods as wicked, in a constantly increasing progression; that mankind have gone on adding trait after trait till they reached the most perfect conception of wickedness which the human mind could devise, and have called this God, and prostrated themselves before it. This *ne plus ultra* of wickedness he considered to be embodied in what is commonly presented to mankind as the creed of Christianity. (26)

The relentlessly constructivist tone of this passage is telling. Mill does not simply denounce God as inherently evil but emphasizes the man-made quality of this object of loathing. He addresses how human ideology has shaped the representation of God and how that representation has evolved historically, as "trait after trait" of his hateful image accrued over the course of time. It is worth pointing out that this is an even more far-ranging attack against divinity than Paine's. Indeed, both father and son Mill have widened the scope of their misotheism to include all gods, Christian and non-Christian. But as in Paine, an implicit deism comes through when John discusses the "ideal conception of a Perfect Being, to which [deists] habitually refer as the guide of their conscience; and this ideal of Good is usually far nearer to perfection than the objective Deity of those who think themselves obliged to find absolute goodness in the author of a world so crowded with suffering and so deformed by injustice as ours" (29). The deistic invocation of an abstract god is subtly blended in with the utilitarian regard for maximizing goodness, which is seen as the culmination of the deistic notion of God. And just as deism has led James Stuart Mill to utilitarianism, so utilitarianism is indebted to Epicureanism: "His standard of morals," writes John Stuart Mill about his father, "was Epicurean, inasmuch as it was utilitarian, taking as the exclusive test of right and wrong, the tendency of actions to produce pleasure or pain" (30). The trajectory of misotheism from Epicureanism on to deism and then to utilitarianism can thus be shown as a continuum in the history of ideas. Now we can move on to the next stage in this chain of thought.

Ludwig Feuerbach

I mentioned above that the deist Thomas Paine kept his revolutionary political agitation and his misotheistic rhetoric running on separate tracks of his subversive agenda. Before the liberation from kings could be seen as logically consistent with the project of liberation from the gods, however, a more rigorously rationalist approach to religion was required to displace the transcendental basis of deistic thinking altogether. Such a model was provided by the German philosopher Ludwig Feuerbach (1804–1872), who during his life moved from being a follower of Hegelian idealism to becoming an anti-Hegelian critic of state and religion. Feuerbach's radicalization began when he joined the Young Hegelians, a group of antiestablishment intellectuals, and continued when he emerged as an outspoken critic of the authoritarian Prussian state during the political turmoil of 1848. He eventually became an atheistic materialist, more interested in studying natural science than abstract philosophy.

Feuerbach's best-known book, a rambling tract titled *The Essence of Christianity* (1841), caused a sensation and was embraced by many rationalist intellectuals of the day. While Feuerbach was not a misotheist, his skeptical empiricism regarding religion provided later enemies of God with rhetorical ammunition. Basically, Feuerbach advanced the development of misotheism by exchanging the traditional roles of God and man: while humanizing God, he idealized man. If Paine sought to demolish the reputation of Yahweh, and James Mill strove to discredit all personalized deities, Feuerbach intended to prove that God was simply a case of idealized man projected onto the figure of God. In other words, God was not so much the maker of man as he was the product of man, as human qualities were abstracted and projected onto an entity given the name of God or Yahweh.

In *The Essence of Christianity*, Feuerbach asserts his key argument again and again, namely, that "religion, at least the Christian, is the relation of man to himself. . . . The divine being is nothing else than the human being, or, rather, the human nature purified, freed from the limits of the individual man, made objective" (14). What is so radical and so blasphemous about this view is the implication that the Christian god is not a transcendent creator god, eternal, preexisting and separate from humanity. The contrary is the case, claims Feuerbach: "the antithesis of divine and human is altogether illusory, that it is nothing else than the antithesis between the human nature in general and the human individual" (14). The resultant bind between God and man is based on the realization that man first externalizes his own essence into an idealized godhead and then turns around to worship that projection: "Man—this is the mystery of religion—projects his being into objectivity, and then again makes himself an object to this projected image of himself thus converted into a subject" (29).

Two major implications arise from this stance for the purpose of our inquiry. First, if God is nothing but the distilled essence of man, then God is dependent upon humanity and would cease to exist if we ceased to collectively project him. God is like a photographic image projected onto a screen that vanishes as soon as we flip the "off" switch on the projector. Secondly, if the projected image is a reflection of man in the abstract, it would seem inevitable that certain human shortcomings are carried over, tainting that projection. Being essentially an idealist, Feuerbach did not exploit this negative possibility of his own theory. But in the hands of a pessimist, the god of Feuerbach may well elicit loathing because of his correlation with imperfect man. If it were true, as Rebecca West said, that "man is a hating rather than a loving animal" (*Black Lamb and Grey Falcon* 302), then what would Feuerbach's god be?

Karl Marx

Feuerbach's influence is pronounced within the circle of socialist and anarchist thinkers who took his theory further. Specifically, Feuerbach is seen as the bridge between Hegel and Marx. After reading Feuerbach, Karl Marx (1818–1883) came to the conclusion that God represents man alienated from himself: "*Man makes religion*, religion does not make man. Religion is the self-consciousness and the self-esteem of man who has either not yet found himself or has already lost himself again" (Marx 301). In this view, projecting an idealized abstraction of humanity onto the figure of God will leave common man feeling deficient and inferior. Moreover, religion accustoms man to seek fulfillment in the realm of idealization rather than achieving it in his own personal life. In other words, religion can be turned into an instrument of oppression because religious projections disguise and distort the relationship of man to the real conditions of his existence.

But compared to the typical God-hater, Marx looked at religion from a systemic point of view, seeing it as an ideology that needs to be overthrown as a whole before prosperity and social justice can be realized. His hatred of religion did not really extend to hatred of God, per se. Indeed, the two stances are not continuous. Therefore, when Quentin Lauer says that "unlike most atheists whom history has known, Marx does not war against a popular or even a current theological conception of God" (48), he confuses atheism with what would be more accurately identified as misotheism. While I agree that Marx was a typical atheist, that is, someone who simply could not muster any belief in God, the formulation that "most atheists whom history has known . . . war against . . . God" seems too imprecise. Such an attitude would represent the paradoxical belief of the misotheist who believes in God but hates him. Marx was incapable of such a conception, but the same cannot be said of his ideological rivals among the anarchists, in whom we can find some of the most fervent misotheists.

When we go from Marxism to anarchism, we move from a belief system that exalts authority, requires submission to doctrine, and fosters a personality cult to a belief system that denounces authority, hierarchy, and leader worship. This has crucial implications with regard to the two systems' respective attitudes toward God. On the one side we have communism, which has historically developed a party apparatus with ecclesiastical characteristics, an organization that endows the writings of its founders with scriptural authority and encourages worship of its exalted "prophets," including Marx, Engels, Lenin, and Mao. Communism, in other words, becomes a surrogate religion even as it advocates the eradication of Christianity. On the other side, we have anarchism which precisely resisted the establishment of a top-down authoritarian system of governance based on charismatic leadership. With the anarchists, therefore, the struggle against religion gets personal. For them, God is not just the symbol of an oppressive religious establishment but a concrete enemy.

Pierre-Joseph Proudhon

The earliest and possibly the most radical and shocking manifestation of such politically inspired misotheism can be found in Pierre-Joseph Proudhon's book *The System of Economic Contradictions; or, The Philosophy of Misery* (1846; *Philosophie de la misère* is sometimes also translated as *The Philosophy of Poverty*). Proudhon (1809–1865) was a French philosopher, a pioneer of alternative banking schemes, and the first elected member of parliament anywhere to call himself an anarchist. After spending his youth in Besançon, he moved to Paris at age twenty, joining radical intellectual circles there and beginning to publish essays on political philosophy and the economics of work. In 1840, he attracted considerable attention with his essay "What Is Property?" (his answer was "theft"), and for a while he became an associate of Karl Marx. But when Proudhon opposed Marx's statist approach to economic management, they became mutual enemies. Proudhon was a mild revolutionary with a pacifist bent who believed in gradual, collective sociopolitical changes. His most lasting contribution to political theory was the working out of a mutualist approach to anarchism according to which voluntary associations and cooperative structures would provide for social security; and, instead of the state owning the means of production, as in Marxism, he envisioned workers' syndicates as the collective owners of the production facilities and the guarantors of a nation's economic viability. Proudhon's views about economic self-management and social mutualism had no room for authoritarian political structures, and they certainly had no room for religious institutions.

Proudhon can be considered as a prototypical modern misotheist because he not only based his polemic against God on the existence of God but also because he advocated pacifist and humanist ideals. In *The Philosophy of Misery*, he goes great lengths to demonstrate that God, or what he calls "the God-idea," is a valid and real hypothesis:

> The hypothesis of God is allowable, for it forces itself upon every man in spite of himself: no one, then, can take exception to it. He who believes can do no less than grant me the supposition that God exists; he who denies is forced to grant it to me also, since he entertained it before me, every negation implying a previous affirmation; as for him who doubts, he needs but to reflect a moment to understand that his doubt necessarily supposes an unknown something, which, sooner or later, he will call God. (20)

But despite such hedging acknowledgments of God's existence, Proudhon is very clear that belief in God does not imply the need to worship him: "the semi-Christian democrats will curse me as an enemy of God, and consequently a traitor to the republic, when I am seeking for the meaning and content of the idea of God" (23). Proudhon's project, which he summarizes as "a complete criticism of God and humanity" (29) is based on the premise that "God is persona, or he does not exist" (316), a belief that, ultimately, leads him to conclude that "God is evil" (322). Proudhon arrives at this insight after dismantling the concept of Providence, which he sees as a monstrous instrument of deception and betrayal.

That betrayal—giving man information that nurtures unfulfilled hopes, and withholding information that would ease his pain and suffering—"is exactly what God, the God of Providence, has done in the government of humanity; it is that that I accuse him of" (318). Proudhon goes on to clinch his argument against the benevolence of the Almighty as follows:

God, whom faith represents as a tender father and a prudent master, abandons us to the fatality of our incomplete conceptions; he digs the ditch under our feet; he causes us to move blindly; and then, at every fall, he punishes us as rascals. What do I say? It seems as if it were in spite of him that at last, covered with bruises from our journey, we recognize our road; as if we offended his glory in becoming more intelligent and free through the trials which he imposes upon us. What need, then, have we to continually invoke Divinity, and what have we to do with those satellites of a Providence which for sixty centuries, by the aid of a thousand religions, has deceived and misled us? (319)

What is new in Proudhon's anti-God rhetoric, compared to his forebears like Paine and Mill, is the peculiar combination of theological sophistication and sociological astuteness that he brings to his subject.

Indeed, Proudhon identifies God as his enemy not only because of the delusional aspect of Providence on a personal level but also because God refuses to let Providence herald the establishment of a just social order:

That this order may be realized, man must discover it; that it may exist, he must have divined it. This labor of invention might be abridged; no one, either in heaven or on earth, will come to man's aid; no one will instruct him. Humanity, for hundreds of centuries, will devour its generations; it will exhaust itself in blood and mire, without the God whom it worships coming once to illuminate its reason and abridge its time of trial. Where is divine action here? Where is Providence? (320)

The charges against God having been laid out in this manner, it is time to read Proudhon's ultimate verdict: "if there is a being who, before ourselves and more than ourselves, is deserving of hell,—I am bound to name him,—it is God" (320). The difference between Job's wife and Proudhon is that whereas she fully expected to die instantly after cursing God, Proudhon betrays no such apprehension. Like Job's wife, though, he feels justified in passing such a harsh judgment not only because he thinks God has passively failed to aid human development and lessen suffering, but also because he suspects God of willful negligence and open animosity against his creation: "God, if he exists, is essentially hostile to our nature, and we do not depend at all upon his authority. We arrive at knowledge in spite of him, at comfort in spite of him, at society in spite of him; every step we take in advance is a victory in which we crush Divinity" (321). This is the basic reciprocity of the misotheist: since God evidently hates us, it is our destiny to hate and despise him in return. As he nears the end of his treatise, Proudhon broadens the scope of his attack against all supreme deities, the monotheistic and polytheistic systems included: "Eternal father, Jupiter or Jehovah, we have learned to know you; you are, you were, you ever will be, the jealous rival of Adam, the tyrant of Prometheus" (321). And from this basis of belief in an evil and tyrannical concept of God, Proudhon delivers a reverse prayer, a curse of God so eloquent that to call it blasphemous is an understatement. In short, Proudhon shoots off his most explosive rhetorical pyrotechnics in a display of heroic defiance against divinity that seeks to destroy, not just to denounce, the idea of the theistic god:

> We were as naught before your invisible majesty, to whom we gave the sky for a canopy and the earth for a footstool. And now here you are dethroned and broken. Your name, so long the last word of the savant, the sanction of the judge, the force of the prince, the hope of the poor, the refuge of the repentant sinner,—this incommunicable name, I say, henceforth an object of contempt and curses, shall be a hissing among men. For God is stupidity and cowardice; God is hypocrisy and falsehood; God is tyranny and misery; God is evil. As long as humanity shall bend before an altar, humanity, the slave of kings and priests, will be condemned; as long as one man, in the name of God, shall receive the oath of another man, society will be founded on perjury; peace and love will be banished from among mortals. God, take yourself away! for, from this day forth, cured of your fear and become wise, I swear, with hand extended to heaven, that you are only the tormentor of my reason, the spectre of my conscience. (322)

One can only imagine that this is what Job's wife had in mind, yet it took several millennia for paper to receive these words and for humanity to bear hearing them without instantly eviscerating the one who wrote them.

Proudhon's intention in such inflammatory passages is to disabuse humanity of its religious misconceptions and to debunk the logic of theism. In his view, God does exist, but if we worship and revere him, we are all committing a huge mistake, acting as the dupes of a long-standing fallacy. But Proudhon goes further than most misotheists in history because he is one of the few who did not suggest to place a new god on the altar of the smashed deity. He was completely averse to any attempt at substituting the new god of science, or art, or socialism for the old god of theism (or deism, for that matter). In fact, it turns out that Proudhon accuses humanism of the same fallacious tendencies that he condemns in Christianity: "Humanism is the most perfect theism" (330) he exclaims. At first sight, this looks like a counterintuitive twist in Proudhon's argument. After all, there was a vast mystical hunger in the nineteenth century aimed at replacing the god of received religion with the inner god of the individual or with the humanistic ideal of man's boundless spirit. Thinkers as diverse as Hegel, Feuerbach, and Emily Brontë put forth their own humanistic theses that identified divinity variously with the Zeitgeist, idealized man, consciousness, or inspiration. As for the latter, Emily Brontë put it best in her well-known poem "God of Visions": "And am I wrong to worship where / Faith cannot doubt nor Hope despair / Since my own soul can grant my prayer? / Speak, God of Visions, plead for me / And tell why I have chosen thee!" (209). Brontë's "God of Visions" is clearly identified with her own imagination as a writer, and hence she finds the transcendent Absolute within herself. In such a view, there is no need to pray to an almighty God looking down on us from heaven; rather, the human spirit is capable of granting its own prayers.

This, in a nutshell, is the agnostic position advanced by James Turner in his study *Without God, Without Creed*. According to Turner, nineteenth-century agnostics, whom Turner calls "unbelievers," were really hungering for a replacement of the conventional god of Christianity: "The faith of many unbelievers set Humanity on the altar in place of God. When progress became a purely human millennialism, reverence for progress was no longer worship of God but veneration of humanity" (251). This attitude was anathema to Proudhon, who thus placed himself not only in opposition to Auguste Comte's positivist "Religion of Humanity," but also, perhaps more importantly, in opposition to Ludwig Feuerbach's assertion that the figure of God was a projection of idealized man: "Man, instead of adoring in God his sovereign and his guide, could and should look on him only as his antagonist. And this last consideration will suffice to make us reject humanism also, as tending invincibly, by the deification of humanity, to a religious restoration" (Proudhon 334). With astonishing foresight, Proudhon warns against the dangers implied in worshipping any idol, be it a religious godhead or the glorification of a man or woman. As an absolute misotheist, Proudhon argues that one must declare war on any deity whatsoever. In his eyes, it is as noxious to worship God as it would be to "worship" Homer, Marx, science, or nature. Worship itself is the problem, and if humanism provides secular objects of worship, even the more abstract notions of truth and progress, then humanism has to be resisted as well.

This attitude clearly contrasts with that of the twentieth-century British journalist and novelist Rebecca West, who elevated the human qualities of courage, compassion, and artistic creation to an almost divine level. In this, she is actually a descendant of nineteenth-century bourgeois agnostics who, according to James Turner, sought in art the uplifting, quasi-spiritual potential that had previously been exclusively the domain of religion: "Unbelievers, needing religion, transformed it into art. . . . As avatar of the human spiritual values, art ascended the throne abdicated by God" (Turner 253). One could argue, in this context, that the struggle against God can have two basic possible outcomes and that Proudhon and West represent the two different poles on this spectrum. On the one side stands West, whose spiritual yearning is such that it sets up an alternative object of worship, in this case art. In her long essay on the meaning of literature, *The Strange Necessity*, West talks of "this crystalline concentration of glory, this deep and serene and intense emotion that I feel before the greatest works of art" (195); she goes on to elaborate on "the intense exaltation which comes to our knowledge of the greatest works of art" (196), and refers to the "transcendent joy" (197) of beholding the works of artists. The language is palpably religious ("glory," "serene and intense emotion," "exaltation," "transcendent"), indicating a strong spiritual engagement with works of art that shows elements of worship. Such idealism contrasts strongly with Proudhon, who declares war against all idols, including God and all man-made god-substitutes. As for art, Proudhon mocks the idealistic view that art is inherently humanizing: "It has been supposed that art can be sufficient in itself and that, all else extinct, it would have the power to revive the dead and ennoble humanity. This is to be misled by the grossest sophistry" ("Art" 387). Proudhon further argues that any humanistic idealization of man, any vision of the perfectibility of his works, constitutes merely a phase of transition, allowing man "to fall back immediately into the arms of religion; so that in the last analysis all that the world will have gained by the denial of God will be the resurrection of God" (333). This is a remarkably perceptive and almost prophetic analysis.

In his comprehensive study of nineteenth-century deicide, A. N. Wilson comes to the very same conclusion, although he does not mention Proudhon. Bent on skewering George Bernard Shaw, whose progressive socialism did not prevent him from admiring Hitler and Stalin in his later years, Wilson broadens his argument to include all the ardent social revolutionaries of Shaw's generation, insisting that "dethroning God, that generation found it impossible to leave the sanctuary open. They put man in His place, which had the paradoxical effect not of elevating human nature but of demeaning it to depths of cruelty, depravity and stupidity unparalleled in human history" (304). As regards fascist and communist totalitarianisms, then, Proudhon's fear seems to be borne out, with a "new god" of ideological absolutism stepping in as a substitute object of veneration. Thus, Proudhon's admonition to get rid of *all* the gods—both human and superhuman—is directed both at religious authorities and at the sway of what would later be known as totalitarian rulers and their ideologies. At the same time, however, Proudhon's warning disregards man's demonstrated need for transcendent ideals and an urge to worship.

Because of his uncompromising and absolute hatred of all divinities, and because he made such an eloquent and detailed case against God, Pierre-Joseph Proudhon is a titan of misotheism. His reasoning for the rejection of God and religion appears to emerge directly from the political ideology of anarchism, of which Proudhon was, of course, an early and influential proponent. He was also, it should be noted, a supporter of pacifist anarchism, dealing with ideas rather than with direct political action, which earned him the scorn of his erstwhile friend, Karl Marx, who rejected the arguments of Proudhon's *Philosophy of Poverty* in his own treatise, mockingly titled *The Poverty of Philosophy*.

It may surprise somewhat that the man who cried "God is evil" was a mild-mannered person of kindly disposition. In Proudhon, we are not dealing with a fiery revolutionary but with a secular humanist who refused to deify humanity, who believed that social order should be voluntary, and who had a passionate—though perhaps impractical—interest in justice and peace.

Mikhail Bakunin

Among Proudhon's fellow anarchists, Mikhail Bakunin (1814–1876) was instrumental in making misotheism part of a more closely circumscribed political and economic rationale. Born into an aristocratic household in a small town 150 miles north of Moscow, Bakunin first embarked on a conventional career as a Russian army officer. But after beginning to study philosophy in Moscow and meeting the political writer and activist Aleksandr Herzen, he became radicalized, and in 1842 he left Russia for Paris, where he associated with the likes of Proudhon, Marx, and George Sand. Bakunin's life was marked by repeated and prolonged imprisonment. He was first jailed in St. Petersburg for his role in the Czech uprising of 1848, and after eleven years of incarceration he was transferred to a prison camp in Siberia from which he escaped in 1862. After making his way to London, he joined the First International, a federation of workers' groups founded in 1864 as the International Working Men's Association, but in a conflict over the association's participation in parliamentary elections, which he opposed, Bakunin lost against the faction of Karl Marx and was excluded from the Second International. In the 1870s, he settled in various places in Switzerland, then a safe haven for anarchists and socialists of various stripes, and began work on his two most influential treatises, *Statism and Anarchy* (1873), which laid out the basis of his collectivist anarchism, and *God and the State* (1871), a prolonged polemic against Christianity's complicity in the state's oppression and exploitation of the people.

Bakunin's book *God and the State* popularized the thesis that divine authority is directly linked to state authority and that both are used as justifications of slavery. While Proudhon's argument with God concerns the nature of Providence, Bakunin's is simply authority itself. His hostility against God is based on the master-slave dichotomy, and he denounces the Almighty in the name of social justice and the liberation of the exploited lower classes. If God is a symbol of top-down hierarchies and if he represents the arrogance of power, then the masses must rise up in struggle not only against the industrial bosses but against the celestial boss as well. Bakunin's struggle against institutional authority is a candle that burns at both ends, since it strives to consume the continuum of state power from both the political and the religious sides. Despite the explicitly socioeconomic basis of his analysis, visceral hatred of God appears to be the force that drives Bakunin's undertaking. Consider this personal attack, which recalls Paine's deistic fury against the Christian personal god:

> Jehovah, who of all the good gods adored by men was certainly the most jealous, the most vain, the most ferocious, and the most unjust, the most bloodthirsty, the most despotic, and the most hostile to human dignity and liberty—Jehovah had just created Adam and Eve, to satisfy we know not what caprice; no doubt to while away his time, which must weigh heavy on his hands in his eternal egoistic solitude, or that he might have some new slaves. (10)

At first sight, this diatribe is almost undistinguishable from the polemics of either Thomas Paine or James Mill. But, in the last resort, Bakunin despised those thinkers' piety, including their notion of a "Supreme Being, the abstract and sterile God of the deists" (80). To Bakunin, deistic idealism was merely a tool in the hands of the capitalist bourgeoisie, whose

> boldly avowed object was the reconciliation of Revolution with Reaction, or, to use the language of the school, of the principle of liberty with that of authority, and naturally to the advantage of the latter. This reconciliation signified: in politics, the taking away of popular liberty for the benefit of bourgeois rule, represented by the monarchical and constitutional state; in philosophy, the deliberate submission of free reason to the eternal principles of faith. (86)

Any vestige of religious belief, then, including the deistic abstraction, is a thorn in the eyes of the anarchist liberationist. Hence, the insistent pairing of religious belief with slavery, as evidenced in Bakunin's emphasis on the exploitative nature of God in his relationship to mankind. This argument is summed up in Bakunin's best-known misotheistic pronouncement: "God being master, man is the slave" (24). In this view, God stands between man and his liberty, which is as much as saying that God becomes anathema to anarchists. Indeed, Bakunin leaves no doubt about the matter: *"The idea of God implies the abdication of human reason and justice; it is the most decisive negation of human liberty"* (25).

Bakunin's misotheistic approach, arguing against a god whom he considered to be the invention of the collective mind, reveals him to be indebted to Feuerbachian rationalism: "Consequently, the religious heaven is nothing but a mirage in which man, exalted by ignorance and faith, discovers his own image, but enlarged and reversed—that is *divinized*. The history of religions . . . is nothing, therefore, but the development of the collective intelligence and conscience of mankind" (23). But if God is merely a collective mental concept, a shared fantasy, then the struggle against God and the struggle for human liberty must also begin in the mind, not in the material conditions of man. As one of the leading French anarchist thinkers and friend of Bakunin, Élisée Reclus, put it: "The external form of society must alter in correspondence with the impelling force within; there is no better established historical fact. The sap makes the tree and gives it leaves and flowers, the blood makes the man, the ideas make the society" (8). That is but one formulation of the anarchist notion of deterministic idealism, a belief that slavery and oppression must be overcome by first changing fundamental habits of the mind, which goes, of course, directly against Marxist materialism. Anarchists argue that the slave mentality *can* be exchanged for the revolutionary mentality if one is sufficiently exposed to the ideas of liberation and social change. While this grassroots approach has proven to be far less effective than the top-down communist party apparatus in the political arena, in spiritual terms, one cannot help but agreeing that the mind is really the principal battlefield of the rebellion against God. Note in this context how Bakunin tries to be all-inclusive in defining the various forms that the figure of God takes in the collective conscious. He rails against

> the fallacies and truly revolting absurdities to which one is inevitably led by this imagination of a God, let him be considered as a personal being, the creator and organizer of worlds; or even as impersonal, a kind of divine soul spread over the whole universe and constituting thus its eternal principle; or let him be an idea, infinite and divine, always present and active in the world, and always manifested by the totality of material and definite things. (13)

This carefully worded catalogue makes it clear that Bakunin's indictment against the God-idea aims to be as sweeping and inclusive as possible. In the final account, it does not matter to him whether the object of his enmity is Yahweh, or the impersonal abstraction of the deists, or whether it is the panentheistic *spiritus mundi*—he declares war on all of these forms of divinity. Thus, although Bakunin does not believe in a personal God, while Proudhon still held a vestigial belief in such a deity, both anarchists agreed in their opposition to any divine object of worship.

But what about Christ? While Proudhon has little to say on this account, Bakunin recognizes Jesus's revolutionary potential, saying that "he was the preacher of the poor, the friend and counselor of the wretched, of the ignorant, of the slaves and women, and that by these last he was much loved" (75). He further acknowledges that originally the Christian "propagandism was directed almost exclusively among the people, unfortunate and degraded by slavery. This was the first awakening, the first intellectual revolt of the proletariat" (75). Of course, Bakunin would not be an anarchist were he to bow down before the apotheosis of Christ. To Bakunin, Christ was a legitimate revolutionary only insofar as he sees in him a kind of protoanarchist preacher of liberty. However, he finds fault with the fact that Christ's message was not specifically directed at the mind "of the ancient proletariat" (77). Moreover, church fathers made sure that Christ's message was modified into an essentially antiworldly dogma, what Bakunin calls "the Christian absurdity," that is, the belief that "the living being, the real world, were considered thereafter as nothing, whereas the product of man's abstractive faculty, the last and supreme abstraction . . . the true nothing, God, is proclaimed the only real eternal, all powerful being. The real All is declared nothing, and the absolute nothing All" (76).

Thus, Bakunin's war against God proceeds on three fronts: first, he attacks "the very brutal, selfish and cruel person of Jehovah" (74); second, he goes on to promote the idea of God as being at the root and heart of human bondage; and third, he theorizes God as being the "true nothing," the supreme void created by collective human fantasizing. This last, rationalist move is crucial to conveying the anarchist doctrine that the struggle for liberation begins in the mind and that the true subversion of authority consists in the recognition that we as individuals create the mental preconditions for the existence of bondage or freedom. From this radical standpoint, civil liberties and social justice are incompatible with the existence of religious belief. Of course, this is a highly partisan take on liberty, and one that is incompatible with the larger view of civic freedom, which includes the right to practice religion.

Peter Kropotkin

If Bakunin came from a prosperous Russian family, then Peter Kropotkin (1842–1921) outdid him in privilege, even carrying the legitimate title of prince, derived from his father's line. He joined a prestigious military school in St. Petersburg as a young adult, abandoned his princely title soon thereafter, and began reading literature about the plight of the peasants, an unlikely preoccupation for a Russian nobleman. He joined the army in 1862, but held mostly administrative posts and participated in geographical expeditions rather than combat missions. From 1872 on, when he joined the International Workman's Union (that is, the First International) in Switzerland, he dedicated the rest of his life to anarchist agitation and propaganda, writing many tracts, among them *Mutual Aid: A Factor of Evolution* (1902), in which he outlined his optimistic determinism, according to which evolution did not select in favor of the fittest but in favor of the species and the individuals who excelled at cooperation. Kropotkin's views were closer to Proudhon's principle of mutual aid than to Bakunin's emphasis on collectivization. Like Proudhon, Kropotkin was mild-mannered, and by some he was considered saintly, while, like Bakunin, he shuttled from place to place, living in Switzerland, France, England, and Russia for years at a time, often harassed or expelled by the government of his current host nation. After the Russian Revolution of 1917, Kropotkin was one of the first to denounce the seizure of power by the Bolsheviks, and he predicted that the Russian Revolution would be betrayed.

Kropotkin's pronouncements on the topic of religion are devoid of the visceral hatred against God—or the idea of God—that Bakunin and Proudhon expressed in their treatises. Still, his critical reflections are suffused by a similar resistance against the fusion of Christianity with the state, and they emphasize the role of Christianity as facilitating the act of enslavement. In "The Shortcomings of

Christianity" (n.d.), Kropotkin echoes Bakunin's categorical rejection of authority by stating that Christianity lost its authentic moorings as a religion of liberty by allying itself with political power: "Christianity dealt itself a blow from which it has not recovered to this day. It became the religion of the State" (133). More central to Kropotkin's argument is his analysis of the institution of slavery. He denounces the fact that "the Apostles St. Peter and St. Paul present as a fundamental Christian virtue the obedience of subjects to the established authorities as to God's anointed with 'fear and trepidation' and the obedience of slaves to their masters" (132). This is a reference to St. Paul's instruction in Ephesians (6:5–9) that slaves be obedient to their masters, an attitude also attributed to St. Augustine. Kropotkin argues that "various people whom the Church included among the saints, approved slavery, and St. Augustine even vindicated it, asserting that sinners became slaves in punishment for their sins" (133). He goes on to give a secular explanation for the end of slavery: "It was the Revolution and not the Church that abolished slavery in the French Colonies and serfdom in France itself. But during the first half of the nineteenth century, trading in negro-slaves flourished in Europe and in America and the Church was silent" (133). This anarchist emphasis on slavery as having been condoned by the church and its god may well be the underlying reason why the African American writer Zora Neale Hurston (1891–1960) wrote in her novel *Their Eyes Were Watching God* a denunciation of divinity that closely resembles Bakunin's dictum that "all religions are cruel, all founded on blood" ("God and the State" 25). And if Hurston was familiar with anarchist literature at all, it is likely that she had read Kropotkin's devastating conclusion that "Christianity proved impotent in the struggle against the greed of the slave-owners and the slave-dealers. Slavery endured until the slaves themselves began to revolt" (133). Of course, it is equally true that Christianity provided slaves with a basis of spiritual faith and hope for redemption that lightened the burdens of their existence. It is hardly to be doubted that Christianity gave some meaning to the suffering of the slaves, but it is also true that Christianity's injunction to bear oppression patiently in hopes of a better afterlife, as well as Christianity's emphasis on seeing hardships as punishment for original sin, created conditions favorable to the maintenance of an exploited slave class, both on the part of the masters and the slaves.

Friedrich Nietzsche

Following the accounts of Proudhon's and Bakunin's politically motivated misotheism, one may be tempted to conclude that God-hatred
is the exclusive domain of leftist ideologues. Obviously, this is not a
hard-and-fast rule since Friedrich Nietzsche (1844–1900), one of the
nineteenth century's most vocal misotheists, was as far from the left
as can be. And because his dominant passion was the death of God,
Nietzsche is an exponent of absolute misotheism. Significantly,
though, the first time the statement "God is dead" appeared in print,
it did so in a literary, imaginative context. In his treatise *The Gay
Science* (1882), Nietzsche elaborates a parable-like episode about a
fictional madman who one day rushes into the town square to shout
at his irreligious contemporaries, " 'Where has God gone?' he cried. 'I
shall tell you. We have killed him—you and I. We are his murderers' "
(181). To Nietzsche, this scene represents a foundational moment in
modern history, and he weaves a fictional screen thin enough to let
the reader see his own likeness behind the madman's antics. According to Erich Heller, "[Nietzsche] is the madman, breaking with his
sinister news into the market-place complacency of the Pharisees of
unbelief" (95).

But Nietzsche was far from complacent about his radical
announcement. Heller comments that "[Nietzsche] never said that
there was no God, but that the Eternal had been vanquished by
Time. . . . It is like a cry mingled of despair and triumph "(93). In other
words, Nietzsche was not an atheist, and neither was he an agnostic.
Heller compared him to a wrestler with god (like Jacob in Genesis 32):
"Nietzsche is just such a wrestler; except that in him the shadow of
Jacob merges with the shadow of Prometheus" (93). The reference to
Prometheus is appropriate in the context of Nietzsche's hatred for the
Almighty. Even as he continued to attack both Yahweh and Christ,
and even after declaring the death of God, he still manifested a powerful spiritual yearning and an admiration for pagan deities. His anti-
Christian hero, Zarathustra, after all, is a religious founder and poet
of spirituality. But Nietzsche goes further than Victorian misotheist
poets such as Swinburne and Thomson who advocated the revival of
older, pagan gods to replace the God of the Bible. Although sympathetic to this project, Nietzsche eventually shifted his allegiance to a
different kind of "new god."

Two years after *The Gay Science*, Nietzsche published what is arguably a kind of anti-Bible—*Thus Spake Zarathustra* (1883–85). The work as a whole is a hybrid mix of dramatic monologue, poetry, and theological treatise, but all in all, we can take it for granted that its protagonist, Zarathustra (named after Zoroaster, the founder of a Persian religious sect), functions as the mouthpiece for Nietzsche's own values and beliefs. Indeed, his rejection of Christian morality, together with his celebration of the will and of power are all at the center of Zarathustra's impassioned pleas for a radical transformation of values. The work once again contains the statement that *"God is dead!"* (6), but it goes further than *The Gay Science* by elaborating the consequences of that event: *"Dead are all the Gods: now do we desire the Superman to live"* (91). The Superman (or "Übermensch," also translated as "Overman") will be able to thrive only after the vanishing of God. The strong man, who is earthbound, true to his physical being, and an incarnation of will and power, becomes the new god of the future. To set up a version of man as the new god, Nietzsche took a gamble, as he himself knew perfectly well. He is reported as saying, "I am terrified by the thought of the sort of people who may one day invoke my authority" (quoted in Heller 92). It is a chillingly prophetic statement, given that, as Karl Jaspers noted, "the Nazis, with whom his turn of mind had nothing in common, took a large part of their vocabulary from him" (vii). But even though Nietzsche was not a protofascist, he certainly did not have any sympathy for the victims of economic or political exploitation.

In fact, he ridiculed the leftist protesters against God mentioned earlier in this chapter. In *Thus Spake Zarathustra*, we encounter the type of misotheist who could be a parody of Proudhon. During his wanderings, Nietzsche's Zarathustra encounters a weak, tottering "man who threw his limbs about like a maniac." The reason for this man's agitation, it turns out, is his enmity against God:

> Thus do I lie,
> Bend myself, twist myself, convulsed
> With all eternal torture
>   And smitten
> By thee, cruelest huntsman,
> Thou unfamiliar—God . . ."
> . . . .

> Not murder wilt thou,
> But torture, torture?
> For why—*me* torture,
> Thou mischief-loving, unfamiliar God?—(307)

It is interesting to note how Zarathustra reacts to this blasphemer: "[Zarathustra] could no longer restrain himself; he took his staff and struck the wailer with all his might. 'Stop this,' cried he to him with wrathful laughter, 'stop this, thou stage-player! Though false coiner! Thou liar from the very heart" (310). Zarathustra thus has no sympathy for the old man's impotent complaints against an overbearing god. Later in the book, Zarathustra encounters another frail old man, the "last pope," but this man's idea of God is directly in line with Zarathustra's own:

> When he was young, that God out of the Orient, then was he harsh and revengeful, and built himself a hell for the delight of his favourites. At last, however, he became old and soft and mellow and pitiful, more like a grandfather than a father, but most like a tottering old grandmother. There did he sit shriveled in his chimney-corner, fretting on account of his weak legs, world-weary, will-weary, and one day he suffocated of his all-too-great pity. (318)

This is a direct reference to Nietzsche's own preference for the Old Testament–style god who represented to him the only desirable attributes of divinity, namely, power, arrogance, and wrath. This is the "young . . . God out of the Orient." By comparison, anything that smacks of loving-kindness of the "old and soft" god is anathema to Nietzsche. In other words, Nietzsche does not side with those misotheists who, like the anarchists, accuse God of being the incarnation of ultimate power and overbearing authority; instead, he attacks the soft, flabby god who has lost his fierce glory.

The last word in this matter is contained in *The Anti-Christ* (1888), Nietzsche's final indictment of Christianity and its god. Note the word-play in the title, which is both a polemic against Christ and Nietzsche's prideful assumption of the role of the Antichrist. In this book, Nietzsche goes completely against Bakunin's antiauthoritarianism by proclaiming "What is good?—Whatever augments the feeling of power, the will to power, power itself, in man" (22). The addendum "in man" is of course crucial, as Nietzsche recognizes none but human superpowers. That there will always be victims of this drive to power is a cost society should be willing to pay: "The weak and the botched shall perish: first principle of *our* charity. And one should help them to it" (22). Evidently, this ethos of the Übermensch has no room for Christian virtues of compassion and charity. Although he calls his treatise the *Anti-Christ*, he takes aim equally at the New Testament conception of God the father. According to Nietzsche, this benevolent deity, "the god as the patron of the sick, the god as a spinner of cobwebs, the god as a spirit, is one of the most corrupt concepts that has ever been set up in the world" (34). From this basis of enmity against the Christian god, he further denounces a Christian bias against the sociopolitical elites and a disdain for the body: "Christian, again, is all deadly enmity to the rulers of the earth, to the 'aristocratic.' . . . Christian is all hatred of the senses, of joy in the senses, of joy in general" (37). He ends this diatribe by mocking the "'equality of souls before God'—this fraud, this *pretext* for the [rancor] of all the base minded, this explosive concept, ending in revolution, the modern idea, and the notion of overthrowing the whole social order— this *Christian* dynamite" (90–91). Thus, rather than condemning Christianity for implanting the slave mentality in its followers, as the anarchists were arguing, here he accuses Christianity of fostering a basis for social revolution. Nietzsche worries that Christianity provides the oppressed with hopes for social equality and gives them the moral high ground over their masters. This is the very opposite of the position taken up by the socialists and anarchists. Bakunin, for example, attacks Yahweh precisely because he represents absolute authority, and he regrets that Christ did not play a more decisive role in advancing the cause of social egalitarianism. By contrast, Nietzsche finds fault with the Christian god for not being powerful enough. He bemoans the fact that the ancient god of wrath has been declawed in the New Testament, and he hates Christ for having implanted ideas of equality and humanitarianism in people. Both Nietzsche and Bakunin see in religion the betrayal of human potentialities and the root cause of the current state of dissatisfaction; however, beyond these basic premises their arguments are driven by entirely antithetical political agendas and philosophical principles.

Nietzsche missed no opportunity to ridicule leftists, as evidenced in a section of *Twilight of the Idols* (1889) titled "The Christian and the Anarchist": "When the anarchist, as the mouthpiece of the decaying strata of society, raises his voice in splendid indignation of 'right,' 'justice,' 'equal rights,' he is only groaning under the burden of his ignorance. . . . To bewail one's lot is always despicable: it is always the outcome of weakness. . . . The Christian and the Anarchist—both are decadents" (86–87). By lumping together Christianity and anarchism as equally decadent, he emphasizes the two ideologies' mission to improve the lot of unfortunate and downtrodden masses, but he is less mindful of the vast differences that exist between the two camps, notably the fact that anarchists were anticlerical to a fault and often misotheists as well. Nietzsche's indiscriminate condemnation of Christians and anarchists reveals his need to distance his God-hatred from the liberal, democratic, and revolutionary program that normally fuels that impulse. This anomalous position has had few, if any, imitators over the course of time.

It has become something of a commonplace to consider Nietzsche's dictum "God is dead" as less an expression of active deicide than as a reflection of the fact that scientific advances and rapid technological developments had already killed God. As Camus put it: "Nietzsche did not form a project to kill God. He found Him dead in the soul of his contemporaries" (*Rebel* 68). However, this view disregards the visceral hatred for the concept of the divine that inspired Nietzsche's tirades. Camus's view that Nietzsche simply gave voice to the demise of a real, vital god in the hearts of men, appears to me a fallacy. But this misinterpretation flared up again in the so-called death-of-God theology of the 1960s (*Time* magazine at Easter 1966 famously printed the question "Is God Dead?" in bold red letters on a black background). Leading exponents of this movement, notably Thomas Altizer (the author of the *Time* article), William Hamilton, and Paul van Buren, took the premise that God is already dead as the starting point for their own theological speculations. Taking God's death for granted, they attempted to construct a new, forward-looking theology on the basis of Christology, that is, a religious position that favors a Christ-centered religious ethic. For them, it is simply a given that God is dead, and they expend no hostility in denouncing Yahweh or lambasting any of his biblical manifestations. They are Unitarian theists insofar as they accept Christ as the divine center of ethics and spirituality, while building a new theology based on a dismantling of the Trinity. Discarding the solution of the "Übermensch," they emphasize, variously, the message of freedom in Christ (van Buren), the social function of Christ's suffering (Hamilton), and the mystical aspect of Christ's eschatological dimension (Altizer).

It must be one of the great ironies in the history of ideas that Nietzsche's misotheism, particularly his loathing of Christ, gave rise to a theological school that not only circumvented misotheism entirely but emphasized Christology above conventional Trinitarianism. Thus, it appears once again that people have a tendency to overlook God-hatred when they come face-to-face with it, or that, at the very least, they pretend that it is nonexistent. The misotheism that underlies Nietzsche's message was carefully anesthetized by the death-of-god theologians who thereby failed to grapple with the most fundamental aspect of Nietzsche's obsession with deicide.

Feminists

After the cometlike appearance of misotheism in the work of deists, utilitarians, and anarchists from the end of the eighteenth century onward, members of another movement can be said to have belatedly thrown down the gauntlet to God toward the end of the nineteenth century: feminists. For first-wave feminism, the pursuit of suffrage, equity, and basic rights for women was a revolutionary undertaking much in keeping with the spirit of Thomas Paine's declaration of human rights and his insistence on individual liberty one hundred years earlier. Also in keeping with Paine's rejection of the church and the Bible as obstacles to the development of full civil liberties, some early feminists similarly linked the oppression of women to the pervasiveness of religious ideas and to institutionalized Christianity. In a memorial speech given in 1906 in honor of Thomas Paine, Julia H. Severance put it this way: "Paine's every word and work has been for Freedom. The church has ever been the relentless enemy of Liberty" (9). On this basis, Severance goes on to indict the role played by the Christian creed in keeping women in bondage:

> Wherever you find a church, I care not under what name it rests, be it Catholic or Protestant, there you find an enemy to Liberty. Woman has ever found in the church her worst enemy and oppressor. In the Bible she is taught that her creation was an after thought and that she was made solely for man's convenience. Moses legalized the sale of

daughters. Paul's contemptible doctrines in regard to women have been used as chains to bind her in her degradation. (9–10)

Significantly, this feminist protest is directed against church and Bible, not against God *per se*. The same holds true for Elizabeth Cady Stanton (1815–1902), one of the most vocal American suffragists of the nineteenth century. In collaboration with Susan B. Anthony, she was largely responsible for turning the drive for women's vote into a tightly organized national movement. As many of her suffragist followers were not aware, she had been an outspoken critic of Christianity, publishing a feminist study of the Bible titled *The Woman's Bible*, in 1895. While Stanton's revisionist reading of the Bible blasts specific misogynistic passages in it, she did not dare openly rebel against God the father. In fact, she states in her introduction, "the only points in which I differ from all ecclesiastical teachings is that I do not believe that any man ever saw or talked with God, I do not believe that God inspired the Mosaic code, or told the historians what they say he did about women, for all the religions on the face of the earth degrade her" (12). Though informed by rational skepticism, Stanton still operates within a properly religious framework. Her impulse is reformist, not iconoclastic, trying to make Christianity conform better with the enlightened, emancipated role of women and aiming to blunt the passages of the Bible that are most demeaning to women. Hence, her attack against the Bible does not so much contradict scripture as it draws attention to its inherent misogyny: "The Bible teaches that woman brought sin and death into the world, that she precipitated the fall of the race, that she was arraigned before the judgment seat of Heaven, tried, condemned and sentenced. Marriage for her was to be a condition of bondage" (7). This is the position of a radical suffragist, who based her struggle on a legalistic basis, even if the law she aimed to reform was God's law.

This is, of course, only the beginning of the feminist critique of religion. As a rule, first-wave feminists did not dare to proclaim open hostility against God. At most, they confided their radical disbelief to private and unpublished musings, while experimenting with misotheistic ideas in the form of fiction. These women needed to tread lightly when it came to misotheism, even during the stormy days of modernism. For instance, one of the sharpest rebukes against God was written by the British socialist-feminist Rebecca West (1892–1983). The essay in question bears the Nietzschean title "The New God," but it remained unpublished and exists only as a corrected typescript, possibly the outline for a speech or the draft for an article that she had thought of submitting. Besides West, a handful of other modernist women also took the liberty of expressing their misotheistic convictions, however veiled. Virginia Woolf (1882–1941), for example, admitted her disbelief in her correspondence, as evidenced in this quote from a letter to her sister, Vanessa Bell: "I mean, there's something obscene in a living person sitting by the fire and believing in God" (*Letters* 3:458). Another private letter exclaims: "How repulsive the Xtian [*sic*] religion as conveyed by the Xtian clergyman is" (*Letters* 6: 196). Of course, such iconoclasm was almost a given in the circle of Bloomsbury, which attracted radicals of almost every stripe, including freethinkers, anti-imperialists, experimental artists, and innovative economists. And although Woolf was obviously influenced by her nonconformist father, Sir Leslie Stephen, her unbelief went further than his. Leslie Stephen, who had been ordained as an Anglican priest, turned agnostic after he could not reconcile his conception of the Christian deity with the problem of evil. In fact, he is credited with having popularized the term "agnostic," coined earlier by the English biologist Thomas Henry Huxley. But while Stephen advocated a secular ethic based on utilitarian principles, Woolf nurtured a deeper, more militant rejection of God and religion. We need look no further than Woolf's novel *Mrs. Dalloway* (1925) to be exposed to the belief that dare not speak its name. To begin with, the novel carries distinctly anti-Christian overtones. The most despicable of all unpleasant characters populating this novel, the aptly named Miss Kilman, is also the only self-declared Christian of the book. Confronted with Clarissa Dalloway's infinitely higher social and intellectual standing, pious Miss Kilman is given over to vindictive thoughts: "If only she could make [Mrs. Dalloway] weep; could ruin her; humiliate her, bring her to her knees crying. . . . It was to be a religious victory" (125). Besides portraying religiosity as compatible with vindictiveness and hypocrisy, Woolf also fires off a broadside against God himself.

One of the central characters of the novel, Peter Walsh, an old friend and still an admirer, ruminates about Mrs. Dalloway's nonconformist religious views as follows: "possibly she said to herself . . . those ruffians, the Gods, shan't have it all their own way,—her notion being that the Gods, who never lost a chance of hurting, thwarting and spoiling human lives, were seriously put out if, all the same, you behaved like a lady. . . . Later, she wasn't so positive perhaps; she thought there were no Gods; no one was to blame; and so she evolved this atheist's religion of doing good for the sake of goodness" (77–78). In this passage, personal antipathy against God precedes the complete rejection of belief in the deity. Thus, in Walsh's recollection, Mrs. Dalloway progressed from contempt for gods to complete disbelief. The relevance of this statement is augmented by the fact that Mrs. Dalloway is in fact a fictional stand-in for Woolf herself; moreover, Walsh's assessment of Mrs. Dalloway's spiritual rebellion is nowhere explicitly contradicted in the novel. In fact, Peter Walsh turns out to be a keen observer and confidant of Mrs. Dalloway, so that his assessment of her attitude needs to be taken seriously. To me, Peter Walsh's recollection of Mrs. Dalloway's religious radicalism allows us a glimpse into the "religious unconscious" of Virginia Woolf herself. Again, as with Zora Neale Hurston, the female writer uses indirection in handling her misotheistic thoughts, having a character sum up the antireligious stance of another character, who, in turn represents Woolf's own aversion to Christianity and its god.

Around the same time, the British feminist writer (Margaret) Storm Jameson (1891–1986) published *The Clash* (1922), a novel whose opening chapters chronicle the intellectual and moral awakening of a girl named Elizabeth who is introduced to Bible study just as tragedy strikes in her neighborhood. Two extraordinarily beautiful and charming children have been killed by lightning, an event that Elizabeth attributes to divine fiat. When the local vicar invokes Job's conventional acquiescence to God's will, intoning the words "God gave and God has taken" (19), Elizabeth suddenly "stepped out of the shadow of the bed curtains. 'He is a beast, that God,' she said" (19). After hearing Elizabeth's blasphemy, the visiting vicar feels compelled to (in Milton's phrase) justify the ways of God to man. His explanation is rendered in indirect speech as follows:

> The capricious Power who intrigued so vigorously in [the Bible's] pages, executing swift vengeance, was the ruling God of this world. . . . The vicar entered upon the tale of divine punishments. It was a long one, and Elizabeth, who remembered many of them perfectly, lost interest. She had, moreover, esteemed lightly enough the deity of

whom it was said that it is not strange He has so few friends. . . .
Elizabeth conceived some dislike of a god who hated defiant beauty
and prepared a burning rod for straight-limbed youth. (19)

What is particularly significant about this passage is the fact that it portrays the "natural" reasoning of an innocent child who is not yet conditioned by ideology and cant. Elizabeth simply compares her experience
to what she had read in the Bible, and the result is misotheism—a child's
misotheism, that is. Also, the novel clearly endorses a heretical point of
view. The casual invocation of divine caprice and the comment about the
long tale of divine punishments, both deliberately irreverent, are not
representing a character's idiosyncratic point of view so much as the
narrator's more authoritative position.

As we have seen, feminism provided a whole new platform for
attacks against God and religion, though not all of the feminists'
attacks were inspired by explicitly gendered analyses of religion and
divinity. Both Woolf and Jameson portray characters whose enmity
against God springs from purely moral considerations. But the feminist critique of God took a new turn under the aegis of second-wave
feminism and feminist theology. Writing in 1979, Naomi Goldenberg
leaves no doubt that the feminist struggle against patriarchy in the
worldly sphere should carry over into the religious sphere as well:
"By challenging the authority of males on earth, feminists make
effective onslaughts on male authority in heaven" (36). Goldenberg
supports Elizabeth Cady Stanton's view that women who embrace
traditional Christianity lend support to their own denigration:
"women are led to perceive it right and natural that men should
rule their earth the way God rules His heaven" (90). And, because of
"the misogyny which smolders within the Christian tradition" (90),
Goldenberg does not see a reform potential within Christianity itself.
Even Christ is denied the power to grant women greater freedom and
justice: "Jesus Christ cannot symbolize the liberation of women. A
culture that maintains a masculine image for its highest divinity cannot allow its women to experience themselves as the equals of its
men. In order to develop a theology of women's liberation, feminists
have to leave Christ and Bible behind them" (22). This clearly
goes beyond Stanton's project, but significantly the impulse behind
Goldenberg's feminist initiative is a departure from the patriarchal
values inscribed into Christianity and not mainly a misotheistic attack

against God. In Goldenberg's analysis, misotheism is merely a temporary phase in the struggle to overcome the sexism of the Judeo-Christian religion: "In contemporary feminist culture and in the next few years ahead, the father will live in the hatred of women who need a god to blame. . . . While we are growing, many women will keep the father-god alive in their need for a psychic figure to represent negative feeling" (83). Goldenberg is aware that continuously "hating the father" (83) of patriarchal monotheism implies a continued belief in his existence and power. Contrary to this misotheistic position, she champions an alternative spirituality that is based on a mystical worship of the female goddess said to dwell in every woman. This mystical spirituality within the female self can be accessed through community-based ritual and incantation, that is to say, through patently non-Christian, shamanistic, mystical practices. The practitioners of this religion "place divinity or supernatural power within the person. In a very practical sense they have turned religion into psychology" (89).

In the eyes of this late-twentieth-century feminist theologian, misotheism is simply not a viable position of resistance against religious misogyny. What is needed, instead, is an affirmative orientation that is feminine, mystical, communal, ecological, and possibly polytheistic. Indeed, when Rosemary Ruether speaks about the need to rediscover that "our kinship with all earth creatures is global, linking us to the whole living Gaia today" (*Gaia and God* 252), she is invoking a modern version of pantheism. This new strain of earth-goddess spirituality ("*Gaia* is the word for the Greek Earth Goddess" [Ruether 4]) is seen as not only an alternative form of female-centered spirituality, but also as a sociopolitical alternative to the outdated patriarchal basis of religious monotheism. In Ruether's candid formulation, "an ecological spirituality needs to be built on three premises: the transience of selves, the living interdependency of all things, and the value of the personal in communion" (251). The notion of a personal god has been removed to make room for the general ecological love of the earth and the care of its complex biological systems. Such a mutualist, pacifist, eco-friendly social philosophy or quasi-theology simply bypasses the misotheist's antagonistic relationship with an oppressive god. On the contrary, Ruether rejects both the premise that "the 'Goddess' we need for ecological well-being is the reverse of the God we have had in the

Semitic monotheistic traditions" (247) and the radical feminist position that feminine values ought to substitute for patriarchal ideology: "Perhaps we need a more imaginative solution to these traditional oppositions than simply their reversal" (247). The solution she refers to is, of course, the ecofeminist healing that stands at the center of Ruether's project: "The goal of this quest is earth healing, a healed relationship between men and women, between classes and nations, and between humans and the earth" (1). The way to bring about these ecological and pacifist changes is to adjust the mental consciousness of the feminist believer. This internalization of the religious and political quests is reminiscent of the radical idealism of nineteenth-century anarchists, who also saw the beginning of significant social changes in the realm of consciousness. Naomi Goldenberg gives this idea the requisite psychological focus: "In the new age of changes for our gods, Christ and Yahweh will no longer behave as egotistical, spoiled children in our psyches. . . . They will remind us of the patriarchal monotheism which we have outgrown but which we will need to remember" (83). This emphasis on the psychological effects of religion and on an outgrowing and leaving behind of the father god (rather than continuing to struggle with him) resonates strongly with the work of the founder of psychoanalysis.

Sigmund Freud

Approaching the relationship between man and God as analogous to a father-son conflict, Sigmund Freud (1856–1939) thought about religion as an Oedipal drama writ large. In his writings on religion, especially *Totem and Taboo* (1913) and *The Future of an Illusion* (1927), Freud argues that religion is not only indicative of a shared mental imbalance but, more importantly, that worship of a deity signals an unresolved Oedipus complex (that is, the usually unconscious desire to possess the parent of the opposite sex and feelings of hostility or jealousy toward the parent of the same sex). He states that "religion would thus be the universal obsessional neurosis of humanity; like the obsessional neurosis of children, it arose out of the Oedipus complex, out of the relation to the father" (*Illusion* 55). In other words, religious practices are an obstacle toward reaching full mental health and intellectual maturity because they constitute a blockage of the Oedipal resolution involving the über-father in the sky. As for the association between God and the image of the father, Freud argues in *Totem and Taboo* that "the psychoanalysis of individual human beings . . . teaches us with quite special insistence that the God of each of them is formed in the likeness of his father, that his personal relation to God depends on his relation to his father in the flesh and oscillates and changes along with that relation, and that at bottom God is nothing other than an exalted father" (147). What that relation with the father looks like, in particular, is spelled out in *The Future of an Illusion*: "The child's attitude to its father is coloured by a peculiar ambivalence. The father himself constitutes a danger for the child. . . . Thus it fears him no less than it longs for him and admires him. . . . When the growing individual finds that he is destined to remain a child for ever . . . he creates for himself the gods whom he dreads, whom he seeks to propitiate, and whom he nevertheless entrusts with his own protection" (30). Thus Freud arrives at his opposition to religion from two separate perspectives: first, he identifies religion as a mild form of insanity because it treats as real that which only exists in the imaginary realm; and second, he accuses religion of retarding the psychosocial development by side-stepping the struggle with the father, which is integral to overcoming the Oedipus complex. According to Freud, the Oedipus complex will be laid to rest only when the boy internalizes the rules of the father and comes to emulate rather than jealously resent him. No such emulation is possible with regard to the Almighty, who inspires in the worshipper a never-ending ambivalence of awed inferiority coupled with a longing for acceptance. A religious upbringing, in this view, defers the completion of a key factor of psychic development and locks believers into pre-Oedipal immaturity. Conversely, a civilization that sheds its religious fear and veneration of the gods will strengthen the role played by the superego (that is, the set of moral standards and rules of conduct internalized by successfully socialized individuals). Freud comments: "Such a strengthening of the super-ego is a most precious cultural asset in the psychological field" (*Illusion* 14). Naomi Goldenberg usefully sums up this dynamic as follows:

> Freud expresses nothing but contempt for Judaism and Christianity
> in all his writings about their effects on contemporary society. To

Freud, religions that worshipped a father-god were the most oppressive institutions in modern culture. In essay after essay Freud inveighed against religions-of-the-father for working to stunt human intellects and for encouraging people to stagnate in Oedipal dependency. (Goldenberg 29)

Obviously, the Oedipal scenario is only a speculative model, evolved in a specific sociocultural context (early twentieth-century patriarchal Viennese customs), whose fine points need not all be taken at face value. Still, in its insistence on the analogy between the heavenly father and the paterfamilias, it certainly has common sense on its side, as well as a good deal of historical evidence. While Freud did not really explore the historical ramifications of his hypothesis about the believer's unconscious rivalry with the deity, we can turn to the work of A. N. Wilson and Albert Camus for an interesting application of Freud's take on religion.

In his book *God's Funeral* (1999), Wilson exactly confirms the Oedipal theory developed above by applying it to the Victorian deicides, that is, those intellectuals, philosophers, and artists including Thomas Carlyle, Thomas Hardy, Charles Darwin, Charles Lyell (the great geologist), Herbert Spencer, Samuel Butler, and many others who contributed collectively to the understanding, summed up by Nietzsche, that the concept of God was either already dead or in its death throes. Wilson skillfully applies Freud's Oedipal drama to the persecution of God by these eminent Victorians. Apropos of Samuel Butler, Wilson writes:

As we read Butler's works and follow his life, we feel that the earthly father is attacked with the same fervour with which he set out to dethrone or disprove the Heavenly Father; and then again, as the wheel comes full circle, we sense that this ineradicable theological obsession, his inability to leave God the Father alone, has something to do with unconscious dramas buried in childhood. (240)

This clearly marks Butler as a misotheist because he did not simply attempt to remove God by disproving his existence; instead, he was consistently drawn back into disputes with God. And that is precisely the characteristic of enemies of God: they cannot "leave God the Father alone," which presumes some form of belief, however adversarial.

In the final analysis, Wilson explains the Victorian desire to slay God with the particular historical form that fatherhood took during this time in England:

> The Victorian Age produced the Victorian Father and the tension, peculiar to its time. . . . So, we might argue, it is in this age that we should expect men to discard belief in the Heavenly Father. . . . But equally, you could argue that the desire to *discard* God is not a rational thing: it is part of one's Oedipal need to assert oneself. We tell ourselves that God is dead, when what we mean is God is Dad, and we *wish* him dead. (249)

Wilson's historicizing of the phenomenon of deicide as a displacement of the patricidal impulse in reaction against the stern Victorian patriarch carries some persuasive weight. And his theory of nineteenth-century deicide does conform to Freud's argument that the relationship between man and the heavenly father is psychologically analogous to a man's relationship with his biological father. But Wilson parts company with Freud by emphatically rejecting the argument that shedding one's religious beliefs is a precondition for mental health. In the final analysis, Wilson does not see the killing of God the father as a milestone of human progress but rather as a temporary hitch in man's evolving religious sensibility. It is by turning to the thought of the existential philosopher of rebellion, Albert Camus, that we can further sharpen our understanding of the relationship both between sons and fathers and between men and gods.

Albert Camus

The sense of struggle with the father is evident in much of the writings by Albert Camus (1913–1960), the French existentialist philosopher, novelist, and member of the French resistance movement during World War II. His writings, especially his essays, betray his fascination with the moral and religious implications surrounding the son's usurpation of the father's throne. But Camus's fascination with the father-son conflict would at first sight seem to be surprising. In fact, his own father died shortly after Camus's birth, leaving him to grow up fatherless. Of course, one can argue that Camus was so drawn toward this topic precisely because he did not have a chance to grapple with and overcome his Oedipal rivalry with the father, and that he worked out through imaginative channels what he could not experience in real life. Whatever the case may be, Camus's fascination with Fyodor Dostoyevsky is based at least in part on Dostoyevsky's own preoccupation with the father-son dynamic. In contradistinction to Camus, however, Dostoyevsky himself was involved in what could be termed an intense Oedipal conflict with his father. When Dostoyevsky's father died (he was killed by his own serfs), Dostoyevsky experienced a strong sense of guilt because he had often wished his father dead during his youth, holding his father responsible for his unhappy childhood.

In an essay titled "Dostoevsky and Parricide," Freud himself explored the Oedipal dimension of Dostoyevsky's work, especially the prominent motif of patricide in *The Brothers Karamazov* (1879–80). And now we can connect the dots: Dostoyevsky was tormented by guilt over his patricidal longings; his great novel *The Brothers Karamazov* is both about an actual patricide (the killing of Fyodor Karamazov) and about the struggle to maintain faith in God, with Ivan Karamazov famously rejecting God because he was responsible for the suffering of innocent children (an argument carried out in the book-within-a-book titled "The Grand Inquisitor"). It would seem, then, that Freud definitely had a point regarding Dostoyevsky, whose unresolved Oedipal conflict with his father appears to have been enacted in his fictional patricide, followed by Ivan's rejection of God. Ultimately, Dostoyevsky's religious doubts can thus be traced to his rebellious sentiments toward his own father.

Albert Camus, in turn, relied heavily on Dostoyevsky to bolster his own theory of metaphysical rebellion, which is really just another name for misotheism. In Part Two of *The Rebel*, Camus insists that "Ivan [Karamazov] rebels against a murderous God" (58) because he is obsessed with the divinity of man:

> Ivan allows us to guess his answer: one can live in a state of rebellion only by pursuing it to the bitter end. What is the bitter end of metaphysical rebellion? Metaphysical revolution. The master of the world, after his legitimacy has been contested, must be overthrown. Man must occupy his place. "As God and immortality do not exist, the new man is permitted to become God." (*Rebel* 58)

Camus would return to this premise again in his discussion of Nietzsche's elevation of the artist to the status of quasi-divine creator. The omniscient narrator, the abstract painter, the bohemian rebel artist—all are in one sense or another marking their rejection of the heavenly order: "The rebel, who at first denies God, finally aspires to replace Him" (73).

But ultimately Camus is conflicted about the moral implications of this proposition. On the one hand, this former member of the *Résistance* during World War II recognizes the nobility of rebellion (21); but, on the other hand, he also understands that "in a certain sense, rebellion . . . ends again in the exaltation of evil" (74). This is the problem with Ivan Karamazov's position: he rebels against God the father but ends up condoning the murder of his own father. A similar problem besets political revolutions, according to Camus: "The prophetic dream of Marx and the over-inspired predictions of Hegel or of Nietzsche ended by conjuring up, after the city of God had been razed to the ground, a rational or irrational State, which in both cases, however, was founded on terror." (177). In *The Rebel*, then, Camus cautions against metaphysical rebellion because he fears that it ultimately is an invitation to nihilism and also that it leads to totalitarianism via the son's wish to inherit the father's authority.[2]

Faced with two unsatisfactory outcomes of metaphysical rebellion—God-hatred that leads to moral nihilism and God-hatred that is the prelude to complete identification with the father's oppressive rules—Camus sought a third way to frame his conviction of man's need to rebel against God. His essay "The Myth of Sisyphus" (1942) can be seen as his attempt to resolve this impasse. In this essay, the emphasis is not so much on the outcome of metaphysical rebellion as it is on the process of the struggle itself. Camus argues that the only way misotheism can be valid and moral is by it remaining incomplete, just like Sisyphus's task of rolling the boulder up the hill remains vexingly incomplete. Passion, hope, self-reflection, and rebellious defiance are the attributes demonstrating "that Sisyphus is the absurd hero. He *is*, as much through his passions as through his torture. His scorn of the gods, his hatred of death, and his passion for life won him that unspeakable penalty in which the whole being is exerted toward accomplishing nothing. This is the price that must be paid for the passions of this earth" ("Sisyphus" 89). It is, then, in Sisyphus's inner attitude, rather than in any external, finite accomplishment, that Camus locates the redeeming power of human rebellion against the divine. Scorn, in particular, is the modus operandi of that noble impulse: "There is no fate that cannot be surmounted by scorn. . . . It drives out of this world a god who had come into it with dissatisfaction and a preference for futile suffering" (91). In the final consequence, Camus advocates radical secular humanism as the engine of perpetual rebellion against the absurd condition of man, a condition he sees as the consequence of God's botched work: "Thus, convinced of the wholly human origin of all that is human, a blind man eager to see who knows that the night has no end, he is still on the go. The rock is still rolling. . . . Sisyphus teaches the higher fidelity that negates the gods and raises rocks" (91). To Camus, then, the secret of human dignity (that quintessential objective of the existentialists) lies in the process of a struggle that is self-conscious, ongoing, and conducted in defiance of the palpably absurd arrangements of the universe.

Alister McGrath argues that "the denial of God can be said to lie at the heart of Camus's understanding of politics and morality" (157). This is quite an accurate description, as is McGrath's contention that "Camus seems to embrace a faith of his own, a rather negative faith, it is true, but a *faith* nevertheless" (158). To be more precise, though, I wish to add that this faith has a name, namely metaphysical rebellion, in Camus's words, or misotheism in my own terminology. In any case, it is a stance that locates the target of rebellion in the realm of the gods, although simultaneously admitting that the rebellion remains incomplete and provisional. In other words, Camus does not reduce the meaning of life to the binary alternatives of faith versus atheism or piety versus misotheism. Rather, he draws the outlines of an antagonistic faith that emphasizes the permanent scorn for the gods and the ongoing struggle with them, rather than their permanent elimination.

Camus is unique among existentialists in terms of the importance that he attached to the whole notion of defying the gods in a continuous state of spiritual revolt. Other existentialists either built their philosophy around more recognizable forms of religious piety, as is the case with Søren Kierkegaard and Martin Buber, or they pursued a plainly atheistic agenda, as in the case of Jean-Paul Sartre and Martin Heidegger. Hence, it cannot really be said that misotheism passed through existentialism as a major twentieth-century stopping point in the ongoing history of God-hatred. A rather more sustained manifestation of misotheism can be traced to left-leaning, progressive, secular humanists like William Empson and Gore Vidal.

William Empson

William Empson (1906–1984) was a preeminent formalist literary critic and an English poet. He wrote voluminously on English Renaissance authors, especially Shakespeare, Donne, and Milton. His first book *Seven Types of Ambiguity* (1930), published when he was twenty-four, is one of the classics of scholarly criticism. Empson was also an enfant terrible in more ways than one. This son of the landed gentry was expelled from Cambridge for having had sex in his dorm room; he was a man of the world with sensual appetites; he was heterodox in his opinions and literary pronouncements; and he was a radical leftist with Maoist sympathies. He also wrote the book *Milton's God* (1961) that has sent shockwaves through the literary establishment. *Milton's God* takes up a prominent place in the history of misotheism, not only because of its radical declarations of God-hatred, but also because of its bold claim that the greatest English poet, John Milton, was not only a covert admirer of Satan, as Blake had famously argued long before, but that he was in fact a closeted enemy of God.

Writing a 320-page book on the figure of God in *Paradise Lost* may seem a bit excessive, yet it shows just what an epic project the denunciation of God can be. In this endeavor, however, Empson functions as a middleman, demonstrating how Milton had already done the job three hundred years earlier. Empson begins his discussion by facing head-on what critics and commentators have grudgingly admitted throughout the centuries since the publication of *Paradise Lost*: "[Milton's] God is somehow 'embarrassing.' . . . C. S. Lewis let in some needed fresh air . . . by saying, 'Many of those who say they dislike Milton's God only mean that they dislike God'" (9). Empson leaves no doubt about where he stands on this issue: " 'Dislike' is a question-begging term here. I think the traditional God of Christianity very wicked, and have done since I was at school, where nearly all my little playmates thought the same" (10). Of course, the correlation between Milton and his god works the other way around as well:

those who dislike the poem tend to be admirers of God. Empson refers to T. S. Eliot in this connection: "[Eliot's] feelings seem to me evidently right; indeed the poem, if read with understanding, must be read with growing horror unless you decide to reject its God" (25). In his assessment of *Paradise Lost*, Empson aligns himself self-consciously with "Blake and Shelley, who said that the reason why the poem is so good is that it makes God so bad" (13). Thus, Empson's argument contains two crucial premises. First, looked at closely, Milton's god comes across as a scheming, selfish, and "wicked" deity and thus as worthy of scorn rather than adoration. Second, Milton's god does not constitute a misrepresentation of the biblical deity but rather a true rendering of the Almighty's actual moral character. In Empson's view, Milton's epic poem, though ostensibly conceived as a theodicy (to "justify the ways of God to man"), is actually presented as a trial of God. The ironic result of this is that Satan, especially in the first half of the epic, comes across as a more admirable and charismatic hero than either God or his son: "Milton's Devil as a moral being is far superior to his God" (20), says Empson; moreover, Milton never quite clears God from the suspicion that he is handling cosmic and human affairs rather wickedly and incompetently.

In other words, Empson deconstructs Milton's text by penetrating through its surface aspect of piety and faithfulness to the Bible to reveal a profound discontent with the orthodox concept of divinity at its heart: "[Milton] is struggling to make his God appear less wicked, as he tells us he will at the start (I.25), and does succeed in making him noticeably less wicked than the traditional Christian one; though, after all his efforts, owing to his loyalty to the sacred text and the penetration with which he makes its story real to us, his modern critics still feel, in a puzzled way, that there is something badly wrong about it all" (11). What is wrong, for instance, is the fact that God-hatred is such a strong and quasi-legitimate affect in Milton's poem: "the reason why Satan can win over his army [of rebel angels] so quickly is that they already hate God, or hate the recent ukase of God. . . . The mind of Mr. Eliot, I submit, totally jibbed at imagining angels who hated God as much as that, whereas Milton thought it only to be expected" (27–28). This comes close to suggesting that Milton was a closeted misotheist, or at least that he recognized the existence of good reasons for hating God, even among the angels in heaven. Indeed, Satan's central article of impeachment, namely, that

God had essentially usurped the throne, finds support among one-third of the heavenly host, not an insignificant turnout. Quoting Herbert Grierson, Empson places this power struggle in a worldly context: "if the third part of a school or college or nation broke into rebellion we should be driven, or strongly disposed, to suspect some mismanagement by the supreme powers" (95). Indeed, Empson's close reading of the general conditions in heaven as presented to us in *Paradise Lost* leads him to conclude that "God had already produced a very unattractive Heaven before Satan fell" (111).

This is reminiscent of reader-response criticism, and notably of Stanley Fish's argument in *Surprised by Sin* (1967) that Milton had laid a trap for his readers to let them experience their own "fall" as pious Christians. In Fish's view, Milton's rhetorical strategies seduce us into admiring Satan's greatness, at least in the early books of the poem, while despising the grim totalitarianism of God and the numbing conformity of his heaven. Fish's claim that Milton tempts the reader into heresy sidesteps Empson's implied question: What if misotheism is the right and moral position to be taken up, and what if defying the Almighty is not so much a cardinal sin as the right stance that leads to the declaration of independence from the heavenly monarch? To Empson, that is the real drama of *Paradise Lost*: "I do not think that anyone . . . will regard Milton's treatment [of God] as due to ignorance or stupidity. The effect is that of a powerful mind thrashing about in exasperation" (115). It would take much more than one century before the idea that lies at the root of Milton's exasperation, and what I would consider to be the stirrings of misotheism, could be voiced openly without fear of ecclesiastical reprisals or worse. Nevertheless, *Paradise Lost* serves as a locus classicus of hidden misotheism, the faith that dare not speak its name, and Milton's epic is one of the great reservoirs of latent resentment against God, of which the textual surface is merely the manifest symptom.

William Empson thus treasures *Paradise Lost* not just for its poetic virtuosity but also for its barely concealed misotheism, which to him is an unavoidable by-product of any honest examination of the Bible. Empson follows his literary discussion of *Paradise Lost* with a polemical chapter summing up his heterodox view that "the Christian God the Father, the God of Tertullian, Augustine and Aquinas, is the wickedest thing yet invented by the black heart of man" (251).

The wickedness he imputes is based mainly on three principles legit-imized by God: the debasement of sex, the celebration of suffering, and tyrannical absolutism. As for the first principle, Empson states that "the fires of unsatisfied sex can be relied upon to stoke the fires of Hell" (252), and that, therefore, "mucking about with people's sex . . . is the epidemic or grass-roots way for Christians to gratify their God" (251). Such rhetoric is, of course, a staple of anti-Christian views since Blake and Swinburne. But, in the hands of Empson, the argu-ment about sex and sin becomes intertwined with the question of sacrifice and torture: "Worship of torture is itself a sexual perversion, oddly and shockingly at home in the human psyche but rather hard to teach without interference with normal sex" (251). In Empson's view, then, "the symbol of the Religion of Love is a torture" (251), not only because of Christ's torture on the cross, which is considered the deed that redeems mankind, but also because God the father is deeply invested in punishment and torture: "All normal and genuinely civi-lized pleasures are low-class; the only high-class pleasure is God's pleasure, the satisfaction of inflicting punishment; and if you do not enjoy this spontaneously you must torture yourself till you do, as in learning to crave for tobacco" (252).

According to Empson, the apex of divine sadism is to be found in the doctrine of divine grace:

> This is what Christians have to regard as Heaven; if they take the vaunted "logic" of their system seriously. They must sit beside God for all eternity and watch almost all the people they have loved on earth being tortured by God . . . and they must incessantly praise God for his mercy. . . . Consider the type of man who would like arriving in Heaven; still half afraid to let God see his cravings and half-incred-ulous that God can share them . . . and then settling down to hold kind God's hand for all eternity and watch old mother being ripped up so much more satisfyingly than he could ever have imagined. This was never stated as anybody's ideal of Heaven, but there is no stopping short of it once the logic runs in that direction. (250)

Empson can hardly be faulted here for flawed or inconsistent rea-soning: for the majority of the faithful, life *is* hard, sinning *is* the inescapable fate of man, God *is* jealous and liable to punish sinners, and, finally, divine grace *is* a highly unpredictable process of selec-tion, rewarding few while leaving most people in expectation of hellish sufferings. On the basis of such an interpretation of some tenets of Christianity, Empson has logic on his side when he conceives of heaven ruled by this God as a kind of dystopia.

The above passage also goes a long way toward explaining Empson's fascination with *Paradise Lost*: obviously he saw in Milton a man whose thinking was running precisely in the direction of envisioning heaven as place of corruption and of considering God as a symbol of wickedness. Yet, Milton's pious heart prompted him to be a Christian apologist. To Empson, Milton did humanity a great service by failing so spectacularly in his intention "to justify the ways of God to man." It is what makes him a true humanist, because by turning Genesis into an epic story of man's liberal impulses in battle with a restraining God, he brought the biblical story down to the level of human experience. This operation, the subjecting of Christian dogmas to the test of logic and letting human experience be the judge of religious claims, is precisely what Empson sees as the most efficient antidote against the religious obfuscations of Christianity: "To guard against being tricked into accepting such a doctrine, and then gradually corrupted by it, one needs not to be prevented by fear from realizing it in terms of human experience" (250). It is to Milton's credit that he did not balk at the prospect of "realizing [biblical doctrine] in terms of human experience," which, in turn, nurtured the rational impulse toward criticism of authority and resistance against injustice in the human realm.

This resistance is particularly crucial because to Empson the Christian doctrine harbors deep within it a totalitarian streak. Empson contends that "[Milton's] God has in any case an authoritarian character, just what one would expect from a usurping angel, which can be felt all the time in Heaven" (103). He is even more outspoken in the conclusion of his chapter on Milton's heaven. In fact, Empson goes so far as to compare God to a terrestrial dictator:

> Perhaps I find [Milton] like Kafka merely because both seem to have had a kind of foreknowledge of the Totalitarian State. . . . The picture of God in the poem, including perhaps even the high moments when he speaks of the end, is astonishingly like Uncle Joe Stalin; the same patience under an appearance of roughness, the same flashes of joviality, the same thorough unscrupulousness, the same real bad temper. It seems little use to puzzle ourselves whether Milton realized he was

producing this effect, because it would follow in any case from what he had set himself to do. (146)

Now, it is not every day that we hear God compared to Joseph Stalin, and this bit of anticommunism is surely a rhetorical hyperbole, a deliberate overstatement. But it is in keeping with prior left-wing denunciations of God. We see behind Empson's Stalin comparison the characterization of God as a tyrant by Proudhon as well as God's indictment as a slave master by Bakunin.

More recently, the linking of the kingdom of God with a secular tyranny has been enacted again by a contemporary public intellectual. In *Letters to a Young Contrarian* (2001), British journalist Christopher Hitchens expressed the same idea as follows: "I touched on the threat of hell with which the devout have always reinforced their ostensibly kindly recommendations, but just consider for a moment what their heaven looks like. Endless praise and adoration, limitless abnegation and abjection of self; a celestial North Korea" (64). This amounts to saying that God is comparable to Kim Jong Il. Hitchens thus continues the leftist trend to discredit God, but his critique of religion is so categorical that it places him outside of misotheism altogether. In other words, Hitchens is an enemy of religion rather than a believer who does not think that God is worthy of worship. Hitchens professes, "I am not even an atheist so much as an antitheist; I not only maintain that all religions are versions of the same untruth, but I hold that the influence of churches, and the effect of religious belief, is positively harmful" (55). The distinction Hitchens is making here, as well as his claim to being an antitheist, places him in the company of antitheists like Emma Goldman rather than of misotheists such as Pierre-Joseph Proudhon.

In her essay "The Philosophy of Atheism" (1916), the anarchist and feminist Emma Goldman takes on the doctrine of theism, which presumes the existence of an eternal, all-powerful, and benevolent creator God, and calls for resistance against this belief. Rather than indicating specifically her contempt for God, she uses the same term Hitchens uses, antitheism, to characterize her rejection of the doctrine of theism in general. Both Hitchens and Goldman see in theistic religion in general a threat to the sanity, prosperity, and peaceful cooperation of humanity. But, in contradistinction to the real misotheists, they see theistic belief *systems*, not their gods, as the number one enemy. In other words, their critique is not aimed at God, but at ecclesiastical institutions and the masses of believers conditioned by their religious indoctrination.

Gore Vidal

Gore Vidal (b. 1925), a left-leaning American public intellectual, actually comes down more on the side of misotheism than antitheism. Indeed, his attacks against God tend to be of the top-down version of the misotheists. He is an especially fitting figure to end this historical overview, as he may well be considered a kind of present-day Thomas Paine. Indeed, Vidal shares with Paine the distinction of being a national pamphleteer, intent on debunking hypocrisy, exposing obfuscation, and denouncing bigotry. Vidal's self-definition as a radical would certainly apply to the writer of *The Age of Reason* as well:

> The word "radical" derives from the Latin word for root. Therefore, if you want to get to the root of *any*thing you must be radical. It is no accident that the word has now been totally demonized by our masters, and no one in politics dares even use the word favorably, much less track any problem to its root. (1048)

This is the start of Vidal's irreligious pamphlet titled "Monotheism and Its Discontents" (1992). This short essay, originally a Lowell Lecture at Harvard University, contains the summation of Vidal's antipathy against the Abrahamic deity. I say "Abrahamic deity" because Vidal takes his attack against God to the level of all major monotheisms: "The great unmentionable evil at the center of our culture is monotheism. From a barbaric Bronze Age text known as the Old Testament, three antihuman religions have evolved—Judaism, Christianity, and Islam. These are sky-god religions" (1049). At this level, Vidal's view of religion closely resembles Hitchens's antitheism. But Vidal goes further by turning his critique into an explicit, top-down expression of misotheism. Take note of how he characterizes the "sky-god," which is Vidal's chosen term to refer to the collective deity of monotheism: "The sky-god is a jealous god, of course. He requires total obedience from everyone on earth, as he is in place not just for one tribe but for all creation. Those who would reject him must be converted or killed for their own good. Ultimately, totalitarianism is the only sort of politics that can truly serve the sky-god's purpose. Any movement of a liberal nature endangers his authority and that of his delegates on earth" (1049). The ideas of Proudhon and Bakunin are revisited here, except that the anarchist byword for god as the ultimate "master" has been substituted with the twentieth-century term "totalitarianism," a word, incidentally, also invoked by Empson in *Milton's God* to describe the conditions in heaven. Despite the terminological difference, the basic idea remains intact: God is the ultimate model of an authoritarian, intolerant, and cruel ruler. Vidal leaves no doubt that this celestial authority is not a god of love; on the contrary, he refers to "the sky-god with his terrible hatred of women, blacks, gays, drugs, abortion, contraception, gambling—you name it, he hates it" (1054). In a typical application of misotheistic thought, Vidal declares his hatred of the hostile deity, citing racial hatred as evidence that the servants of God are especially good at sowing discord and cruelty. This echoes Zora Neale Hurston's view that racism is an offshoot of religious attitudes and that a god who creates the conditions for racial tensions is a god of hatred: "We must live—presumably forever—with a highly enervating race war, set in train by the One God and his many hatreds" (Vidal 1051). Vidal thus fights a rhetorical war on two fronts, both against "a highly primitive sky-god" (999) that is grimly presiding over three major world religions, and against the ministers and televangelists on earth who sing his glories and fill their pockets (as he accuses Jerry Falwell of doing) with income made from bogus millennial predictions and sensationalist stories of Armageddon.

Does such misotheism constitute a constructive approach to humanity? The answer depends on one's deepest convictions, and those are often at root ideological tendencies. Both Vidal and Hitchens claim that their radicalism is a function of pure, enlightened, humanistic values. Vidal identifies himself as a "radical" in the original sense of the word, meaning a person who goes to the root of problems and exposes the causes of strife and unhappiness. The central, master root from which all other problems branch out is monotheism. Hitchens, similarly disinclined to religion, emphasizes that his kind of "radicalism is humanism or it is nothing" (115). These two radical icons of anti-religious agitation are examples of the rhetorical, essentially peaceful nature of that struggle: their enemy is a belief, their weapons are words, and their battlefield is public discourse. They do not inflict any wounds on anybody or cause manifest harm. On the contrary, harm may come to misotheists, whose opinions are so radical and, until quite recently, so unmentionable that they can become targets of religiously motivated retribution.[3] The fact that misotheistic ideas echo the tenets of philosophical anarchism may only aggravate the position these radicals put themselves into. But arguably, anarchism is the most misunderstood of all political theories. Although it is sometimes aligned with concepts of nihilism and terrorism, the philosophical anarchism of Proudhon, Kropotkin, Bakunin, and the Reclus brothers is essentially a pacifist, utopian, and liberal theory of voluntary association and mutual aid. The "propaganda by the deed" is not at all a recipe for terror, although some isolated anarchists have invoked this principle to justify their resort to violence, especially in Russia in the later part of the nineteenth century and in the Spanish Civil War. In general, however, anarchism's rejection of centralized state power and institutionalized authority has ironically limited the political effectiveness of this philosophy, which stands in direct contrast to communism and socialism, both of which have traditionally embraced hierarchical structures of power.

Thus, while misotheism had its first great efflorescence in the writings of radical nineteenth-century thinkers, this antagonistic religious view continued to be relevant to twentieth-century writers, influencing the likes of Rebecca West, Zora Neale Hurston, Albert Camus, William Empson, and Gore Vidal. However, these thinkers were not drawn to the idea of God-hatred for the sake of revolutionary agitation or as a motive for the overthrow of government. Misotheism was attractive to them because it offered an outlet for immense frustrations over the condition of humanity and because it made good philosophical and spiritual sense. After witnessing the horrific wars of the twentieth century, after seeing their hopes of social justice dashed, and after learning of the Holocaust, many artists and thinkers couldn't help implicating a supernatural agency in the unprecedented surge of evil that they saw as swamping the globe. Either because they were brought up to believe in God or because they recognized that the God-idea was an actual force in the lives of a majority of their contemporaries, thinkers such as Camus, Empson, West, Wiesel, and Vidal did not profess atheism in reaction to their sobering understanding of the universe. Instead, their anger at the unabated reign of sickness, poverty, crime, famine, corruption, and war in many parts of

God's own world prompted them to want to shake their fist at the Almighty. Hence, fundamentally the impulse to denounce God is born from a moral imperative.

This is obviously not a new impulse. In fact, what surprises about the story of misotheism is that it is precisely not susceptible to the vicissitudes that have shaped the histories of atheism or fundamentalism, both of which seem to fluctuate on a cyclical pattern. Instead, misotheism remained a surprisingly constant bass line in the history of dissent during the last two centuries. It is my contention that there is relatively little development in the intellectual and philosophical trajectory of misotheism, a fact that is due precisely to misotheism's lack of acknowledgment in the wider public sphere. Notwithstanding Camus's singular attempt to trace the history of misotheism, there is not much awareness that such a history even exists. Most of the individuals I discuss in this book think and write as if they were criers in the wilderness. Gore Vidal does not mention William Empson, who does not mention Rebecca West; she does not mention Proudhon, and so on, yet they were all engaged in a comparable enterprise: they were all enemies of God for similar political, philosophical, moral, and spiritual reasons. The same goes for the creative writers such as Philip Pullman, Elie Wiesel, Peter Shaffer, and others who display an equal lack of awareness that they are part of an ongoing history of ideas or that one of their principal concerns, God-hatred, is shared by others. When asked about it in a private letter, Philip Pullman marveled at having been placed among fellow misotheists like Nietzsche and Bakunin. But once we have at our disposal the outline of a tradition of misotheism, it will be unnecessary to reinvent the wheel every time this idea comes up. Once this hidden history is brought into the daylight, it will not only take on a greater degree of public relevance, but it might actually begin to spawn new ideas and to lead to different spiritual and philosophical arguments that will contribute to making misotheism an evolving system of ideas rather than a static, reiterative position. By defining the history of misotheism, we not only give it reality and relevance but also a life, perhaps even a sort of self-consciousness, and that, by implication, leads to process, development, critique, and invention.

PART TWO

Six Case Studies in Literary Misotheism

Absolute Misotheism I

Paganism, Radicalism, and Algernon Swinburne's War Against God

We who worship no material incarnation of any qualities, no person, may worship the divine humanity, the ideal of human perfection and aspiration, without worshipping any God, any person, any fetish at all. Therefore I might call myself if I wished a kind of Christian (of the Church of Blake and Shelley), but assuredly in no sense a Theist.

—Algernon Charles Swinburne (1874)

I BEGIN THIS SERIES OF CASE STUDIES WITH ALGERNON CHARLES Swinburne (1837–1909), partly in response to Denis Saurat's open invitation, dating back to 1938, when he encouraged critics to explore the tradition of God-hatred starting from Swinburne's reference to "The supreme evil, God!" Looking at the development of misotheism, one cannot help but realize the crucial role played by Swinburne in this process. The novelty about his discourse of misotheism is the complete candor with which he announced his enmity against God in print. True, Blake had preceded Swinburne as an anticleric and opponent of

Yahweh. But instead of insulting God directly, Blake invented a new pantheon of eccentrically named deities and then singled out the god most resembling Yahweh, whom he dubbed Urizen or Nobodaddy, and aimed his poetic wrath against him. As discussed in the Introduction, Shelley used different methods to deflect censure for his anti-God rhetoric, first by severely limiting the distribution of *Queen Mab,* and then by using the guise of Greek mythology in *Prometheus Unbound* to get around the official guardians of religious propriety.

Swinburne's trajectory was significantly different from that of these predecessors: although he began his misotheistic career in a Shelleyan fashion by seeming to aim his attacks against Jupiter in *Atalanta in Calydon* (1865), he then became progressively more explicit in his blasphemy against the Christian God. Moreover, he was simply more centrally invested in the war against deity, turning out poem after poem on this subject and becoming notorious for his anti-devotional attitude. Finally, Swinburne anticipated Nietzsche by invoking the death of God and the rise of man from the ashes of the deity. Thus, while Blake and Shelley made sporadic forays into the territory of misotheism, Swinburne strode into this terrain and settled down on it in broad daylight.

Of course, Swinburne did not have an easy time of it when he decided to cast off religious decorum and declare himself a poet against God. He invited censure for offending Victorian morality in more ways than one. Besides being openly misotheistic, he also presented himself as a political radical and a sensualist. "The prudery of a whole epoch," writes Clyde K. Hyder, "found expression in a long series of attacks which permanently damaged the poet's reputation" (xx). Especially the publication of his two most risqué collections, *Poems and Ballads* (1866) and *Songs before Sunrise* (1871), created a minor scandal. After a public outcry caused by *Poems and Ballads,* Swinburne's publisher withdrew the offending poetry collection from the market, and Swinburne felt obliged to write an apologia, titled *Notes on Poems and Reviews* (1866) to refute the charges of immorality brought against him. To his credit, Swinburne remained undeterred from the virulent attacks against *Poems and Ballads* and went on to pen further poems that were even more explicit in their opposition to God and their transgression of conventional mores.

Swinburne broke down a barrier that had been dented and cracked by Blake and Shelley before him. By setting a strong precedent of neo-pagan and misotheistic poetry, he created a breach that other radical poets such as James Thomson and Thomas Hardy could step into more easily. Although Thomson (1834–1882) claimed not to have read Swinburne (Armstrong 464), it is rather unlikely that he would have published his misotheistic verse narrative *City of the Dreadful Night* (1874) without the precedent set by Swinburne's anti-devotional poetry. Thompson's poetry is replete with verses such as these:

> The vilest thing must be less vile than Thou
> From whom it had its being, God and Lord!
> Creator of all woe and sin! abhorred,
> Malignant and implacable! (24)

This not only echoes the fierce diatribes against God in *Queen Mab*, but it also resonates with the anti-God rhetoric of Swinburne's *Atalanta in Calydon*. However, by comparison with Swinburne and Shelley, Thompson has withstood the test of time less successfully and is mostly remembered today as a precursor for modernist depictions of the city as a depressing, drab environment. Swinburne, on the other hand, has been consistently in print and still commands critical interest, not just because of his eccentric lifestyle, passionate neo-paganism, and irreligiousness, but also because of the vigor of his exuberant diction and the mastery of his versification.

Before we proceed with detailed analyses of Swinburne's poetry, it is necessary to shed some more light on the trajectory of ideas that came to such a radical flowering in his work. Swinburne grew up in an aristocratic home and was at first a devout Anglican, imbued with Christian lore and intimately familiar with church liturgy. What then, one wonders, happened to turn this erstwhile Anglican believer into such a fervent misotheist? Margot Louis speculates as follows about the process of Swinburne's religious turnaround:

> Swinburne lost his faith at Oxford, in 1858 or 1859, and never regained it. We have almost no documentation for the period in question—Swinburne's letters, otherwise so frank about his thoughts and feelings, say as little about his loss of faith as they do about his "lost love" (John Nichol's mixture of Carlylean and Millite liberalism was probably the main contributing factor). (10)

While Louis justifiably traces Swinburne's loss of faith to Carlyle and John Stuart Mill, she overlooks the more obvious roots. For one thing,

Swinburne was a devotee of Epicurus. In one of his youthful (posthumously published) poems, titled "Epicurus," Swinburne emulates the Greek philosopher's disdain for the gods:

> Who tells ye of the Gods ye cry on? No,
> There is no help but man's for man below;
> And he shall work and triumph and be strong
> In wisdom solely by his proper might;
> The rest is darkness, though ye call it light. (*Hyperion* 162)

In his commentary to this poem, Georges Lafourcade states that "the lines seem to be a half-didactic, half-lyrical exposition of *De Rerum Natura*. It should be noted that Swinburne's metaphysics are on the whole similar to those of Lucretius, and this poem, Epicurean though it may purport to be, is interesting as an early and violent expression of its author's life-long anti-theism" (159). Particularly noteworthy about this comment is not only the connection between Swinburne's misotheism (what Lafourcade calls anti-theism) and his early exposure to Epicureanism, but also Lafourcade's contention that the "violent" nature of Swinburne's attack against God goes really beyond Epicureanism. Indeed, while Epicurus inspired contempt for the unresponsive, distant gods, Swinburne eventually went beyond this detached attitude to become a more militant proponent of absolute misotheism or deicide. And so, the story of Swinburne's misotheism doesn't begin with *Atalanta in Calydon*. Rather, it begins with Lucretius (whose disdain of worship he enjoyed), with Victor Hugo (whose anticlerical fury and compassion for the working class he emulated), with Blake (whose attacks against deity he relished), and perhaps most of all with Shelley (with whom he shared more than a penchant for blasphemy, being also an aristocratic scion who had attended Eton).

As for his relationship with Blake, Swinburne was one of the early critics to recognize the significance of William Blake as a supremely gifted, though obscurely mystical, poet. His influential study *William Blake: A Critical Essay* (1868) depicts Blake as a rebel, a "heretic and mystic" (44) and yet a "poetic genius" (2). Swinburne did not relish what he calls the "insane cosmogony, blatant mythology, and sonorous aberration of thoughts and theories" (209) that characterize Blake's prophetic works, but he surely appreciated the underlying anticlericalism and Promethean rebellion evidenced in Blake's poetic works:

"Rational deism and clerical religion were to him two equally abhorrent incarnations of the same evil spirit, appearing now as negation and now as restriction. He wanted supremacy of freedom with intensity of faith. Hence he was properly neither Christian nor infidel: he was emphatically a heretic" (210). From this recognition of Blake's intense spirituality and subversive faith, Swinburne goes on to identify Blake as both a Christologist and a misotheist: "He believed in redemption by Christ, and in the incarnation of Satan as Jehovah" (210). This combination of Christology with misotheism (directed against Yahweh) did not appeal to Swinburne's own brand of neo-pagan misotheism. But despite this reservation and despite Swinburne's rejection of Blake's idiosyncratic mysticism, Blake had a powerful hold on his imagination, as we will see below.

As for Shelley, his influence on Swinburne eclipsed even that of Blake. Swinburne directly invoked Shelley in defense of his own practice of blasphemy when he wrote to a friend that "I do not deprecate, but demand for all men freedom to speak and freedom to hear. . . . After many alternate curses and denials of God, a great poet [i.e., Shelley] talks of Christ 'veiling his horrible Godhead,' of his 'malignant soul,' his 'godlike malice.' Shelley outlived all this and much more; but Shelley wrote all this and much more" (*Notes* 53). It is significant that of all the intensely blasphemous statements in *Queen Mab*, Swinburne should focus on Shelley's attacks against Christ. This is, in fact, the most shocking of all the antireligious aspects of *Queen Mab*. The angry words against Christ are spoken by Ahasuerus, a Jew condemned to eternal wandering for mocking Jesus during his passion: "Indignantly I summed / The massacres and miseries which his name / Had sanctioned in my country, and I cried, / 'Go! Go!' in mockery. / A smile of godlike malice reillumed / His fading lineaments" (Canto VII, 176–81). In his rejection of both Christ and Yahweh, Swinburne followed the example set by Shelley rather than Blake. Indeed, Blake's misotheism was tempered by his reverence for Christ's humanistic message.

Queen Mab, the poem that made such a deep impression on Swinburne, runs the gamut of antireligious sentiments. The main speaker of the poem, the eponymous Fairy, is a representative of rational atheism and a predecessor of Feuerbach. In Canto VI, the Fairy explains that "the God of human error" (199) is a man-made construct, and in the following Canto, she broadens her attack to target any supreme deity whatever "The name of God / Has fenced about all crime with holiness, / Himself the creature of his worshippers, / Whose names, and attributes, and passions change, / Seeva, Buddh, Foh, Jehovah, God, or Lord, / Even with the human dupes who build his shrines, / Still serving o'er the war-polluted world / For desolation's watch-word" (Canto VII, 26–33). Ahasuerus further condemns Moses as "the murderer" (Canto VII, 127), and utters words of unmitigated misotheism: "[I] resolved to wage unweariable war / With my almighty tyrant, and to hurl defiance at his impotence to harm / Beyond the curse I bore" (Canto VII, 198–201).

An impressionable young Algernon Swinburne took his cue from Ahasuerus's resolve to continue "Mocking my powerless tyrant's horrible curse / with stubborn and unalterable will" (Canto VII, 256–57). Indeed, Swinburne's work is a continuation of Shelley's blasphemous attacks against Yahweh and Christ. But, unlike Shelley, who based his misotheism on a categorical rejection of anthropomorphic deities, Swinburne distinguished himself from his predecessor insofar as his religious devotion ran in the direction of paganism. Swinburne developed an increasingly fervent reverence for the Greco-Roman deities of passion, love, and fertility. Thus, Swinburne selectively adopted Shelley's Promethean misotheism while disregarding the secular humanism underlying Shelley's radicalism.

Such Prometheanism is clearly evidenced in Swinburne's verse play *Atalanta in Calydon*. The often-quoted outburst against "The supreme evil, God!" comes from the lips of a Greek chorus, ostensibly condemning the doings of Zeus (or Jupiter) but actually serving as a denunciation of the Judeo-Christian god. As in Shelley's *Prometheus Unbound*, Swinburne's attack against God is here veiled behind a screen of classical mythology. However, the following verses can easily be recognized as an insult against omnipotent Yahweh,

> Who makes desire, and slays desire with shame;
> Who shakes the heaven as ashes in his hand;
> Who seeing the light and shadow for the same,
> Bids day waste night as fire devours a brand
> Smites without sword, and scourges without rod;
> The supreme evil, God.
> Yea, with thine hate, O God, thou hast covered us
>
> . . . .

> Yet have men praised thee, saying, He hath made man thus,
> And he doeth right. (1146–1152; 1156–57)

In this formulation, Swinburne's chorus invokes God's hatred of mankind as the cause of man's own dislike of the deity. This divine hatred expresses itself in different ways: the members of the chorus are outraged that God would first create the pleasures of the body and then declare their satisfaction to be a sin—a reference to Christian views of sexuality; and they also blame God for being cowardly by meting out punishment via remote control, as it were, instead of taking matters into his own hands (by wielding a sword and rod). The result of this list of grievances is the baffled realization that humanity insists on worshipping what is essentially an unloving and unlovable divinity.

Atalanta in Calydon is only one among Swinburne's numerous anti-God poems based on a mythological scenario. Increasingly, though, he invoked pagan deities in a comparative manner to demonstrate their superiority over the deities and saints of the Christian tradition. "Hertha" and "Hymn to Proserpine" are examples of that tendency. The latter dramatizes the spiritual and cultural upheavals after Christianity became Rome's state religion in the fourth century AD. Swinburne's speaker in "Hymn to Proserpine" is identified as the "last pagan" in Rome, and he comments on the changing of the guards, religiously speaking. This imagined scenario offered Swinburne an opportunity to dramatize the historical contingency of religious systems and to cast doubt on the ethical and spiritual superiority of Christianity. First he gives a depiction of the recently overthrown pagan system:

> O Gods dethroned and deceased, cast forth, wiped out in a day!
> From your wrath is the world released, redeemed from your chains,
>   men say
> New Gods are crowned in the city; their flowers have broken your rods
> They are merciful, clothed with pity, the young compassionate Gods.
> But for me their new device is barren, the days are bare. (13–17)

While there is little grief over the departure of the old pagan gods, the speaker does not muster enthusiasm about the newly installed Christian Trinity. This lack of enthusiasm for the Christian message is further dramatized in the often quoted line "Thou has conquered, O pale

Galilean; the world has grown grey from thy breath" (35). Here, Christ (the "pale Galilean") is shown not so much as the redeemer of humanity but as someone who has cast a pallor over the world. The speaker then makes a rather shocking prophetic prediction: "Yet thy kingdom shall pass, Galilean, thy dead shall go down to thee dead" (74). Here Swinburne lampoons the Gospels by twisting the language of Matthew ("thy kingdom come"), and by denying Christ the power to resurrect the dead. There is no atonement, and no second coming in this vision of terminal Christianity.

Swinburne then contrasts the fleeting success of Christianity with the vital permanence of Proserpine, goddess of the natural cycle of the seasons and powerful symbol of life, death, and rebirth. Compared with the vibrant aspect of Proserpine, the Virgin Mary cuts a poor figure, and Swinburne makes the best of this opportunity to devalue the Christian ethos: "Not as thine [like the mother of Christ] was our mother," he says, referring to Proserpine,

> Clothed round with the world's desire as with raiment, and fair
>   as the foam,
> And fleeter than kindled fire, and a goddess, and mother of Rome.
> For thine came pale and a maiden, and sister to sorrow; but ours
> Her deep hair heavily laden with odour and colour of flowers
> . . . .
> Bent down unto us that besought her, and the earth grew sweet
>   with her name. (78–84)

While the male gods of the pagan pantheon are quite easily overmastered by Christianity, Proserpine retains her splendor and remains the only divinity worthy of ongoing worship after the Christian conquest. In fact, Swinburne's religious sensibility here points toward the ancient roots of religion in the mysteries of sex and procreation.

Of course, such an affirmation of female sensuality laced with mockery of male divinities made it rather hard for many fellow Victorians to accept this poetry. If they were shocked by Proserpine's alleged superiority over Mary, they must have been aghast at the celebration of the goddess as whore in "Laus Veneris" ("praise of Venus"). The poem is a latter-day adaptation of the medieval Tannhäuser legend, which runs like this: Tannhäuser, a Christian knight, has found the abode of Venus underneath Hörselberg (also Venusberg, or Mount Venus, in Thuringia, in central Germany).

There he spends a full year with Venus, enjoying the pleasures of sensual love. But after eventually tiring of the voluptuousness, he makes a pilgrimage to Rome to apply to the pope for forgiveness and begin reforming himself. The pope, however, rejects him and claims that it is more likely for his staff to break into bloom than for God to forgive Tannhäuser's transgressions. Miraculously, the papal staff starts blooming three days later; immediately, the pope dispatches messengers to bring Tannhäuser back to him, but it is too late—he had already returned to the embrace of Venus. Swinburne undercuts the normative sexual implications of this tale by siding openly with the knight and by supporting his choice of eros, or erotic love, over agape, or divine love:

> Lo, she was thus when her clear limbs enticed
> All lips that now grow sad with kissing Christ
> Stained with blood fallen from the feet of God
> The feet and hands whereat our souls were priced.
> Alas, Lord, surely thou art great and fair.
> But lo her wonderfully woven hair!
> And thou didst heal us with thy piteous kiss;
> But now see, Lord; her mouth is lovelier. (13–20)

The discourse of staining, of sadness and piteousness, associated with Christ, is contrasted with the more attractive and wholesome attributes of Venus's "clear limbs," "wonderfully woven hair," and "mouth [that] is lovelier." Swinburne here boldly celebrates the erotic realm of beauty and desire, despising the ideas of purity, holiness, and repentance that come with Christian worship. The poem continues to qualify and limit the blessing of the Judeo-Christian god compared to the bliss bestowed on man by the goddess of love. The poem ends with a repudiation of the promise of divine salvation and instead exalts the figure of Venus:

> And lo my love, mine own soul's heart, more dear
> than mine own soul, more beautiful than God
> Who hath my being between the hands of her
> . . . . .
> And I forgot fear and all weary things,
> All ended prayers and perished thanksgivings
> . . . . .

> Yes, these that know not, shall they have such bliss
> High up in barren heaven before his face . . . ? (386–88, 401–2, 412–13)

Here Swinburne makes it clear that Tannhäuser made the right choice—Venus *is* greater than the Christian God, by virtue of her greater affection and beauty. Swinburne further subverts customary Christian ideas by denigrating prayer as a weary and wasteful act and by portraying heaven as a sterile place. In particular, he repudiates the Christian association of sexuality with sin and guilt.

"Laus Veneris" celebrates the power of erotic passion at the expense of Christ's passion, and it contrasts the life force of Venus with the morbidity of the Christian atonement and self-denial. Although Nietzsche apparently knew nothing of Swinburne, and vice versa, it is quite clear that Swinburne's poem is in fact performing just the kind of "transvaluation of all values" that Nietzsche was demanding of his contemporaries. Although hailing from opposing ends of the political spectrum, both intellectuals saw in Christianity a religion in decline and both advocated the extermination of God in order to infuse new vitality into the spiritual life of European culture.

The subversive potential of Swinburne's "transvaluation" is made obvious in a poem that pits physical and spiritual love against each other. In "The Leper," Swinburne discredits claims about God's love. The poem opens by asserting that "Nothing is better, I well think, / Than love; the hidden well-water / Is not so delicate to drink" (113). But the kind of love the poet has in mind—eros—is not only different from but incompatible with divine love, or agape. In fact, God's love for humanity turns out to be a form of hatred in this poem. Swinburne's speaker insists that "God hateth us" (89), and he goes on to say:

> Yea, though God always hated me,
> And hates me now that I can kiss
> Her eyes . . .
> Nothing better, I well know,
> Than love; no amber in cold sea
> Or gathered berries under snow. (14–16; 21–23)

In the dramatic situation of the poem, the speaker expresses his love for a woman who is a leper, a person who is not fit to return his ardor and therefore rejects him. The blame for this paradoxical condition is squarely laid at the feet of

> God, that makes time and ruins it
> And alters not, abiding God,
> Changed with disease her body sweet,
> The body of love wherein she abode
>
> . . . . .
>
> They cursed her, seeing how God had wrought
> This curse to plague her, a curse of his.
> Fools were they surely, seeing not
> How sweeter than all sweet she is. (45–48; 53–54)

There are intriguing parallels to the Book of Job here: the God who "makes time and ruins it" recalls the God who hectors Job: "Where wast thou when I laid the foundations of the earth?" (38:4), and the leper's skin disease, blamed on God, recalls Job, who is covered with boils and sores as a result of God's wager with the devil (7:5). But Swinburne precisely inverts the pious implications of the Jobian reference: he condemns God for making the woman sick, and he calls fools those who believe that God acted righteously. In other words, the scenario is pagan, but the implied reference is Biblical, and the meaning derived from both is anti-Christian.

While Swinburne's earlier works derive their anti-God thrust from their pagan subject matter and their celebrations of sensuality, the poetry of his middle phase is distinguished by politically motivated attacks against Christianity and by an increasingly secular humanism. Swinburne's poem "Before a Crucifix" is typical of this trend, combining fervent misotheism with a hefty dose of leftist radicalism. It's the kind of poem that might have resulted from a hypothetical collaboration between Feuerbach, Proudhon, and Nietzsche. Devoid of arcane mythological references, this rather simple and rhetorically effective poem begins by describing a rural scene of worship, before turning the seemingly peaceful setting into an occasion for bitter commentary on the misguided faith of the pious masses:

> Here, down between the dusty trees,
>   At this lank edge of haggard wood,
> Women with labour-loosened knees
>   With gaunt back bowed by servitude,
> Stop, shift their loads, and pray, and fare
> Forth with souls easier for the prayer
>
> The suns have branded black, the rains

> Striped grey this piteous God of theirs;
> The face is full of prayers and pains,
>   To which they bring their pains and prayers;
> Lean limbs that show the labouring bones.
> And ghastly mouth that gapes and groans.
>
> God of this grievous people, wrought
>   After the likeness of their race,
> By faces like thine own besought,
>   Thine own blind helpless eyeless face,
> I too, that have nor tongue nor knee
> For prayer, I have a word to thee. (1–18)

This is reminiscent of Shelley's "Men of England" or "England 1819," insofar as it has the rhythmic quality of a protest song. From the beginning, the fact of the women's hard—too hard—labor, their servitude and exploitation are causally linked to the women's religious piety. They are described as having "labour loosened knees," "gaunt backs," and a distorting "ghastly mouth that gapes and groans." The blasphemous implications of the poem turn on the mirror effect between the laboring masses and the effigy of Christ. Rather than being invested with dignity and the promise of redemption, the figure on the cross merely confirms and reinforces the weariness and forlornness of the worshipping crowds. Like that crowd, Christ is "branded" and "striped grey"; and, again like the crowd itself, Christ is "piteous" and "grievous," "wrought after the likeness" of his worshippers. The economy of mutual reinforcement and mirroring is most clearly delineated in the chiastic lines "The face is full of prayers and pains / To which they bring their pains and prayers." This weary and pointless circularity denies Christ's agency as a savior. Moreover, the argument that the "God of this grievous people [was] wrought / After the likeness of their race" goes beyond even the argument of Ludwig Feuerbach who at least had argued that the godhead is the sum total of humanity's projection of *ideal* qualities. In the Swinburnian version of this constructivist argument, the godhead is the symbol of man's downtrodden state, quite the opposite of the ideal.

Looking at the scene of desolation and weariness, the speaker of the poem shifts from diagnosis to attack by stating:

> It was for this, that men should make
> Thy name a fetter on men's necks,

> Poor men's made poorer for thy sake?
> And women's withered out of sex? (25–28)

Here in short order are three major accusations against Christianity: first, that Christian doctrine becomes a severely limiting, "fettering" force, presumably because it teaches puritan values; next, in extension of this accusation, Christianity specifically saps women of their sexual energies, with the effect of "withering" their life force; and, third, Christianity aids in the exploitation of the poor. In this claim, Swinburne goes even beyond Marx, who had famously critiqued the alienating force of religion by speaking against Christianity as the palliative ("Opium des Volkes," as he put it, or "opiate of the masses") that made the condition of the unhappy, exploited working classes more bearable. Swinburne's point is more radical than that, claiming that Christianity not only furnishes an exaltation of suffering, thereby keeping the proletariat in line, but that it also can be used as a direct instrument of exploitation by agents who have the church's blessing.

Even Christ, Swinburne argues, has become the dupe of the clergy, the church, and the monarch, all of whom turn his mission into fodder for furthering their own interests. He accuses the clergy of opulence ("the toothéd thorns that bit thy brows / Lighten the weight of gold on theirs"), he blames the church for luxury ("Thy nakedness enrobes thy spouse"—here the church is represented as the spouse of Christ), and he maintains that kings ultimately derive their power from the sufferings of Christ ("The blinding buffets on thine head / On their crowned heads confirms the crown" [61–62]). The monarchy, as a metonymy for exploitative power, is said to "bind the people's nail-pierced hands / They hide the people's nail-pierced feet" (69–70). Contrary to the wealthy class, who are smiled upon by God, the poor "have not the rich man's grave / To sleep in when their pain is done. / These were not fit for God to save" (73–75). These "tombless crucified," also known as the proletariat, have three nails driven through them:

> Through the left hand a nail is driven
> Faith, and another through the right,
> Forged in the fires of hell and heaven,
> Fear that puts out the eye of light:
> And the feet soiled and scarred and pale
> Are pierced with falsehood for a nail. (85–90)

If there is a familiar ring to this, it's because Blake and Shelley appear to be speaking directly to us through these lines. Shelley's analogy for religion in *Queen Mab*, "falsehood," is transformed into the nail that pierces Christ's feet; moreover, echoes of Shelley's protest song "Men of England" resonate throughout "Before a Crucifix." But Swinburne's poem also invites comparison with "The Human Abstract" in which Blake introduces the symbolical "tree of religion" as a construct of cruelty, fear, humility, and deceit. These qualities correspond directly to Swinburne's evocation of the cruelty endured by the faithful ("humility" in Blake's poem), as well as the falsehood of religious hypocrisy (called "deceit" by Blake). The allusion to Blake's "tree of religion" becomes explicit in the lines "The tree of faith ingraffed by priests / Puts its foul foliage out above thee" (163–64). There are other Blakean echoes in the poem, such as the riff on "The Tyger" in Swinburne's lines "And what man or what angel known / Shall roll back the sepulchral stone?" (71–72). These resonances, together with allusions to the Gospel of Matthew (regarding the rich man's grave) are designed to lend authority and gravity to Swinburne's argument by anchoring it in a web of preexisting commentaries on the status of religion, Christ, and the poor.

"Before a Crucifix," with its explicitly anti-Christian, anticlerical, antimonarchic, republican amalgam of ideas, is cut from a different cloth than the earlier, more obscure, arcane, and mythical poems of pagan subject matter. In "Before a Crucifix," Swinburne's blasphemy has morphed from a more speculative misotheism, as expressed in the pagan poems, to a more pragmatic form of protest against a god who is either powerless or unwilling to alleviate the suffering of workers "with labour-loosened knees." Swinburne's focus on women laborers makes his plea for social justice even more poignant, as he combines the attack against church and monarchy with an attack against the patriarchal logic underpinning these institutions. Not surprisingly, in addition to charges of "bitter antitheism" (Hyder xix), Swinburne came in for criticism of a specifically political sort. An anonymous reviewer, obviously having read "Before a Crucifix," complained: "much as he delights in what used in our younger days to be called blasphemy, he delights still more, if that were possible, in the reddest of Red Republicanism" (Anonymous 136).

But Swinburne's critique of religion and divinity was not purely negative. In "Before a Crucifix," he attempts to work out an alternative myth of socioeconomic salvation by substituting the working classes for Christ. In another poem, titled "Genesis," he rewrites the biblical account in order to provide a new story of creation. Swinburne starts out by blasphemously insinuating that God came into existence only after creation and by placing God and man on the same footing: " . . . before any world had any light, / Or anything called God or man drew breath / Slowly the strong sides of the heaving night / Moved, and brought forth the strength of life and death" (5–6). Invoking a familiar motif of creation myths around the world, Swinburne writes about the beginning of the cosmos as involving the separation of darkness and light:

> The very darkness that time knew not of,
> > Nor God laid hand on, nor was man found there,
> Ceased, and was cloven in several shapes; above
> > Light, and night under, and fire, earth, water, and air.
> . . . . . .
> And death, the shadow cast by life's wide wings,
> > And God, the shade cast by the soul of man. (13–20)

Contrary to religious creation myths that picture a divinity separating the realms of light and darkness, Swinburne's version does not feature a prime mover. The separation happens spontaneously, as it were. And not only has God nothing to do with the genesis of the cosmos per se, but he is merely the "shade cast by the soul of man," which recalls Shelley's *Queen Mab*, where God is referred to as "the creature of his worshippers" (VII. 28). The animating principle of the universe, according to Swinburne, is not a God creating the cosmos ex nihilo but rather a Blakean war of opposites:

> The mild antiphonies that melt and kiss,
> > The violent symphonies that meet and kill,
> All nature of all things began to be.
> But chiefliest in the spirit (beast or man,
> Planet of heaven or blossom of earth or sea)
> > The divine contraries of life began. (27–32)

This, of course, invokes the lines from *Marriage of Heaven and Hell* that "Without contraries there is no progression." But Swinburne's alternative creation myth has another dominant element that cannot be overlooked, namely, its almost explicitly Manichaean theogony:

> For in each man and each year that is born
>> Are sown the twin seeds of the strong twin powers;
> The white seed of the fruitful helpful morn,
>> The black seed of the barren hurtful hours. (45–58)

Swinburne's Manichaeanism emerges not only from the explicit dualism in which he casts his vision but also from the moral qualities he attaches to the two principal forces of light and darkness. Like a Manichaean, Swinburne recognizes the inherent virtue of duality, seeing the codependence of the two warring elements as the prime movers of existence:

> And he that of the black seed eateth fruit
> To him the savour as honey shall be sweet;
> And he in whom the white seed hath struck root,
>> He shall have sorrow and trouble and tears for meat.
> . . . .
> And of these twain, the black seed and the white,
> All things come forth, endured of men and done;
> And still the day is great with child of night,
> And still the black night labors with the sun. (49–60)

This emphasis on the absolute value of dual forces recalls the chorus in *Atalanta in Calydon*, which critiques God's imperious attempt to expand the domain of light at the expense of darkness: "Who, seeing the light and shadow for the same, / Bids day waste night as fire devours a brand" (1148–49). By condemning God who favors light at the expense of darkness, the chorus of *Atalanta in Calydon* justifies the dignity of Blakean dualism at the expense of an imperious and life-denying monism.

This light-dark dichotomy represents the master binary from which all other dichotomies spring, including the one between male and female. Dorothea Barrett put it like this: "for [Swinburne] pleasure and pain are *intrinsic* to sexual and poetic experience, are indeed essential to them, since pleasure is perceived only in contrast to pain. Swinburne's is a relative world in which all opposites are embraced because perception is impossible without difference" (113). It is noteworthy that in promoting the idea that dualism is the essence of existence, Swinburne is both a disciple of Blake and a forerunner of Rebecca West, another prominent British misotheist. West, too, was an inveterate Manichaean, and she, too, believed that dualism was a more profound and powerful force than any power God might claim. But West held with Blake rather than with Shelley and Swinburne because she revered Christ. This gave her misotheism a different complexion. Being on the side of Christ made her shrink from deicide, and she never crossed from protesting God to seeking to destroy him. Such differences indicate the range of possible positions that can be taken up by people who are otherwise united in their enmity against the Judeo-Christian deity.

As for Swinburne, his absolute misotheism hardened over the years. His most radical testimony to that kind of God-hatred is the rarely printed poem "Hymn of Man" (1871).[1] This elaborate parody of devotional poetry goes to the very heart of misotheism by treating God as a criminal who is judged and condemned by a jury of men:

> By the dread wherewith life was astounded and shamed out of
>   sense of its trust,
> By the scourges of doubt and repentance that fell on the soul
>   at thy nod,
> Thou art judged, O judge, and the sentence is gone forth
>   against thee, O God.
> Thy slave that slept is awake; thy slave but slept for a span;
> Yea, man thy slave shall unmake thee, who made thee lord
>   over man. (*The Best* 178)

In *Swinburne and His Gods* (1990), Margot Louis demonstrated that "Hymn of Man" skillfully parodies several passages of the Bible to subvert the biblical meaning and to turn God's word against himself (105). The above extract is no exception, invoking the words of Matthew 7:1 ("For in the same way you judge others, you will be judged, and with the measure you use, it will be measured to you") while radically departing from the evangelist's meaning. As Louis further argued, the passion and eloquence of Lamentations, of the Psalms, and of other parts of the Bible are directly transposed to the branding and cursing of God in this most ardent of Swinburne's condemnations of divinity: "By the crimes of thine hands unforgiven they beseech thee to hear them, O Lord" [177]). In keeping with the title of the hymn, the poem ends with the apotheosis of man, an act of triumphant humanism that is conditioned upon the killing of God:

> Shall God then die as the beasts die? who is it hath broken his rod?
> O God, Lord God of thy priests, rise up now and show thyself God.
> They cry out, thine elect, thine aspirants to heavenward, whose
>   faith is as flame;
> O thou the Lord God of our tyrants, they call thee, their God, by
>   thy name.
> By thy name that in hell-fire was written, and burned at the point
>   of thy sword,
> Thou art smitten, thou God, thou art smitten; thy death is upon
>   thee, O Lord.
> And the love-song of earth as thou diest resounds through the
>   wind of her wings—
> Glory to Man in the highest! for Man is the master of things.
>   (*The Best* 182)

With such blasphemous prophecies, Swinburne established himself as a British Nietzsche: radical to a fault, super-humanist in his belief in man's godlike ability to renew himself and the world, poised to commit deicide on the Christian Trinity, and endowed with a religious sensibility that was inspired by neo-pagan fervor. Also like Nietzsche in his early phase (the *Birth of Tragedy* is heavily indebted to Greek mythology), Swinburne was so enamored of classical mythology that William Rossetti proclaimed him "a manifest pagan" (64). Swinburne's "killing" of God and the deification of man in "Hymn of Man" anticipates Nietzsche's *The Gay Science* and *Thus Spake Zarathustra* by more than a decade, and it would be easy to conclude that Nietzsche drew inspiration from Swinburne, except that no evidence exists that he ever read Swinburne.[2] Theirs was a kindred spirit far more radical than mere atheism would imply, so radical, in fact, that it left contemporary commentators baffled.

Few critics of Swinburne's poetry quite understood that he was not an atheist. An anonymous reviewer for the *London Review* was one of the few who fully grasped the significance of Swinburne's anti-God stance. He wrote very perceptively that

> the strangest and most melancholy fact in these strange and melancholy poems is, not the *absence* of faith, but the presence of a faith which mocks at itself, and takes pleasure in its own degradation. Mr. Swinburne apparently believes in a God, for he makes use of his

name in unnecessary frequency; but, quite as often as not, it is to revile him for suffering the merest riot of the senses to end in disappointment and satiety. He seems to have some idea of heaven. . . . He speaks of hell. . . . To such faith as this we prefer blank atheism. (Anonymous 36)

By naming Swinburne's negative attitude toward the gods a type of faith, this reviewer got it right. The same reviewer is representative of the general mood by confessing that atheism is vastly preferable to Swinburne's perverse faith, for which he tellingly lacks a proper term. Indeed, the reviewer keeps groping for a fitting name or definition for the phenomenon at hand: "But a faith that laughs at itself, that insults its own deities and defiles its own temples—this is the wildest and the dreariest aberration of all" (Anonymous 36). With the benefit of some historical context, Swinburne's stance does not look quite so "aberrant." He was neither the first to write in the vein of absolute misotheism, nor the last, as the subsequent chapters will show.

However, not all misotheists have adopted his style of God-hatred. Equally, if not more, common than absolute misotheism is the attitude of agonistic misotheism, where there are doubts about one's enmity against God, where one tries to enter into dispute with God, and where one literally agonizes over the sad necessity to resent the very God who is recognized as the supreme power in the universe. This negative worship is indeed a paradox, but it is not true, as the anonymous reviewer of Swinburne surmised, that "this kind of writing is so alien to the spirit of our country that it can obtain no root in the national soil. Men may wonder at it for a time; they will cast it out and forget it in the end" (Anonymous 37–38). Hindsight has disproved this view, as the line of misotheists running from Blake through Shelley to Swinburne was not extinguished with the death of Swinburne. Others followed to pick up the slack, including individuals as disparate as Philip Pullman, Peter Shaffer, Rebecca West, and William Empson, to name just a few other British misotheists. They may not always have been as aware of their misotheistic forebears, and certainly not all of them were fully conscious of belonging to a stream of heretical thought that reaches as far back as the Book of Job, but they nevertheless made sure that although the public might want to "forget it in the end," misotheism was there to stay.

Agonistic Misotheism I
Faith, Doubt, and Zora Neale Hurston's Resistance to God

All gods who receive homage are cruel. All gods dispense suffering without reason. Otherwise they would not be worshipped. Through indiscriminate suffering men know fear and fear is the most divine emotion. It is the stones for altars and the beginning of wisdom. Half gods are worshipped in wine and flowers. Real gods require blood.

—Zora Neale Hurston, *Their Eyes Were Watching God* (1937)

ON FIRST SIGHT, THERE IS LITTLE COMMON GROUND BETWEEN Algernon Charles Swinburne—a white, male, British, aristocratic, Victorian *poète maudit*—and Zora Neale Hurston—a black, economically struggling female novelist from the American South. But despite their radical differences in culture, nationality, race, and socioeconomic background, there is one thing that the two artists shared: they were both misotheists. But while Swinburne wore misotheism on his sleeve, so to speak, Hurston kept hers mostly hidden in the closet. Both artists also drew their inspiration from two different strands of influence. The major precursors that shaped Swinburne's developing antireligious outlook included radical poets, especially Blake, Shelley, and Victor Hugo, as well as utilitarian and republican thinkers such as John Stuart Mill, Walter Savage Landor, and Giuseppe Mazzini. Because Swinburne was so outspoken about his influences and referenced his predecessors both in his expository and poetical works, the genesis of his misotheistic outlook can be fairly easily traced. The situation is different with regard to Hurston, who took care to conceal the fact that she harbored secret feelings of bitterness and resentment against God. Not only did she cleverly disguise her misotheism in her published works, she was equally evasive about the major figures who might have influenced her negative view of divinity. According to Deborah Plant, Hurston very likely drew inspiration from Nietzsche: "Though Hurston never mentions or directly alludes to Nietzsche in her work, it is highly probable that she studied him as well as discussed him in her intellectual circles" (52). Of course, Nietzsche is not the only unacknowledged influence contributing to Hurston's unconventional world of ideas. Specifically, her dissenting religious views draw on a range of sources, including Epicurus's bias against the gods, the deistic denial of a personal god, and the anarchist's rebellion against divine tyranny. These Epicurean, deist, and anarchist influences on Hurston have been largely neglected because Hurston scholarship has not come to terms with the anti-devotional aspect of her work.

However, I shall begin this treatment of Hurston's misotheism from a biographical rather than a philosophical perspective. Indeed, besides a host of ideas and thinkers, it was her own father who strongly contributed to Hurston's negative outlook on God. Stephen Finlan has argued that the perception of a tyrannical deity is often the result of parental influences: "The harshness of God is largely a byproduct of the harshness of parents and other authorities. As parents become less frightening figures, God becomes less frightening" (82). And what can be more frightening to a child, especially a girl, than the prospect of being rejected by her father? As we learn from Hurston's biographical writings, she had reason to see in her father a source of anxiety and fear. A crucial passage in her autobiographical musings *Dust Tracks on a Road* (1942) concerns the story of how her fear of the father came to be linked with her doubt about God's benevolence. Concerning the idea of God's infinite goodness, she admits that even as a child "it seemed to me somebody had been fooled"

(*Dust Tracks* 268). When she confided her doubts about God to her father, a Baptist minister and carpenter, she was promptly beaten for her audacity. After this experience, she says,

> my head was full of misty fumes of doubt. Neither could I understand the passionate declarations of love for a being that nobody could see. Your family, your puppy and the new bull-calf, yes. But a spirit far away off who found fault with everybody all the time, that was more than I could fathom. When I was asked if I loved God, I always said yes because I know that that was the thing I was supposed to say. It was a guilty secret with me for a long time. (*Dust Tracks* 268)

It is a guilty secret that Hurston only half reveals even in these lines. Although she describes her disaffection from God as a child, she does not state explicitly that her lack of love might have amounted to an active dislike of God. And what does the pronoun "it" in the last sentence stand for? Its antecedent is surprisingly vague, comprising the whole attitude of the preceding passage rather than a specific noun. I see this as an indication that the guilty secret, that is, the feeling of misotheism, doesn't quite dare to speak its name even in these lines.

As for Hurston's relationship with her father, John Hurston, biographers suggest that there was mutual resentment and that this unhappy situation strongly shaped her attitude toward male-centered authority: "depicted more as a negative force, in Hurston's life as well as in the life of Hurston's mother, John Hurston symbolizes the various faces of patriarchal oppression" (Plant 144). It is not far-fetched to construe a rejection of God from the daughter's experience of being rejected by her own father. Rebecca West underwent a similar fate: she also felt betrayed by her father and then developed a hostility against the divine patriarch. Admittedly, the circumstances of the two women's feeling of abandonment by their respective fathers are different, and I will discuss the specific background of West's problems with her father in the next chapter. In the case of Hurston, Deborah Plant informs us that "she was the second daughter, unwanted, ill treated, and even abandoned by her father. . . . Such treatment of a child by a parent, of a daughter by her father, leaves its marks" (Plant 145). One particularly profound consequence of paternal abandonment, I think, is Hurston's subsequent rebellious attitude to God.

Such a claim resonates with Freud's thinking about the Oedipal implications of man's religious sensibility. In *Totem and Taboo*, Freud theorizes that the figure of God is essentially a symbolical placeholder of the father, after being eliminated by his son (or sons): "The psycho-analysis of individual human beings, however, teaches us with quite special insistence that the god of each of them is formed in the like-ness of his father, that his personal relation to God depends on his relation to his father in the flesh and oscillates and changes along with that relation and that at bottom God is nothing other than an exalted father" (147). From this fundamental premise, Freud proceeds to inquire into the inherent ambivalence of many believers with regard to their God. He found that man's relationship to God was made up of equal parts reverence and guilt. God must be placated, hence the image of the wrathful deity, but at the same time he is wor-shipped with ardor. To Freud, this ambivalence originates in the pri-mal act of patricide, spurred by the son's desire to vest himself in his father's authority, while at the same time trying to assuage his guilt about that act of aggression: "The elevation of the father who had once been murdered into a god from whom the clan claimed descent was a . . . serious attempt at atonement" (149). Taken to its radical conclusion, this view suggests that worship is codependent upon dei-cide; in other words, worship is merely the other side of the coin of God-hatred. Certainly in the work of Peter Shaffer this premise is borne out with surprising precision, as we shall see in another chapter.

But even in a mitigated form, Freud's linking of God with the father figure has the benefit of empirical evidence on its side. In the words of one critic, "poets who could fairly be called antitheistic, Shelley, Swinburne, and James Thompson" have in them a feeling "of actual hostility to the Creator as the source of all evil. . . . The root of this vehement anger . . . is easily traceable to an unsatisfactory relationship between father and son, the source of a burning feeling of injustice, which led them first to project their indignation on to the Creator and then to declare that He did not exist" (Vertue 61). This explanation makes good sense in the context of Freud's assertion that "the religious problem" consists mainly in "the son's sense of guilt and the son's rebelliousness [against the father]" (*Totem and Taboo* 152). Of course, this theory is aligned with Freud's Oedipus complex and, hence, is particularly suitable to explain a man's relationship to God.

Interestingly, though, a similar effect of guilt mixed in with aggres-sion against God can be found among women. For instance, Sylvia Plath's poem "Daddy" is replete with the simultaneous love and hatred for the father. The poem even erases the boundary between God and the father altogether: Plath's daddy is described as a fascist ("Panzer-man, panzer-man, O you—/ Not God but a swastika" [161]) while she also invokes the father as "marble-heavy, a bag full of God" (160). Plath later rationalized her poem as "spoken by a girl with an Electra complex. Her father died while she thought he was God" (quoted in Wagner 196). Thus, resentment for her father vies for prominence with the love she felt for him. It appears, then, that God as a father figure elicits different responses from men and women: men tend to base their aggression against God on feelings of rivalry, whereas women base their hostility more on feelings of frustrated love. Therefore, I venture the hypothesis that there are more men among the deicidal misotheists than women. Women who oppose God seem not so much to work for the extermination of God as they seek to provoke him into showing his affection to them; they keep taunting him with provocative accusations and by lamenting his lack of protectiveness and care. These women are caught in an ambivalent, agonistic relationship with the über-father, wishing that he would turn out to be affectionate but knowing from experience that he is (or can be) rather capricious and mean.

In the case of Zora Neale Hurston, her apprehension about God as an untrustworthy father was compounded by doubt about how God could have permitted slavery. As Stephen Haynes has demonstrated in *Noah's Curse: The Biblical Justification of American Slavery* (2002), God's word had often been invoked as a stock defense for the practice of slavery, usually with references to Noah's curse of Ham's son, or in regard to Apostle Paul's admonition "Slaves, be obedient to them that are your masters" (Ephesians 6:5). As a critic of both Christianity and the institution of slavery, Hurston would have found powerful backing for her outrage had she read the work of European anarchists, especially the Russians Peter Kropotkin and Emma Goldman. Although these Russian anarchists did not have in mind exactly the same kind of slavery that Hurston was thinking of (they were mainly concerned with the "enslavement" of the proletariat), their argument that Christianity was either ineffectual in stopping slavery or actively conducive to its justification would have resonated with Hurston.

In his essay "The Shortcomings of Christianity," the Russian anarchist Peter Kropotkin states that Christianity lost its moral moorings as a religion of liberty by allying itself with the state. More central to Kropotkin's argument, though, is his analysis of slavery. He denounces the fact that "the Apostles St. Peter and St. Paul present as a fundamental Christian virtue the obedience of subjects to the established authorities as to God's anointed with 'fear and trepidation' and the obedience of slaves to their masters" (132). Against the perception of Christianity as a religion of freedom, Kropotkin argues that "various people whom the Church included among the saints, approved slavery, and St. Augustine even vindicated it, asserting that sinners became slaves in punishment for their sins" (133). He further argues that slavery did not end because any religious qualms existed about it: "It was the Revolution and not the Church that abolished slavery in the French Colonies and serfdom in France itself. But during the first half of the nineteenth century, trading in negro-slaves flourished in Europe and in America and the Church was silent" (133). These critical attitudes toward the Bible and the church regarding their complicity with the institution of slavery would have found a sympathetic hearing in Zora Neale Hurston. And while we cannot be sure that Hurston had actually read these sources, indirect evidence suggests that she did, as I will demonstrate later on.

In any case, Hurston's negative attitude toward God is indicative of an ongoing internal struggle about the meaning of the Bible. In the words of one critic, she mocks Christian morality and "dethrones the notion of an omnipotent, omniscient, and intervening God. . . . The supreme being who oversees the affairs of humans is cast out in favor of an indifferent universe" (Plant 29). At the same time, however, her imagination always reverts back to the Bible as a major source of inspiration. Most of her book titles make Christian references, from *Jonah's Gourd Vine* (1934) and *Their Eyes Were Watching God* (1937) to *Moses, Man of the Mountain* (1939) and *Seraph on the Suwanee* (1948). One of her last book-length projects, a manuscript titled "The Golden Bench of God," indicates her continuing obsession with the deity even as she approached her death. The last project she labored over at the time of her death, an epic life of Herod the Great, revolves again around biblical subject matter.

However, the subversive valence of her religious orientation has not been given its due. In fact, one can even argue that her troubling, critical, and at times hostile religious views have been downplayed. Given the massive attention devoted to her masterpiece, *Their Eyes*

Were Watching God, one might expect that readers are stopped in their tracks by the passage quoted in the epigraph, as well as by other similar expressions of anti-God sentiment sprinkled throughout that novel. But such is not the case. My college students never select this passage for commentary, and, when I point it out to them, they have difficulty comprehending it. More surprising still, after scanning some twenty-five scholarly essays and monographs on this novel, I found only one that quotes this extraordinary passage at all, while another one refers to it in passing. The rest is silence. Even Dolan Hubbard's treatment of the novel's religious implications studiously avoids any discussion of the fact that the novel's narrator pronounces that "all gods who receive homage are cruel" (*Their Eyes* 145). Instead, Hubbard affirms somewhat incongruously that Janie eventually "come[s] to terms with the impenetrable majesty of the divine" (111). But the novel's religious subtext can be read very differently, by emphasizing Janie's religious disillusionment. After all, the brutally destructive hurricane at the end of the novel is presented as "a road crusher on a cosmic scale" (161). And after the death of her lover, Tea Cake, Janie is convinced that "God would do less than He had in His heart" (178). Janie has every right to be bitter: the first man in her life to make her truly happy (though they have their occasional fights), Tea Cake is infected with rabies because of a dog bite he sustained while rescuing Janie from a storm that looks very much like a divine scourge. When Tea Cake becomes literally rabid and tries to kill Janie, she shoots him in self-defense. It is not a sequence of events that inspires faith in the smooth workings of Providence. And while Janie is not exactly Zora Neale Hurston, it is clear that Hurston identified with her heroine. For one thing, Hurston had grown up in the same town (Eatonville) that she chose as the setting for the main part of the novel; for another, "the impetus for the tale came from Zora's affair with a man of West Indian parentage whom she had first met in New York in 1931" (Hemenway 231). Beyond those obvious parallels, both Janie and Hurston grapple with the implications of their unconventional religiosity, as their spiritual yearning and familiarity with the Bible mingle with anti-Christian rebellion and blasphemous pronouncements on God. This is the basis of Hurston's agonistic misotheism.

Although this attitude remained mostly hidden, those looking for evidence of Hurston's negative assessment of God will find it everywhere. Specifically, *Their Eyes Were Watching God* identifies God as the capricious force who, without provocation, lets loose death and destruction on the peaceful Everglades and its harmless inhabitants. That the novel is written in a Jobian "trial-of-God" genre is made clear on the very first page. There we are told that Janie had "come back from . . . the sudden dead, their eyes flung wide open in judgment" (1). This implies that the victims of the storm were judging God's action, and that the judgment is not favorable, given the ferocity of the dead people's expression. The eponymous eyes are silent accusers of God. This motif comes back toward the end of the novel ("six eyes were questioning God" [159]), as Janie, Tea Cake, and one of their friends observe signs of the approaching hurricane. The biblical scale of the disaster, together with insistent references to God's will, suggest that God is ultimately responsible for the storm.

But again, Hurston's narrator both blames God for the mayhem and deflects possible charges of blasphemy. The passing of the apocalyptic storm is summed up as follows: "And then again Him-with-the-square-toes had gone back to his house. He stood once more and again in his high flat house without sides to it and without a roof with his soulless sword standing upright in his hand. His pale white horse had galloped over waters, and thundered over land" (168). Who is this allegorical figure of death? The image of Death as a square-toed deity may well have originated in southern legend. But the association of death with the pale white horse rings more familiar. For one thing, James Weldon Johnson invoked this image in "Go Down Death: A Funeral Sermon" (1927). In Weldon's poem, God summons Death to fetch him the soul of a girl who was dying in Savannah, Georgia. Death doesn't refuse the request, and "loosed the reins on his pale, white horse, / And he clamped the spurs to his bloodless sides, / And out and down he rode" (23). Although there are parallels between Weldon's and Hurston's pale white horses, Weldon's rider cuts a rather benevolent figure: "Death didn't frighten Sister Caroline; / He looked to her like a welcome friend" (23). Hurston's personification of Death is more sinister. Not only does he wreak destruction on a large scale, but he appears plainly malevolent with his "soulless sword."

But what about the relationship between allegorical Death and God? Obviously, we need to turn to the Book of Revelation for an answer. There, the pale horse is one of the four Horsemen of the

Apocalypse: "Behold, a pale horse. And the name of him who sat on it was Death" (Rev. 6:8). Significantly, though, the *pale* horse of death in Revelation 6:8 is not the same as another apocalyptic horse, namely the *white* one, representing conquest (Rev. 6:2). To complicate matters, another white horse (which may or may not be the same as the one mentioned in Revelation 6:2) is introduced in Revelation 19, mounted by Christ at the Second Coming: "Now I saw heaven opened, and behold a white horse. And He who sat on him was called Faithful and True and in righteousness He judges and makes war" (Rev. 19:11). Hurston's invocation of the "pale white horse" in *Their Eyes Were Watching God* is thus a heavily overdetermined figure: it invokes both the Fourth Horseman of the Apocalypse (death) as well as the First Horseman (conquest); and it relates, moreover, to Jesus (at the Second Coming). Hurston's use of this complex motif erases the distinctions between these two (or potentially three) different horses, fusing Christ and Death into one symbolical unit. She even encourages such an identification between Death and God (or Christ) by capitalizing the third-person pronoun in "Him-with-the-square-toes." Normally in Christian usage, capitalized pronouns are reserved for the deity alone. All this suggests that while Hurston ostensibly invoked the Fourth Horseman of the Apocalypse as an allegory of death, she actually hints at the identity of Death and God (or Christ). Again, Hurston points toward misotheism, while protecting herself against the charge of open blasphemy. Although in Hurston's case, God-hatred is the faith that dare not speak its name, there are murmurs of it throughout *Their Eyes Were Watching God*.

The few commentators who did tackle Hurston's statement that "all gods who receive homage are cruel" tend to see it as an expression of one character's racist mindset. Indeed, Mrs. Turner, a minor character of mixed race, worships racial whiteness to the point of obsession, thereby paradoxically repudiating part of her own racial heritage. By identifying the statement about the cruel gods with supremacist bigotry, critics follow a decoy thrown out by Hurston. On some level, the anti-God polemic does indeed suggest a connection between the idolization of whiteness and religion: "Mrs. Turner, like all other believers had built an altar to the unattainable—Caucasian characteristics for all. Her god would smite her, would hurl her from pinnacles and lose her in deserts, but she would not forsake his altars. Behind her crude words was a belief that somehow she and others through worship could attain her paradise" (*Their Eyes* 145). On the surface, that comment targets Mrs. Turner's perverse racism, which has elevated whiteness to the status of a quasi-religious idol. Because Janie (who is one-quarter white) is more light-skinned than even Mrs. Turner, the latter's "worship of Janie's mixed-race features borders on self-hatred" (Lamothe 173). But surely, the passage in question has a broader significance beyond the pale of racism. For one thing, the plural "all gods" is conducive to a wider application of Hurston's critique of worship and divinity. For another, the passage does not argue that Mrs. Turner's belief is an exceptional case, a travesty of authentic, dignified religious practices. Instead, there is again this insistent generalizing tendency. Just as the expression "all gods" includes by necessity the persons of the Holy Trinity, the words "like all other believers" suggests that what Mrs. Turner is doing, worshipping a cruel and tyrannical god, is the fate of all worshippers, no matter who their deity is.

There is, however, another racial implication to Mrs. Turner's twisted devotion, and one not often commented on: the white skin tone she adores is consistent with the iconic image of Yahweh in Western pictorial traditions. God is, after all, traditionally depicted as a white male figure. Thus, worship of Yahweh could, from a racial point of view, be seen as worship of a specifically "Caucasian" god. This is an uncomfortable implication that has been rather shunned (or not noticed) by commentators of Hurston's work. But it is quite obvious that here Hurston lets down her guard and opens the door a crack to let us peer into what forms the basis of her condemnation of God (or, as the case may be, of the gods; she often didn't bother to distinguish between mono- and polytheism). Hurston brings to our attention the realization that Mrs. Turner's racism really has a religious subtext, and her narrator is so incensed about religious worship because the (white) gods arranged the world in such a way that it supports the existence of racism, sexism, and slavery.

But another problem bedevils the argument that the statement about divine cruelty is a "critique of Mrs. Turner's misplaced faith in whiteness" (Lamote 168). In saying this, Lamote mistakenly attributes the anti-God statement to the mind of Mrs. Turner. But a careful reading of the whole passage reveals that we are not privy to Mrs. Turner's thoughts but rather to the narrator's own meditations—a narrator who is sometimes identified with Janie and sometimes with an implied author close to Hurston herself. According to Harold Bloom, Hurston herself is "quite likely the omniscient narrating voice" (7) in this novel. Significantly, the passage in question is free of vernacular and is worded in the same kind of elevated diction normally reserved for authorial intrusions in this book. It may seem a point of little consequence initially, but the attempt to pin the indictment of the gods on Mrs. Turner reveals one's constitutional resistance to Hurston's suggestion that Yahweh, too, requires blood.

Some critics of Hurston, however, have rightly acknowledged the deeply conflicted nature of her ideas and worldviews. For instance, Robert Hemenway says that "Hurston was a complex woman with a high tolerance for contradiction.... Her personality could seem a series of opposites" (5). Still, the misotheistic implications of this agonistic world view have so far escaped critical attention. Like Janie in *Their Eyes Were Watching God*, Hurston is torn between the impulse "tuh go tuh God" (*Their Eyes* 192), while at the same time knowing that people are obliged "tuh find out about livin' fuh theyselves" (*Their Eyes* 192), a proposition that bespeaks a fierce Nietzschean individualism. Plant argues indeed that "her orientation toward individualism and achievement seem invigorated by the Nietzschean 'will-to-power,' a concept that translates in Hurston's philosophy as self-mastery and complete autonomy" (177). Like Spinoza, whom Hurston revered, she believed "in the divinity of humankind and the power of reason" (Plant 176). This philosophy is the underlying principle of her daring novel *Moses, Man of the Mountain* (1939).

In Gloria Cronin's opinion, *Moses, Man of the Mountain* constitutes "a full-scale dismantling of the very foundation of Judeo-Christianity" (14). Another critic argues that "*Moses* questions the judiciousness of blacks in embracing the Judeo-Christian God" (Plant 139–40). Hurston's highly subversive procedure in this book is based on her casting Moses not as the servant of God but as an Egyptian-Asian conjurer, a nonwhite culture hero, and an almost Nietzschean Superman (or "Übermensch"). This bold rewriting of Exodus is based on Hurston's highly critical view of the biblical Moses. In one of her letters she insists that "in every move, he [Moses] shows himself as feeling superior to the people, and his scorn for them. There is not one word of love anywhere" (*Life in Letters* 530). By holding "Moses responsible for the actual death of at least a half million ... people" (*Letters* 529), Hurston contradicts a long-standing tradition of African-American identification with Moses as a benevolent savior from bondage. In her own version of Exodus, she deemphasizes the role of God as the ultimate lawgiver. Thus, compared to her negative assessment of Moses in the letter quoted above, Hurston's fictional retelling of the Moses story is more affirmative. Still, her procedure is quasi-heretical in that she "demystifies God" (Plant 139). By rewriting Exodus, she aims to overwrite and thereby efface the biblical account of Moses's accomplishments as a divinely ordained series of events. As Plant put it, "Hurston thus places human destiny in human hands, removing God, the Presence, from the center of human affairs" (140). This is not only the outcome of a secularizing project, it is another veiled attack against the deity itself.

If one combs Hurston's work for expressions of resentment against God, one is bound to find similar, though more or less shrouded, passages. Nobody can blame her for being so circumspect about her misotheism. After all, her goal was to publish her work, and she had troubles enough competing in the relatively small market for African-American letters that included the luminaries of the Harlem Renaissance, most of them males. With the exception of *Their Eyes Were Watching God*, most of her books were greeted with mixed reviews. Especially *Mules and Men* (1935), *Moses, Man of the Mountain*, and *Dust Tracks on a Road* elicited a good deal of unfavorable review attention (Hemenway 218, 273, 308). Indeed, Hurston's writing career never led to prosperity. Her biographer Valerie Boyd refers specifically to "Hurston's growing gang of black male critics" (336), which included Richard Wright and Alain Locke, as well as to a lesser degree Langston Hughes and Ralph Ellison. Henry Louis Gates Jr. summed the situation up as follows: "What we might think of as Hurston's mythic realism, lush and dense within a lyrical black idiom, seemed politically retrograde to the proponents of a social or critical realism. If Wright, Ellison, Brown, and Hurston were engaged in a battle over ideal fictional modes with which to represent the Negro, clearly Hurston lost the battle" (211). Writing during the heyday of the urban black protest novel in the 1930s and 1940s, Hurston's lack of interest in this genre did little to enhance her success as a writer. It is understandable, therefore, that Hurston did not fancy the idea of stoking the flames of criticism by coming out openly with what would have been a shocking rejection of God.

Such a rejection would have almost certainly incensed the black community. In *Jesus, Jobs, and Justice: African American Women and Religion* (2010), Bettye Collier-Thomas documents just how deep religiosity ran among black women: "African American women have been sustained by their faith in God" (508). During slavery, "many women viewed the Bible as a source of inspiration. It became an instrument of freedom and survival, a tool for development" (Collier-Thomas xxv). And in the nineteenth and twentieth centuries, "many black women leaders were deeply imbued with religious convictions and saw their work as a way of implementing their Christian faith" (xviii). The pervasive influence of Christianity is not limited to black females either: "Historically, the church has been more than just *a* community. Rather, for many it represents a way of life and has been at the center of black life" (xxix). Given the centrality of Christian faith in African American culture and the paramount role played by religion in black women's lives, is it any wonder that Hurston kept her religious dissent and misotheism to herself? Throughout her life, she only hinted at the unacceptable facets of her belief. For the rest, she confessed in *Dust Tracks on a Road* that "whatever I do know, I have no intention of putting but so much in the public ears" (189). Life was difficult enough for her as it was, and she was not keen to make it hell by damning God publicly.

However, avoiding public proclamations of religious dissent is not the same as self-censorship. As Darlene Clark Hine has argued, black female artist were resourceful in circumventing cultural norms designed to silence them. Specifically, their social marginality "enabled subordinate Black woman to craft the veil of secrecy and to perfect the art of dissemblance" (915). This mode of dissembling, according to Hine, is the Black woman's technique of resistance since it allows subversive ideas to find expression, albeit not explicitly. Cronin agrees with this assessment, stating that "Hurston was a warrior in disguise who produced an encoded response to racism by reinventing facts, withholding information, blurring history and fiction, wearing masks, changing hats, lying as a celebration of the human voice, and contradicting herself to prevent closure" (18). What goes for racism and sexism, also goes for hoodoo. In Hurston's own admission, "[hoodoo] is not the accepted theology of the Nation and so believers conceal their faith" (quoted in Boyd 177). It is my contention that the technique of concealment extended from hoodoo

practices to misotheism. Had she dared to come out openly as a misotheist rebel, it is doubtful that Hurston would have had even the
limited success that she enjoyed during the 1930s. More likely, she
would have alienated practically her entire black audience, and she
would have nonplussed her limited white readership as well.

That is why the misotheistic undercurrent of her writings must be
carefully disentangled from a host of seemingly conventional Christian thematics. This is especially the case in her first novel, *Jonah's
Gourd Vine* (1934). There, the misotheistic passage from *Their Eyes
Were Watching God*, quoted in the epigraph of this chapter, can be
found in its incipient form. But to make the substance of her meditations on the immoral character of God more palatable, Hurston's narrator in *Jonah's Gourd Vine* does not attack God directly, but rather
shows how warped the normal believer's attitude to the deity is,
which suggests that the deity itself might not be worthy of worship.
Pious people, we are told in *Jonah's Gourd Vine*, are "ever eager to
break the feet of fallen idols" (166). Hurston here imputes to her gods
a blind destructiveness that needs to be resisted. In a style that recalls
what we have seen of the anti-God rhetoric in *Their Eyes Were
Watching God*, Hurston's narrator states that "gods show feet—not
faces. Feet that crush—feet that crumble—feet that have no eyes for
men's suffering nor ears for agony. . . . If gods have no power for cruelty, why then worship them? Gods tolerate sunshine, but bestir
themselves that men may have storms" (166). The theme of the
storm, combined with the emphasis on divine cruelty as the cause for
religious veneration, clearly anticipates the narrator's protest against
divinity in *Their Eyes Were Watching God*.

But, again, we must be mindful that Hurston was "a textual
trickster, a shape-shifting African-American Hoodoo woman writer
and scholar" (Snyder 173) because we are not given the misotheistic draught straight up. While *Their Eyes Were Watching God*
allows us to misread Hurston's statement about divine cruelty as an
expression of Mrs. Turner's racist mindset, *Jonah's Gourd Vine*
allows us to read (or misread) Hurston's meditation about the brutal aspect of divinity as a female character's attack against patriarchy. Hattie, who accuses the local preacher of adultery, is said to be
"a goddess for the moment. She sat between the Cherubim on the
altar of destruction" (167). At her feet sits the fallen idol, the town's
charismatic preacher, John Pearson. This situation either allows for

an antireligious reading, in which Hattie plays the role of the human triumph over a vanquished god, or it can be taken to mean that Hattie is merely mocking the idol of masculinity. Again, it is important to read this passage from *Jonah's Gourd Vine* in its full context. That passage comes directly after one in which religious faith is characterized as depending on human self-abasement: people need to worship a cruel deity because no other kind of deity would compel worship. There is no love between humans and their gods, only fear, distrust, and hatred. That is why, after the rare overthrow of a god, humanity gathers to trample on the remnants of the deity: "No fury so hot as that of a sycophant as he stands above a god that has toppled from a shrine"(166). Thus, while Hattie apparently addresses the village's idolized preacher (an idol of masculinity), she is really talking about the patriarchal god of Christianity.

I am basing this argument not only on the context of the passage, but also on a startling turn of phrase that points directly to a precedent in the history of misotheism. As Hurston's narrator informs us, the "goddess," Hattie, declares that "those who held themselves above me shall be abased. Him who pastored over a thousand shall rule over none. His name shall be a hissing" (167). Although Hattie ostensibly refers to John Pearson, the exalted preacher of Zion Hope, this man is really just a conduit for her feelings about the Almighty. Throughout this passage, the image of the preacher is fused with the image of deity, as the narrator makes sweeping generalizations about the nature of God based on the nature of his servants. And the conclusion she arrives at, i.e., that John Pearson's name "shall be a hissing," is practically indistinguishable from a curse hurled at God. Interestingly, Hurston's discourse of broken divinity and the phrasing of her curse ("his name shall be a hissing") distinctly invokes similar language used by Pierre-Joseph Proudhon (in English translation), some eighty-eight years earlier:

> And now here you are dethroned and broken. *Your name,* so long the last word of the savant, the sanction of the judge, the force of the prince, the hope of the poor, the refuge of the repentant sinner,—this incommunicable name, I say, henceforth an object of contempt and curses, *shall be a hissing among men.* For God is stupidity and cowardice; God is hypocrisy and falsehood; God is tyranny and misery; God is evil. (322, my emphasis)

Proudhon's *The Philosophy of Misery* (1846) is quite possibly the only other work on record in which the clause "[God's] name shall be a hissing" appears, and hence Hurston's use of that conspicuous phrase strongly suggests that she was acquainted with the Frenchman's misotheistic anti-prayer. The parallel between Proudhon's blasphemous polemic and similar language in *Jonah's Gourd Vine* reinforces my claim about Hurston's animosity against God. This is not surprising, given that "the ideas of Nietzsche, like those of Freud and Marx, had wide currency during the first decades of the twentieth century. They proffered much food for thought for America's 'lost generation,' many of whom were associates of Harlem's Black intelligentsia" (Plant 52). It becomes increasingly likely, therefore, that Hurston drew her inspiration not only from the pantheistic Spinoza, the deicidal Nietzsche, and the anti-religious Freud, but also from a political misotheist like Proudhon.

The novel's title, by the way, has its own relevance in this regard. The protagonist, John Pearson, is ostensibly modeled on Jonah, and hence a comparison between Hurston's story and the biblical Book of Jonah is called for. Not surprisingly, Hurston's narrative deviates significantly from the original, Old Testament version. In the biblical story, Jonah is a reluctant prophet. After foretelling the wholesale destruction of Nineveh, he refuses to preach repentance in order to placate God and to possibly avoid the catastrophe. Moreover, when God has a change of heart because the people of Nineveh appear capable of being reformed after all, Jonah refuses to relate the revised prophecy to his people and instead tries to flee God's command. His futile escape lands him in the belly of a whale, an experience that convinces Jonah that it's time to obey God's command. He goes back to Nineveh, tells people to mend their ways, which they do, and thereby placates God's wrath.

How did Hurston, who was obsessed with questions of divine justice (or injustice), handle this story material? Interestingly, she did not emphasize a merciful god or depict a reluctant prophet who is eventually brought back into the fold by accepting God's will. Just like the biblical Jonah, the protagonist of Hurston's novel, John Pearson, is at first blessed by good fortune and serves as the town's prophetic preacher. However, contrary to the biblical version, Hurston's "Jonah" does not deliver a successful sermon that causes the town to become virtuous in the end, and neither is he saved by God's inescapable grace. He tries to abandon his permissive lifestyle, voluntarily lays down his church office, and marries a good woman. But God's grace is blunted by Pearson's dominant cravings, and the protagonist's reformation is short-lived. He soon falls prey to lust again, and after another bout of adultery he is run over by a train on a level crossing. While Jonah came around to save Nineveh, even at the cost of contradicting his earlier doomsday prophecy, John Pearson does not serve as his people's messenger of redemption. It hardly surprises that such a pessimistic and subversive rewriting of the Bible should be biographically motivated. It is worth noting that Hurston's own father, who had little investment in his daughter's well-being, serves as the model for John Pearson, even sharing the same first name with him. The collision with the train is also biographical: Hurston's father died in 1918 when his car was struck on a level crossing. Thus, the novel can be seen as working through more than one painful aspect of Hurston's religious life. In it she dramatized her negative view of the father as an unworthy prophet, even as she called into question God the father as a benevolent patriarch, whose grace, when dispensed, is supposed to be inescapable.

By contrast to Hurston's negative twist on the Jonah story, Graham Greene later in the same decade published a version that portrayed a more orthodox providential message. His 1939 novel *The Power and the Glory* also revolves around a sinful preacher who tries to escape the will of God. Although the "whisky priest" in Greene's novel doesn't realize it, it is God's will that he continue fulfilling the duties of the cloth throughout the period of religious persecution during Mexico's revolutionary years. In Greene's novel, God's will finally catches up with the fugitive priest, and he dies under circumstances that imply a full redemption for his life and the lives of his fellow believers. While Greene's alcoholic priest dies as a martyr, Hurston's philandering priest dies as an unredeemed sinner. Not only is the operation of Providence absent in Hurston's novel, but the story also contains a subversive core of doubt about the pleasure God takes in crushing people and things, and about the self-abasing nature of religious worship. Unlike Jonah's god, the god of Hurston's story is curiously impotent in effecting good, ultimately failing to make an impression on Pearson and his townspeople. God only lives in the mouth of the sinful preacher, and if the car crash in the end is the result of divine inter-vention, then it is reactionary, resolving nothing and redeeming no one.

My claim that Hurston should be read into the history of miso-theism can be bolstered by reference to her book of memoirs, *Dust Tracks on a Road*. Although her biographical writings tread carefully around her own contrarian religious views, the scope of Hurston's spiritual doubt is a good test case for the whole history behind this blasphemous idea. Indeed, Hurston's attitudes can be traced to vari-ous ideologies of liberation and dissent, notably to philosophical anarchism and deism, and even back to Epicureanism. As for the lat-ter, the Epicurean roots of Hurston's religious outlook are most clearly evident in her essay "Religion" (1942). When she states that "I do not pray. . . . Prayer seems to be a cry of weakness, and an attempt to avoid, by trickery, the rules of the game as laid down" (278), she echoes Epicurus's rejection of prayer over two millennia ago: "It is senseless to ask the gods for what a man is able to provide for himself" (*Remains* 117). Like Epicurus, Hurston rejects prayer out of respect for human self-reliance and because she laughs to scorn the idea that God or the gods are fearsome. The absence of fear vis-à-vis divinity corresponds to the first principle of Epicurus's *Tetraphar-macos* (or the "four-part cure"): "God is not to be feared" (Rist 147). The second principle of the *Tetrapharmacos*, summed up in the words "death is not to be feared," also features in Hurston's philosophy: "When the consciousness we know as life ceases, I know that I shall still be part and parcel of the world. . . . Why fear? The stuff of my being is matter, ever changing, ever moving, but never lost; so what need of denominations and creeds to deny myself the comfort of all my fellow men?" (*Dust Tracks* 279). Hurston here not only recalls Epicurus's *Tetrapharmacos*, but she also adopts the principle of Epi-curean "atomism." Epicurus put the same principle as follows: "Death is nothing to us. For what has been dissolved has no sense-experience, and what has no sense-experience is nothing to us" (*Reader* 33). According to Epicurean materialism, human beings, including their minds, are made up of tiny particles or atoms; hence, death is com-plete annihilation since the atoms of the body simply disperse, caus-ing whatever is called soul or spirit to disperse as well. In other words, Epicurus does not believe in either Providence or an afterlife beyond the preservation of the atoms that survive after the complete decay of the physical body. Hurston shares these materialist premises when she asserts in *Dust Tracks* that the most fundamental element of her being is not spirit but matter (279).

Epicurus did not cross the threshold into plain atheism, but instead assigned the gods insignificant roles, convincing his disciples of the disconnected, disinterested, self-involved existence of the gods. In the true sense of the word, these gods are apathetic to human existence. Hurston engages this concept directly by saying "it is futile for me to seek the face of, and fear, an accusing God withdrawn somewhere beyond the stars in space" (323). This notion of a withdrawn, distant God has passed from Epicurus into the theology of deism. According to this view, God did initially create the world, but then withdrew and left his creation to its own devices, just as a clock-maker releases his mechanism into the world, where it continues to function independent of its maker. Thus, Hurston's religious outlook shares some traits with deistic principles as well. This aspect is further evidenced in the Appendix to *Dust Tracks on a Road*, published posthumously: "If I have not felt the divinity of man in his cults, I have found it in his works. When I lift my eyes to the towering structures of Manhattan, and look upon the mighty tunnels and bridges of the world, I know that my search is over and that I can depart in peace" (232). The same principle finds expression in Thomas Paine's deistic treatise *The Age of Reason* (1794): "the Creator of man is the Creator of science: and it is through that medium that man can see God" (181). Both Hurston and Paine make rationalist inferences, judging divinities by the greatness of the works created by them. At times, this rationalism shades into pantheism. When Hurston writes that "the springing of the yellow line of morning out of the misty deep of dawn is glory enough for me" (279), she not only makes a covert reference to the Lord's Prayer ("the Power and the Glory"), but she also validates Spinoza's identification of the physical universe with the reality of God. Indeed, one of Hurston's few acknowledged influences was the pantheist Baruch Spinoza. But it is my contention that Hurston was more Epicurean than Spinozan, and that not only because some of Spinoza's key ideas can be traced to Epicurus: "Spinoza was an Epicurean in repudiating a transcendent God and religious awe and fear" (Hampshire xxxiii). In addition, Epicurus seems to take precedence over Spinoza in Hurston's mind because she derived her disdain for the gods from Epicurus, not from Spinoza. Finally, Hurston's cynical exposure of divine folly in the Bible (especially in the posthumously published "Seeing the World as It Is") follows directly in the tradition of utilitarian and deistic jeremiads against the cruelty and unreason of the Judeo-Christian god.

Besides Epicurean, Spinozan, and deistic elements in Hurston's work, it appears that anarchism can also be traced as one of her influences. Just as it is likely that Hurston had read Proudhon's *Philosophy of Misery*, it is quite possible that she was acquainted with the work of another vocal God-hater of the nineteenth century, the anarchist Mikhail Bakunin. When Hurston's narrator declares in *Their Eyes Were Watching God* that "All gods who receive homage are cruel. . . . Real gods require blood" (145), she echoes a sentence from Bakunin's *God and the State* (1871) in which he says, "all religions are cruel, all founded on blood" (25). These anarchists would have appealed to Hurston not only because of their anti-God rhetoric, but also because of their linking of slavery with religion, as indicated above. I am obviously not arguing that Hurston was an anarchist. But the state of affairs that prevails "on the muck" in *Their Eye Were Watching Gods*, with a kind of voluntary trade association, a society free from taxation, policing, and coercive laws, has more than a passing similarity with the anarchist collectives envisioned by the likes of Proudhon or Kropotkin. Also, the fact that "Hurston's intellectual standpoints . . . culminated in an uncompromising individualism" (Plant 177) and that "Hurston's greatest legacy is that of resistance" (Plant 182) testifies to an underlying anarchist sensibility. However, such tendencies remained latent, as Hurston's professed politics weren't anywhere near the far-left spectrum represented by anarchism. In fact, she had gained a reputation as a "black conservative" by, among other things, openly supporting a conservative GOP presidential candidate, Senator Robert Taft, in 1952 (Boyd 411), and by speaking up against school de-segregation in 1954, arguing that black children would not necessarily learn better in a mixed-racial environment (Boyd 423–24). Her anti-God sentiment was a facet of her belief system that jarred with those publicly endorsed, conservative positions.

Moreover, she had tasted the bitterness of public accusations of immorality and did not relish the prospect of giving her detractors further ammunition with which to question her integrity. In 1948 she was arrested on charges of sexual transgressions involving minors. These trumped-up charges were gleefully taken up by some of her enemies in the black community. The Baltimore paper *Afro-American* used the false allegations against Hurston to conduct a vicious smear campaign against a writer they considered as having written sexually permissive fiction (Boyd 394–400). One can only imagine what the *Afro-American* would have had to say if Hurston had openly cursed God in print. The scandal caused by the sex charges brought against her drove Hurston to the brink of suicide (Boyd 397). Hurston complained that "my country has failed me utterly. My race has seen fit to destroy me without reason, and with the vilest tools conceived of by man so far" (*Life in Letters* 572). She knew that stepping openly into the shoes of misotheistic forebears like Swinburne, Shelley, or Proudhon would mean facing even more censure and hostility. Therefore, she opted for a form of self-restraint that agreed with her creative talents insofar as it allowed her to subvert conventional religious piety without causing too much alarm. Using clever disguises and oblique modes of attack, she subverted the tenets of the Judeo-Christian tradition without seeming to be overtly blasphemous.

That open blasphemy was not an easy choice even for very popular authors in American culture can be verified by reference to an American *man* of letters who equally withheld the truth about his anti-God sentiments from his published works. Most people are not even aware of the fact that Mark Twain (Samuel Langhorne Clemens) was a vehement enemy of God. Only those familiar with Twain's apocrypha know about his explicit and searing indictments of God. His "Reflections on Religion" (a posthumous title given to a series of diary entries written toward the end of his life) were suppressed by Clemens himself and, after his death, censored by Twain's literary executor and by his daughter, Clara (Neider 2). The subject matter of Twain's reflections on religion was deemed far too explosive to see the light of day, amid fears that they would taint his literary legacy. In fact, it is a small miracle that these musings were not destroyed outright. Here is a passage from Twain's remarkable secret "Reflections":

> The real God, the genuine God, the Maker of the mighty universe is just like all the other gods in the list. He proves every day that He takes no interest in man, nor in the other animals, further than to torture them, slay them and get out of this pastime such entertainment as

it may afford—and do what he can not to get weary of the eternal and changeless monotony of it. It is to these celestial bandits that the naïve and confiding and illogical human rabbit looks for a Heaven of eternal bliss. (47)

This is obviously not far from Zora Neale Hurston's dictum that "all gods dispense suffering without reason" (*Their Eyes* 145). The similarity between Twain's misotheistic fury and key passages in *Their Eyes Were Watching God* extends to the motif of the rabbit helplessly watching God. Twain's "confiding and illogical human rabbit" is reminiscent of the terrified rabbit seeking shelter during the hurricane in Hurston's novel: "Six eyes were questioning *God*. Through the screaming wind they heard things crashing and things hurtling and dashing with unbelievable velocity. A baby rabbit, terror ridden, squirmed through a hole in the floor and squatted off there in the shadows against the wall" (*Their Eyes* 159). And, like Hurston's rabbit, expecting the worst alongside its three human occupants of the cabin, Twain does not look to God to find "a Heaven of eternal bliss" (Twain 47). The reference to the rabbit in both texts invokes the idea of man as a helpless, frightened prey of God. But unlike the anarchist treatises on God, which Hurston may well have read, she could not have known about Twain's misotheistic "Reflections on Religion," which were not published until 1963 (in *The Hudson Review*), three years after her death. The parallels between the two passages are incidental, documenting a similar vision of two kindred spirits, rather than a direct intertextual relationship.

Instead of entrusting her nonconformist ideas to secret diaries, as Twain did, Hurston communicated her religious doubts in letters to her friends, including Carl Van Vechten, Langston Hughes, and Herbert Sheen, among others. Interestingly, these letters are rather more restrained when compared to the traces of anti-God rhetoric with which her fiction is laced. For instance, she confessed to her former husband, Herbert Sheen, feelings of a resentful nature: "Why cannot His will be as freely revealed since it is so important? And why allow Himself to be so easily misconstrued" (*Life in Letters* 699). But she deflects any stronger expressions of revulsion by invoking a Feuerbach-like rationalism ("God made in man's image" [*Letters* 699]), and by revealing her deistic inclination: "I have no belief in any bearded divinity sitting on a cloud. . . . To me there is LAW to which

all things in the universe must conform" (*Life in Letters* 599). However, she also admitted that because of being subject to racial discrim-
ination, "my god of tolerance has forsaken me. . . . I have become
what I never wished to be, a good hater" (*Life in Letters* 475). This
statement can be seen as simply invoking a metaphorical "god," and
certainly it appears to have been intended that way. However, the
reference to Jesus's words on the cross ("why hast thou forsaken
me?"), as well as Hurston's awareness that the racial state of affairs in
America appears to be part of God's ordained order, undercut any
innocent metaphoricity. In this light, even casual words betray a sim-
mering resentment, and the object of Hurston's hatred seems to be as
much the effect of racism in America as God's tolerating (and perhaps
even encouraging) racially motivated injustice.

Compared to Twain, then, Hurston had a more complicated relationship to religion and spirituality. Surely, religious inspiration was
closer to Hurston's heart than it was to Twain's. She made religion
regularly the focal point of her writings, be it in the form of anthro-
pological field work, collecting folktales with a religious slant, record-
ing the poetic sermons of black preachers, or basing her stories upon
episodes from the Bible. At the same time, she read the Bible with a
critical eye, and she declared "christianity [*sic*], as practiced, an atten-
uated form of nature-worship" (*Life in Letters* 139). Besides approaching religion and its rituals with the rationalism of a trained
anthropologist, she also had an abiding need for spirituality, as manifested in her fascination with, and involvement in, hoodoo practices.
Her resistance to God, which could modulate into hatred, was founded upon her yearning for a cooperative, nonauthoritarian, and toler-
ant form of social organization, a goal she did not see achieved or
even advanced by the agents of Christianity. As Gloria Cronin puts it:
"Hurston's persistent feminocentric theological revisions of the
Judeo-Christian narrative were her attempts to heal the divisions
between blacks and whites, paganism and Judeo-Christianity, men
and women, divisions that had deeply marked her life" (24).

There were glimmers of hope in this endeavor, as when Hurston
wrote in a private letter late in her life that "God balances the sheet
in time" (*Life in Letters* 754), but one wonders whether, as her death
was approaching, she was trying to reassure herself (or the recipient
of her letter), against her better judgment. Thus, rather than ending
this chapter on such a note, as Valerie Boyd ended her biography

with the sentence quoted above, I would like to place the emphasis differently. In an earlier letter, Hurston had written "I know I cannot straighten out with a few pen-strokes what God and men took centuries to mess up" (*Life in Letters* 286). This critical, protesting attitude outweighs in my view any expressions of conventional piety in Hurston's work. She even alluded to the possibility that her notion of a tyrannical and opposable god is shared more generally among the black population. As she wrote in *Mules and Men*, "God is the supposedly impregnable white masters, who are nevertheless defeated by Negroes" (224). But here she probably went too far, assuming an attitude in others that she found well formed within herself. As Robert Hemenway commented, she tried to persuade others of a very difficult proposition: "If God is a white man, the symbol of oppression, then white Christian claims to a God of love are dubious. Moreover, if the white man's power can easily be circumvented or defeated, often without punishment, the white man's God can hardly be a figure commanding instant, ungrudging obedience" (224). This is the essence of Hurston's misotheistic attitude toward God, but it is not the case that this position was widely shared or even understood by her contemporaries, black or white. In her antagonistic faith, Hurston was walking on thin ice, and she was largely alone. Only a woman of Hurston's stalwart determination, spiritual fortitude, and utter lack of self-pity could remain so poised, so graceful, and so positive, knowing what she knew and enduring the agony of her negative belief without flinching. This is her claim to heroism and, ultimately, what puts such a distinctive mark on her life and work.

Agonistic Misotheism II

Bad Fathers, Historical Crises, and Rebecca West's Accusations Against God

> ... the human will should [not] be degraded by bowing to this master criminal. One hates our fathers for having committed themselves to such a worship and wonders how they could have fancied God was kind.
>
> —Rebecca West, "The New God" (1917)

R EBECCA WEST (1892–1983; DAME CICELY ISABEL ANDREWS, NÉE Fairfield) was one of Britain's leading public intellectuals and an outstanding literary humanist of the twentieth century. While still in her early twenties, she was considered a prodigy by the likes of George Bernard Shaw, Ford Madox Ford, and H. G. Wells. Among her prodigious output is the first novel by a woman about World War I, *The Return of the Soldier* (1918), a psychological biography of Saint Augustine, a magisterial book about Yugoslavia titled *Black Lamb and Grey Falcon* (1941), and reports about the Nuremberg Trials for *The New Yorker* (reprinted in *A Train of Powder* [1955]). Besides all this, Rebecca West was also one of the rare female opponents of God.

Along with Zora Neale Hurston, West belongs to the vanguard of modern, emancipated, and self-confident women who threw down the gauntlet to God. Yet, during her own lifetime West's rebellious religiosity went virtually unnoticed, a sign either of how well she concealed her religious radicalism or of how inconceivable and, hence, unreadable her stance really was for her contemporaries. The first explicit recognition of West's resentment against God is buried deep inside Victoria Glendinning's biography of West, published in 1987: "God for Rebecca West was the ultimate intimate enemy. She pitted herself against Him as if she were a critic and He a recalcitrant artist whose performance did not live up to its reputation" (224). But, as Glendinning noted perceptively, West did not always situate herself in the position of superior critic of God's botched creation. The relationship could easily turn into something closer to victimhood: "She felt like Job, persecuted by God (and by man, woman, and child), and any friend who played the part of Job's comforter got short shrift from her" (Glendinning xvii). Rather than imitate Job's meek attitude to God's persecution and instead of praising the name of the Lord after experiencing disillusionment, West's reaction to God was closer to the curse spoken by Job's wife, with the difference that West did not expect to be struck dead as a result of her defiance. Rather, her will to live and her ability to face adversity gained additional strength from her anti-devotional outlook.

By studying West's antagonistic faith, we can revisit a set of thought systems, composed of Epicureanism, utilitarianism, anarchism, and Nietzschean ideas, that had predisposed others toward misotheism, including Swinburne and Hurston; but in addition to reinforcing misotheism's general trajectory of ideas, West's example also allows us to explore the fluctuations of this outlook over her lifetime. In West's case, the force of history, notably the experience of the Blitz, overruled for a while the misotheistic tendencies of the above-mentioned philosophies, making room for a more conventional form of piety. Indeed, West's misotheism came full circle during her life: her hostility to God was particularly pronounced in the early and late phases of her life. But during her middle years, from about 1940 to 1955, she made strides toward embracing a more affirmative kind of faith. In the long run, however, West could not keep the misotheistic impulse in check, and it reaffirmed itself again toward the end of her life. This curious trajectory of her religious views traces the inverse pattern of Elie Wiesel's spiritual journey. As we will see in the next chapter, Wiesel went from being a pious Hasidic Jew, to becoming an outspoken opponent of God, only to return again into the fold of a more affirmative Jewish belief in his later years. It will be interesting to inquire into the grounds for this contrasting pattern.

As Carl Rollyson has pointed out in his biography of West, the young Cicely Isabel Fairfield (before she took the pen name Rebecca West) grew up in a household dominated by an irreligious, disputatious father. Despite being a devoted follower of Herbert Spencer's economic liberalism, Charles Fairfield was happy to bring home radicals of every stripe, including anarchists, Fabians, and social Darwinists, whom he encouraged to indulge their political rhetoric freely in front of his wife and daughters. This precipitated a remarkable political precocity in Fairfield's daughter. Rebecca West later remarked that during her early youth "the various varieties of anarchism, and the conflict between pacifist and terrorist anarchism, were frequently the subject of conversation" (*Letters* 256). West's relationship to anarchism had a personal coloring, as her father had been tutored by Elie Reclus, one of the two famous Reclus brothers who had been instrumental in nineteenth-century French anarchism. As a lifelong Liberal (with a capital "L"), West always drew some of her inspiration from the creed of philosophical anarchism, although she also looked at their radical ideas with some mild bemusement. Notably her late travel book *Survivors in Mexico*, written between 1966 and 1970 (published posthumously in 2003), brims with anecdotes and comments about the French and Russian anarchists of the second half of the nineteenth century. Thus, it is easier to trace the influence of anarchist theories in West than in the case of Zora Neale Hurston, although, as discussed earlier, Hurston's use of specific misotheistic formulations which echo anarchist tracts is a good indication that she had read Proudhon's *The Philosophy of Misery* and Bakunin's *God and the State*.

An even stronger parallel between Hurston and West than this possibility of a shared exposure to anarchist ideology is the fact that both women were disappointed with their fathers. As with Hurston, West's resentment of God was in part a reaction to her father's abandonment of her. Charles Fairfield mysteriously departed from the family in 1901, when she was just eight years old. The circumstances of his disappearance are not entirely clear, but the biographers basically agree that he went in for a speculative business venture in West Africa, was bankrupted in the process, and returned to Liverpool, where he took up lodging in a cheap boardinghouse until his death in 1906. Rebecca West was traumatized by the sudden and quite inexplicable disappearance of her father. One does not need to be a devotee of Freud to recognize the fundamental impact that the father's withdrawal would have on a young girl's psychology (she was the youngest of three children, all daughters). In much of her writing, she goes almost obsessively over the same ground, reenacting the drama of the father's withdrawal. This theme is particularly prominent in the novels *The Judge* (1922) and *The Fountain Overflows* (1956), and it surfaces repeatedly in *Black Lamb and Grey Falcon* (1941). What matters for the purpose of discussion here is the fact that she saw in her father's abandonment a fitting emblem of parental irresponsibility on a cosmic scale. Indeed, when Marion, the unwed mother in *The Judge*, pronounces that "every mother is a judge who sentences the children for the sins of the father" (346), she ostensibly responds to the behavior of men who shirk the responsibilities of (unwed) parenthood. Implicitly, however, she is really addressing the sins of God the father, for which every human life is a form of expiation.[1] The statement implies that the heavenly father is the origin of sin and that simply being born means to pay the price for God's own immorality.

But as much as West's and Hurston's personal experience and worldview share similarities, there are some crucial differences between these two women of letters. West was not confronted with the wounding reality of racism; at the same time, Hurston was spared the utter disillusionment of the Great War, which traumatized British culture (not to mention the rest of Europe) in a way American life was not affected. West, who during the Great War wrote radical journalism for the socialist paper *The Clarion*, for the feminist *The Freewoman*, and for the leftist American magazine *The New Republic*, was horrified by the carnage, especially the indiscriminate slaughter on the battlefields of Flanders. Learning of the suffering, the mutilation, and the killing that happened on an unimaginable scale during trench warfare, Rebecca West looked up to the sky and shook her fist at the hidden, merciless, grim deity whose silence during the massacres amounted for her to an outright hatred of man.

West sketched the outlines of such an unsavory creator god in her first novel *The Return of the Soldier* (1918), which is set in the midst of World War I. The novel takes place far away from the battlefields, among the quiet and decorous milieu of Britain's social upper crust. But the peace of this privileged setting is disrupted by the return of a soldier suffering from shell shock. Chris Baldry, home on sick leave after a bursting shell left him amnesiac, cannot remember the last fifteen years of his life and, as a result, he does not recognize his wife, Kitty, a society woman who wears sparkling jewelry and dresses in fashionable clothes. Instead, he wants to be reunited with his first love, an earthy working-class woman by the name of Margaret, who is outwardly unsuitable for him but offers the kind of matronly warmness and sexual responsiveness that Chris needs. Although the ensuing love triangle is engrossing for its social class tensions, its feminist implications, and its overall romantic interest, I am skipping over these elements to focus on the heretofore overlooked theme of misotheism in this novel.

Throughout *The Return of the Soldier*, West suggests a causal connection between the horrors of war and the existence of an uncaring god. Although the war is never explicitly depicted in the novel, there are indirect glimpses of the conflict, mainly through remembered sequences of newsreel footage, showing the ghastly devastation of no-man's-land, with soldiers sprinting across a desolate landscape pockmarked by craters from artillery shells. These brief flashes of the warfare are relayed through the novel's narrator, a bystander named Jenny. This character is also the conduit for a lengthy visionary passage in which she imagines that, instead of merely losing his mind, Chris had actually died on the battlefields of Flanders. In this strange and quite fantastical interlude, Chris's ghost is seen walking the countryside in what can only be described as an existentialistic dream vision:

> There, past a church that lacks its tower, stand a score of houses, each hideous with patches of bare bricks that show like sores through the ripped-off plaster and uncovered rafters which stick out like broken bones. There are still people living there. A slut sits at the door of a filthy cottage, counting some dirty linen and waving her bare arms at some passing soldiers. And at another house there is a general store with strings of orange onions and bunches of herbs hanging from the roof, a brown gloom rich with garlic and humming with the flies that live all the year round in French village shops. . . . It is there that Chris is standing, facing across the counter an old man in a blue blouse, with a scar running

> white into the grey thickets of his beard, an old man with a smile at once lewd and benevolent, repulsive with dirt and yet magnificent by reason of the Olympian structure of his body. I think he is the soul of the universe, equally cognizant and disregardful of every living thing. (66)

The seedy figure of "Olympian structure" introduced at the end of this passage is none other than God himself. The divine apparition, "repulsive with dirt and yet magnificent" holds the fate of the world in his hands, as Chris, or rather the disembodied spirit of Chris, is soon to realize: "He is looking down on two crystal balls that the old man's foul strong hands have rolled across to him" (66). One crystal ball shows him Margaret and her world and the other one Kitty and Jenny; as Chris eagerly reaches for Margaret's globe, his sleeve catches on the other ball and sends it crashing to the floor: "The old man's smile continues to be lewd and benevolent, he is still not more interested in me than in the bare-armed slut; and Chris is wholly enclosed in his intentness on his chosen crystal. No one weeps for this shattering of our world" (67). This bizarre sequence is Jenny's way of constructing an explanatory narrative to account for the state of disorder and anomie created by the war and its effects, notably Chris's delusional love affair with Margaret.

At the bottom of Jenny's (and of West's) deepest belief stands the conviction that the unhappy state of affairs on this earth, ranging from the horrors of warfare to the subversion of family relations, to sickness, is the work of a god who is insensitive, incompetent, and coarse. It is surprising how few critics—if any at all—have taken note of the above scene in *The Return of the Soldier*. The one critic who quotes the entire passage doesn't seem to "see" its religious implications at all, commenting on it as follows: "This story is intended as an explanation of Chris's amnesia, a metaphorical interpretation that would access his deepest spiritual reality. It serves instead as an explanation for Jenny's own trauma, the shattering of her world caused by Chris's rejection" (Bonikowski 527). Not a word is said about the fact that Jenny has just given us a lewd, dirty, careless god, who cannot keep his world in order. One is reminded of the way the misotheistic scene in *Their Eyes Were Watching God* ("all gods who receive homage are cruel") has failed to register properly. In both cases, readers understand the words on the page but fail to grasp their import as a frontal attack against God.

The Return of the Soldier contains more than one passage that obliquely reveals the misotheistic bent of its author. When Jenny thinks about Margaret as "a patron saint . . . whose kindliness could be daunted only by some special and incredibly malicious decision of the Supreme Force" (77), we see the flickering of anti-God sentiment, and when we read Jenny's summing up of the human condition, we may as well be reading West's own mind: "I had of late been underestimating the cruelty of the order of things. Lovers are frustrated; children are not begotten that should have had the loveliest life, the pale usurpers of their birth die young. Such a world will not suffer magic circles to endure" (78). This existentialist protest against the order of things, anticipating the explicit and heroic pessimism of West's later writings, is prompted by the memory of the early and unexplained death of two children in *The Return of the Soldier*, that is, Kitty's and Margaret's sons, who both died at the age of two. Margaret, more down-to-earth than the high-strung Jenny, has this to say about the tragedy: "I prayed and read the Bible, but I couldn't get any help. You don't notice how little there is in the Bible really till you go to it for help" (86). That is, of course, an explosive statement, but it is introduced casually into the conversation and elicits no protest from Margaret's interlocutor, Jenny. Again, critics have not picked up on that aspect of the novel, as most commentators have been preoccupied with the psychoanalytical and historical dimensions of the story. Of course, the sting would be taken out of such anti-God musings if we simply assumed that they are the brainchild of the novel's narrator, Jenny. However, we can actually trace the misotheism inherent in these statements to the author herself because there exists an unpublished manuscript of an essay that West had written even while she was working on *The Return of the Soldier*.

The manuscript in question, titled "The New God," looks like a continuation of Jenny's dark musings about the coarse, lewd god of her fantasy world. In all likelihood, West did not seek publication of "The New God" because it would have been too shocking, too radical, and altogether too blasphemous an essay to be put into print. So, it remained as a typewritten, corrected draft in the papers of the West Collection at the University of Tulsa, seen only by a handful of scholars. West's searing indictment of God in this essay betrays a deeper reservoir of anger against God than one could guess from reading her published works. She begins the essay by stating that "He [God] never did much for his people. Always it was his delight to receive rather than to give. The one clear motive in his mysterious ways was his hatred of the common man" (1). Here we have the very root of agonistic misotheism: a feeling that because God hates mankind, man has the right to hate him back. This text, which constitutes Rebecca West's secret misotheistic "manifesto," is a direct reaction to the unprecedented carnage on the battlefields of World War I. Rather than denying God's existence, West indicts the deity for insufficient benevolence. And rather than tinkering with an explanatory theodicy that could help to justify the ways of God to man, West instead goes on the attack against God.

She establishes her credentials as a person familiar with scripture by prefacing her essay with a biblical passage about man's value being infinitely greater than the worth of sparrows (Matthew 10:29–31). But, as the course of World War I has shown, God appears to have mixed up his priorities, because

> the ground of Europe is thick with the bodies of those who are of more value than many sparrows, and God has not said one word. God who blessed the merciful has let mercy and kindness be driven out from the world. God who made Heaven and Earth lets Earth be swallowed up in Hell. God who is Love has given the world as food to Hate. . . . Since God has declared that he is omnipotent, omniscient, omnipresent, he must take the responsibility of all crimes committed in his name. (1–2)

The horrors of World War I convinced West that the Epicurean view of a detached bystander God was not commensurate with the scale of the catastrophe. Rather, for such an unspeakable tragedy to unfold, God would have to be complicit in some way. West's angry rhetoric has no patience for Jobian questioning about the justice and mercy of God. Instead, she wonders why "we have forgiven him all these things" and continues, with implied reference to Job, that "there has been nothing so wonderful since the world began as man's infinite patience towards God" (2). West gives her blasphemy another turn by suggesting that "we should pray 'Forgive us our trespasses as we forgive thee thine'" (2). But such is not really an option, since "the hurt that God has done to the world is too great for any forgiveness" (2).

From righteous indignation, West shifts to bitter cynicism, as she imagines a company of German soldiers stalking a Belgian farm, intent on rape and murder:

> Unmoved he [God] looked upon the grey men who crept like rats through the yellow Belgian harvest that was never reaped. From his secure skies he looked down on the blue smoke curling from the Flemish farmstead and smiled in his beard, well content at the murder he knew would defile its hearth. He who on earth had nothing to say in praise of earthly love and permitted his servants to defame it did not move while men made from the sexual mystery a new torture and prelude to blood. (2–3)

With remarkable literary skill, West here invites us to contemplate the lurking soldiers from the distance of a godlike narrative perspective, only to elicit our sympathy immediately afterward by her indignant paraphrase for rape. In this passage, dense with allusion and symbolism, West consistently anthropomorphizes God. First, she applies human standards of moral conduct to God, thereby disregarding the conventional theological position that God's motives are inscrutable and that his reasons are beyond human ken; she further imputes a hypocritical sexual morality to God, accusing him of requiring his priests to teach that sex is unclean and sinful, while he himself takes an almost perverse interest in rape.

Her debasing of God culminates in the reference to him as a "master criminal" (3). As for the matter of worshipping such a god, West exclaims that "one hates our fathers for having committed themselves to such a worship and wonders how they could have fancied God was kind" (3). Note the telling slippage between her hatred of "our fathers" and the hatred she feels at that moment for God, as if the two hatreds are related. On one level, it is possible to see this text as expressing wishful thinking—if only God were humanlike so that one could call him to task for the crimes that go on under his watch. Even Christ seems powerless to bring relief to a humanity wronged by God, and atonement is a futile act, carried out by the untold victims of the war. Indeed, millions of fathers have "sent out their sons to die and it must be from love of the world, for there is no profit in a dead boy" (5). West goes so far as to claim that the sons who are thus sacrificed are in fact undergoing worse tortures than the agony endured by Christ: "In those days there were not the tearing wounds of shrapnel or poison gas that shriveled up the lungs. And while they die a longer death, lying there between the trenches for three days and three nights, they have no sustaining promise of a quick resurrection" (5). For West, knowledge about the ferocity of human suffering during the Great War eclipsed any belief in the redeeming sacrifice of Christ, and it trumped any theological explanation about the grace of God.

But the essay is not entirely without hope. After discrediting the grace of God, she raises man and his works to the status of a "new god": "Then let us worship humanity" (5) she demands, and continues: "If we go on believing there is a God who wills all these things we must believe in a God who willed this war, and all hope runs from the universe. But if we believe that all that was good in divinity is in humanity too, struggling towards courage and power and peace out of baseness and fear, then it seems possible to face life" (5). The new god, whom she imagines as rising phoenixlike from the ashes of the war, has more than a bit of Feuerbach and Nietzsche mixed in. First West follows Feuerbach by emphasizing the basic correspondence between God and man; second, she emphasizes the Nietzschean attributes of this "new god," including strength, valor, and willpower: "A God will come to us born of the human will. Today in every act of splendour at the front, in the very presence of the armies, we have a sign that he will come. Let us believe in the new God of humanity, who has ransomed us from the old unkindly God by the price of many scars" (5–6). Any act of human decency in this war, she suggests, happens not because of the biblical God but despite of him. Man must look to humanity for guidance, not to Yahweh.

Whether it was through malice or incompetence, it appears certain to West that God has given humanity a conflicting set of instructions: "It was his will that certain passions should be as strong and natural in man as the desire to breathe, and his teaching that they should be cut out of him as some Eastern tyrant might order the excision of a subject's heart and lungs" ("The New God" 1). This looks like a more eloquent version of a verse in Swinburne's *Atalanta in Calydon* where the Chorus protests that "[God] makes desire, and slays desire with shame" (1146). It is further reminiscent of Blake, who similarly condemned Yahweh, or Nobodaddy, for associating the physical, bodily, and sexual aspects of life with shame and degradation. That notion is expressed in Blake's poem "The Garden of Love," where the speaker encounters a cold, repressive ecclesiastical building right in the middle of a burgeoning garden of blossoming affections. This apprehension of religious repression and morbidity gives rise to a veritable hatred of divine omnipotence. Blake's poem "Earth's Answer" in *Songs of Experience* contains one of his notorious attacks against divinity. Here, the deity, who is ostensibly Yahweh, is exhorted by Mother Earth for being a "Selfish father of men, cruel, jealous, selfish fear! . . . / Selfish! Vain! Eternal bane!" (28). Blake did not mince his words when it came to attacking the Old Testament deity, whom he referred to in *America* as "God, a tyrant crowned" (46).

Rebecca West was thinking along similar lines, and just like Blake in "The Human Abstract," she also expressed her doubts about the viability of the Christian virtues of mercy, pity, peace, and love. West attributed the relative ineffectiveness of these qualities to the caprice of a vacillating, indifferent, or plainly sadistic god. Evidence for this view can be found throughout West's work, beginning with her teenage novel *The Sentinel*, whose quasi-mythical invocation of a brooding, malevolent deity is Blakean to boot. Adela, the novel's protagonist (and West's alter ego) affirms that there exists

> an Injustice invulnerable behind the skies. As clearly as if the vaults were rent she saw the face of this spirit convulsed with mockery of the present peoples, heavy with brooding hate of the future. . . . Better let humanity fester and rot into nothingness than bruise body and soul in this futile war against sneering Omnipotence. Adela lost her hope and desire of the war of redemption. She surrendered to this Injustice who is the Law of Life. (54–55)

The capitalization of "Injustice" and "sneering Omnipotence" indicates that these are merely alternative terms for the god Blake had earlier referred to as "Nobodaddy" or "Urizen." Surely, Blake's rebellion against what he considered the life-denying principles of the Christian dogma are continued in Rebecca West's agonistic misotheism. In both cases, the god of wrath has earned their wrath in return.

Significantly, though, both Blake and West largely exempted Christ from their antireligious polemics. Blake's mild representation of Christ in "The Lamb" ("he calls himself a Lamb; / He is meek and he is mild" [*Innocence* 53]) is nowhere directly subverted in the *Songs of Experience*, or in any other part of Blake's work. Rather, the companion piece to "The Lamb," the famous poem "The Tyger," targets the Old Testament god of wrath, who is likened to a savage beast. In his *Vision of the Last Judgment,* Blake puts his Christological ethic rather bluntly: "Thinking as I do that the Creator of this World is a very Cruel Being, and being a Worshipper of Christ, I cannot help saying: 'The Son, O how unlike the Father!' First God Almighty comes with a Thump on the Head. Then Jesus Christ comes with a balm to heal it" (quoted in Erdman, 565). In contradistinction to the Old Testament god of power and glory, whom Blake sought to exorcise, Christ is "the human form divine," a hybrid of humanity and divinity.

The same Christological approach can be found, by and large, in Rebecca West's work. In her masterpiece *Black Lamb and Grey Falcon* she writes a veritable paean to Christ:

> A supremely good man was born on earth, a man who was without cruelty, who could have taught mankind to live in perpetual happiness; and because we are infatuated with this idea of sacrifice, of shedding innocent blood to secure innocent advantages, we found nothing better to do with this passport to deliverance than destroy him. There is that in the universe, half inside and half outside our minds, which is wholly adorable; and this it was that men killed when they crucified Jesus Christ. (827)

West's reverence for the legacy of Christ, whom she regarded in the spirit of German rational theology as either an exemplary human being or an abstract manifestation of "goodness itself" (*Black Lamb and Grey Falcon* 914), gives evidence of a religious conception that deviates significantly from the conventional, Trinitarian Christian doctrine. By regarding Yahweh as a separate entity, different and apart from Christ, both West and Blake betray a quasi-polytheistic approach to Christianity. Of course, Blake consistently blurs the boundaries between mono- and polytheism anyway. For one thing, his polytheistic inventions such as Urizen, Los, and Thel are paradoxically counterbalanced by invocations of a monotheistic divinity, as evidenced in the two "Chimney Sweeper" poems, which invoke a singular deity ("God & His Priest & King" [*Experience* 32]). By comparison, West also invokes a singular God, such as the "sneering Omnipotence" referred to above or the "God" condemned in "The New God," and yet she frequently uses "gods" as a plural noun. The mono- and polytheistic frameworks may even, on occasion, be employed in the very same sentence, as in this passage from *Survivors in Mexico* (2003):

> All over Mexico there are the images of the cruel gods who impose cruelty on us as our duty, as our fate; and people come out of the city and cross the stone square on their knees, asking forgiveness of a kind God, claiming that it is we who impose cruelty on the world, that there is another interpretation to the apparent facts. (93)

Note the easy slippage between plural Aztec gods and the singular "God" worshipped by Catholics at the shrine of Guadalupe in Mexico City. The elision is no coincidence, I believe, since West saw direct parallels between the Abrahamic god and the gods of wrath and bloodshed that dominated the religious imagination of Mesoamericans. In another example of this phenomenon, West wrote: "I had to remind myself that if one believed in a god or gods who habitually sent one communications which were never clearly intelligible but almost always disagreeable, in a sadistic code, in fact, one might feel obliged to answer him in the same code."[2] Again, "god" and "gods" are interchangeable and both are associated with obscurity, caprice, and sadism.

As indicated above, West not only recalls Blake but also the neo-Blakean poet Swinburne who mocked "God, the shade cast by the soul of man" ("Genesis" 155). The connection between West and Swinburne is made explicit in her youthful novel *The Sentinel*. In the very scene where Adela denounces "sneering Omnipotence," the narrator invokes the "pale Galilean" (54), which is, of course, an allusion to Algernon Charles Swinburne's "Hymn to Proserpine." Although West did not embrace Swinburne's contempt for Christ ("O pale Galilean; the world has grown grey from thy breath" [*Major Poems* 101]), she did employ the motif of crucifixion, just as Swinburne did, to express the plight of oppressed and persecuted segments of humanity. We recall that this notion is central to Swinburne's poem "Before a Crucifix," where he suggests that the exploited working classes are tortured on the cross of industrialism. In his view, kings and bosses "bind the people's nail-pierced hands, / they hide the people's nail-pierced feet" (*Major Poems* 151). A similar image is conjured up in *The Sentinel*, only here the sacrificial victim is not the laborer per se but rather the abused, force-fed suffragette. One of these victims of patriarchal violence, Rosie Essletree, is a "a crucified girl" (59), and another one is described as "stretch[ing] out her arms towards the high little window, trying to find knowledge in the light. Long before she could reach it she fell to the floor and lay stark with her tears staining the stone. Inarticulate pity for crucified humanity rent her with sobs" (56). It is indicative of West's quasi-existential worldview that she eventually associated not only suffragettes as victims of figurative crucifixion but all of humanity.

There is an almost Gnostic emphasis on facing the unpleasant knowledge that the world is imperfect. Accordingly, the concept of divine Providence has lost its consolatory potential: "the redemptive power of divine grace no longer seemed credible, nor very respectable in the arbitrary performance that was claimed for it" (*Grandfather* 30). West's protagonist in *The Judge*, a suffragette by the name of Ellen Melville, feels similarly compelled to "disprove all idea of a just Providence" (*Judge* 177). With this idea, Ellen professes her own misotheism. The world as seen by Ellen is devoid of divine care and instead bespeaks a cold and hostile order of things. In one scene she muses that the setting of the sun means that God takes pleasure in depriving the world of heat and light: "there was something awesome and unnatural about this quiet hour in which there was so much light and so little heat, in this furnace of the skies from which there flowed so glacial a wind" (*Judge* 115). Under the metaphorical extravagance lies a core of blasphemy. Indeed, the glacial wind invoked above is an emanation from God because the narrator feels that "the sun's descent was the last piece of carelessness of the part of a negligent universe" (*Judge* 150). If one adds to this the sobering recognition that "there was no hope, things never went well on this earth" (*Judge* 345), then one is in the presence of a rather heretical religious skepticism.

This categorical denial of a just Providence lies at the core of West's agonistic misotheism. How deep that disbelief ran can be gleaned from an unpublished draft of her autobiography, written probably after her husband's death in 1968. A despondent West muses about the disappointments of her life, especially about the men who had betrayed her, including her father, her son, and Lord Beaverbrook, with whom she had an unhappy relationship:

> Because of Anthony and X [presumably Lord Beaverbrook], I had almost no possibility of holding faith of any religious kind except a belief in a wholly and finally defeated God, a hypothesis which I now

accept but tried for a long time to reject, I could not face it. Now I see that if Christ has failed to make his point with the universe, so much the worse for the universe, and there is no helping it, but that it is good to know the truth and I am willing to know that.[3]

Again, there is the assertion that knowledge, even of a bleak kind, is better than self-deceptive faith. Besides the peculiar insistence on placing her failed relationships with men on the same footing as her resentment against God, what stands out here is West's emphasis on the defeat of Christ (presumably the "finally defeated God"), rather than on his atonement, resurrection, and triumphant return. By extension, one can infer that the defeat of Christ also implicates Yahweh, who is not powerful enough to secure his son's victory.

This emphasis on the divine weakness is a reminder of West's Manichaean propensity. Indeed, the defeat of God's son is a central motif in Mani's theogony. According to this myth, the realms of light and darkness used to coexist peacefully for eons, until a "disturbance" at the separation between the two regions encouraged the Prince of Darkness to launch an incursion into the region of light. At this point the supreme god (or Father of Greatness) emanated a son to do battle against the Prince of Darkness. But the Son of Light was defeated in the fight, and the essence of his soul, light, was swallowed up by the essence of evil, that is, gross matter. A complicated sequence of events follows, according to which the battle between light and darkness turns into an attempt to retrieve the particles of light incorporated into the dark, physical substance of the universe. At first, further emanations from the Father of Greatness defeat some of the forces of darkness, and the stars are fashioned out of the vanquished demons. Next, these stars are sexually stimulated, and the seed spilled from male stars fertilizes the earth, causing vegetation to spring forth; at this point, female stars have abortions, which are let loose upon earth to eat the plant life and thereby to accumulate the light particles trapped inside the vegetation. In order to acquire the portion of light that has accumulated in these animals, two powerful demons then eat all the animals and copulate with one another. The offspring resulting from this union are Adam and Eve.[4]

It is not hard to see why the early Roman Catholic Church discouraged the spread of these ideas—indeed, defenders of Christian orthodoxy persecuted Manichaeans with fire and sword. After all, this version of the creation myth teaches that humanity is the spawn of demons and that heavenly bodies are made from devil's matter, a cosmic vision that is not entirely flattering to human self-esteem, nor does it support the tenets of theism in the Judeo-Christian tradition. Indeed, the Manichaean god is not a creator-god, and he obviously does not control the forces of evil, hence his first son's defeat at the hands of the Prince of Darkness. Moreover, the notion of Providence and omniscience are all called into question in this religious myth, which holds that the outcome of the battle between light and darkness cannot be predicted.

Some of these ideas appealed to West's dualistic temper. Indeed, she highlighted the fact that "Mani created a myth that would show the universe as a field for moral effort" (*Black Lamb and Grey Falcon* 172), a vision she approved of, calling it "an extremely useful conception of life" (*Black Lamb and Grey Falcon* 172). Despite such support for Mani's dualism, however, West could not fully endorse the Manichaean god. At best, she saw him as the lesser evil compared to the Judeo-Christian god. By comparison with tyrannical Yahweh, the Manichaean god probably struck her as both reactionary (because he keeps bodying forth new manifestations to deal with crises that he did not foresee) and as ineffective and bumbling (because he relies on human beings to collect the particles of light that were absorbed into matter when his son was defeated). Such a god did not fill her with confidence in the divine plan. Still, Manichaeanism was attractive to her because its underlying dualism appeared to be the best account of the working principle of the universe.

But West was not only beholden to the philosophy of dualism in an abstract, philosophical sense. To her, dualism pervaded every aspect of life: she saw it at work in the difference between the genders, and even in national dualisms, such as in the difference between the Slavic and the British national characters. Equally dualistic was her own religiousness, as she oscillated between the poles of blasphemy and piety. So far we have considered the aspects of her religious sensibility that are at odds with the tenets of traditional Christianity. Her hatred of God, her protests against divine cruelty, and her sympathy for Manichaeanism all bespeak a highly unorthodox, irreverent religious stance. But this is not the whole story.

The agonistic element of her misotheism asserted itself in a prolonged effort to abandon her rebellion against God and to join with

faithful believers. Despite all her misgivings and ambivalences regarding the Christian god, she never entirely abandoned the will to
believe nor the hope that a new understanding of the world and its
creator might emerge from changed private circumstances and
improved public affairs. After her marriage in 1930 and especially
with the advent of World War II, West gradually turned into a more
devout Christian, admitting in 1945 that "I do myself accept the belief
of the Christian Church" ("Christian Faith"). She was prompted to
this new faith, paradoxically, by the deprivations and dangers of
World War II: "I have been astonished since the beginning of the war
at the wonderful way people have come forward to help each other. . . .
[The war] was been a strain for many of them. And, of course, it was
a strain that brought out their finest characteristics, and a lot of the
Christian virtues as well" ("Christian Faith"). This attitude culminated in her 1952 essay "Goodness Doesn't Just Happen," in which
she proclaimed that "I must orientate my writing towards God for it
to have any value" ("Goodness" 41).

Two years earlier, West had made an attempt to convert to Catholicism while traveling through France. It was a closely guarded experience that she only revealed to her husband and her American
friends, Margaret and Evelyn Hutchinson. In a letter to the Hutchinsons, dated 1950, West relates a strange series of coincidences that led
her to believe that she had received a divine summons: first, she had
a dream in which she and her husband drove off a cliff in the mountains; the following day she slipped on a patch of oil next to the church
but was miraculously unhurt, causing her to wonder whether she and
the church "suddenly were in a new spatial relationship"; finally, she
was approached by a Franciscan monk who told her bluntly, "You are
certainly in need of help, I think you ought to be a Catholic."[5] She
goes on to say, laconically, "obviously I cannot do *nothing* about this.
So I am being instructed for the purpose of being received into the
Catholic Church."[6] West hastens to add that "it is not anything like
the acceptance of faith." Her objective, rather, is "to get a technique
which will enable me to come into contact with God, with infinite
goodness. This is still over the hill, I cannot think how it will be
achieved, I suppose it will come about when I practise the observances
of the Roman Catholic Church—obviously the rites of the Orthodox
Church were too remote from me to be a useful technique."[7]
The very same wording is used in her essay "Goodness Doesn't Just

Happen" (1952), where she states that "there is a God and I know that religion offers a technique for getting in touch with Him, but I find that technique difficult" (41).

So difficult was the process, in fact, that it proved ultimately unfeasible. In another letter to the Hutchinsons, dated June 22, 1952, she admits to the failure of her conversion experiment: "I could not go on with being a Catholic," she writes.[8] The reason she gives for abandoning the conversion process, i.e., too much contact with sexually repressed and homosexual priests, might seem spurious. It surely appears to be a smokescreen for her fundamental difficulty in achieving a genuine sense of religious faith and worship. West had reached the apex of her attempt at religious piety, and from this point onward, once again her irritability toward God would grow.

What could have prompted this erstwhile enemy of God to become temporarily pious? Certainly the direct threat to her life and property during World War II, combined with the solidarity and compassion she experienced among her fellow Britons, resulted in a greater respect for Christianity in the years leading up to her "epiphany" in France in 1950. At that point, she had come a long way from her condemnation of God as "the master criminal." In an interview for the *Daily Express*, published in January 1945, she said, "I believe if people are looking for the truth, the truth of the Christian religion will come out and meet them." But ultimately she would turn her back on such religious optimism and return to her blasphemous attitude toward Christianity and its god. In the late 1960s, she wrote these militant words: "The case against religion is the responsibility of God for the sufferings of mankind, which makes it impossible to believe the good things said about Him in the Bible, and consequently to believe anything it says about Him" (*Survivors* 81). If West's religious journey is a pilgrim's progress of sorts, its trajectory is circular.

In this connection it is interesting to note that West always remained on good terms with the Slavic Orthodox faith. She felt that the Orthodox churches were less corrupted by the dogmas of church fathers like Saint Augustine and Jerome than their Western Catholic and Protestant counterparts: "Contact with the Eastern Church, which is many centuries nearer primitive Christianity than the Western Church, have made it clear to me that the life of Christ should have been an incomparable blessing to man and a revelation of the way he must follow if he is not to be a beast" ("I Believe" 32). Compared to the "services devised by the early Church [which] commemorated the beauty of the virtue [i.e., Christ] that was slain," West states that in the course of its two-thousand-year history, the Western "Church has poured as much of the draft as possible down the drain by its attempts to develop a doctrine to account for the crucifixion of Christ as an atonement" ("I Believe" 33). On the rare occasions that West sought consolation from a priest, she favored representatives of the Eastern Church. For instance, after the sudden death of her adored great-grandson, Barnabas, in 1979, West fell into a deep depression. According to her secretary at the time, Elizabeth Leyshon, West called for a Serbian Orthodox priest to give her solace in this hour of despair. It would be interesting to know what passed between them during this interview, but no information exists, other than Leyshon's impression that West had emerged somewhat calmed from the session. Whether it was the priest's spiritual message or his national identity as a Serb that gave her solace remains a matter of speculation.[9] In any case, West maintained a warm relationship with the Serbian Orthodox Church of St. Sava in London in the last years of her life.

No matter how hard she tried to know the true nature of divinity, there was little sense of spiritual solace in her final hours. She experienced no sudden descent of grace comparable to the miraculous death-bed conversion of Lord Marchmain in *Brideshead Revisited* (1945) by Evelyn Waugh. Carl Rollyson gives a harrowing account of her final days in his biography. Apparently, her last words were, "I'm lost. It's wrong" (*Rebecca West* 427). West's niece, Alison Selford, who stayed at the author's bedside during her last illness, remembers her aunt's anguish and feeling of abandonment as she approached the end. West especially agonized over the absence of her son, Anthony West (whom she had had with her former lover, the novelist H. G. Wells). Tellingly, Selford links this anguish with a larger sense of retribution. "Meanwhile," writes Selford, "my aunt's complaints about God, as she summed them up for me, were that he had so made her that she could not possibly refrain from committing sins and then punished her horribly for committing them."[10] This idea can be traced throughout West's writing and is indeed a cornerstone of her critique of God, as summed up in her essay "My Religion" (1926): "That a father should invent the laws of a game knowing that they must be broken, force people to play it, sentence the players to punishment for breaking them, and accept the agony of his son as a substitute for the punishment, was credible enough to people who believed that hate might be the ultimate law of life" (38). As for punishment being an inevitable result of the human condition, Selford writes, "indeed her punishment was horrible—not to see her son when she was dying. I waited for a lucid moment and asked her whether I should send for him. She said: 'Oh, what's the use, if he hates me so much?' When she wasn't lucid she would scream in terror, imagining that Anthony had got into the flat."[11] This sharp anguish, which is part psychological anxiety, part spiritual terror, is based on West's deep apprehension of betrayal. She felt indeed betrayed by her father, by her son, Anthony, by many of her lovers, including H. G. Wells and Lord Beaverbrook, by members of the British Left, and by the American liberal establishment (who turned against her because of her anticommunism), not to mention the actual spies and traitors she dealt with in *The Meaning of Treason*, including William Joyce, Kim Philby, and Stephen Ward. But at the top of this sliding scale of traitors stands God himself. West has often suggested that human affairs were so imperfectly arranged because God had no loyalty to mankind.

To illustrate this principle one need only turn to one of her best short stories, "Parthenope" (1959). The eponymous character in this story has been dealt a harsh fate, being forced to navigate the treacherous waters of madness, patriarchy, unwanted marriage, exile, and loneliness. In addition, she faces betrayal on multiple levels. As Parthenope nears her death, she looks back upon an unhappy life, concluding "there is a force outside the world that hates me and all my family" (91). One could imagine Rebecca West thinking along very similar lines toward the end of her life, although she was beset by different problems. Parthenope leaves no doubt about the nature of that "force": "Something has happened which can only be explained by supposing that God hates you with merciless hatred, and nobody will admit it" (87). West was not one to shirk that admission herself, just as she speculated in her autobiographical musings about the ultimate defeat of Christ.

To sum up, West's agonistic misotheism has an existentialist and a psychological slant. It is existentialist because West saw the universe as inherently cold and hostile, and she believed that humanity was faced with the heroic job of wresting meaning from the hand of an uncaring God. This view is indebted to Epicurus, since the god she resents as the originator of such an unpleasant cosmic arrangement is essentially an absentee landlord, although one with the whimsical propensity of occasionally turning his attention to his underlings on earth to torment them for his pleasure. This attitude ultimately differentiates her rebellion against God from that of the anarchists. West hesitated to portray God as an active tyrant and dictatorial master of the universe. Instead, she insisted on his ineffectiveness in the face of evil and occasionally hinted at a dark strain of passive sadism. Finally, the psychological dimension of her quarrel with God is rooted in her critique of incompetent fathers who abandon their paternal duties and disappoint their charges. To West, God was the ultimate model of an irresponsible and capricious father. And, like her own father, the heavenly father failed to live up to his promise of being a protector for his human family.

Agonistic Misotheism III

Divine Apathy, the Holocaust, and Elie Wiesel's Wrestling with God

> *God comes in here and there in my books. I oppose Him. I fight Him. I quarrel with Him.*
>
> —Elie Wiesel (Interview, 1978)
>
> *Man prefers to blame himself for all possible sins and crimes rather than come to the conclusion that God is capable of the most flagrant injustice. I still blush every time I think of the way God makes fun of human beings, his favorite toys.*
>
> —Elie Wiesel, *The Accident* (1962)

ELIE WIESEL'S WORK IS ONE LONG MEDITATION ON THEODICY, OR the question of how to reconcile God's mercy with the manifest reality of genocide, chaos, catastrophe, and injustice on earth. This question has prompted different responses over the course of this concentration camp survivor's life, with misotheism being the most extreme of a range of religious positions he has taken up. Although in recent years Wiesel has found his way back to a more pious regard for God, in the middle phase of his life his work is dotted with astonishing bursts of blasphemy and with angry denunciations of God. As was the case with Rebecca West, Wiesel's misotheism is both deeply agonistic and also periodic. But the trajectory of his fluctuating misotheism is the inverse of West's development. As we recall, West started her career as a prosecutor of God, before adopting a more pious attitude toward God in midlife, only to revert once again to an anti-God stance during her last decades. By contrast, Wiesel started his life as a pious Jew raised in a Hasidic community in Romania. However, his traumatic experiences during the Holocaust first turned him into a doubter of divine justice and then, intermittently, into an agonistic misotheist.

Thus, World War II affected West and Wiesel in exactly opposite ways as regards their misotheistic tendencies. West's experience of World War II was marked by the trauma of the Blitz in and around London (1940–41). During the war (and until 1969), she lived on an estate in the Chiltern Hills in Buckinghamshire, some thirty miles northwest of London, where the threat of German bombardment was constant, though less acute than in the city itself. West used to go up to London during the war to visit her sister who was living there right through the Blitz, and she thus witnessed the destruction firsthand. She also took in Eastern European refugees, sheltering them in her blacked-out mansion, Ibstone House. During those trying times, West was impressed by the decency of people and by how they pulled together, showing true solidarity and fortitude under pressure. This sense of community awakened in her a new confidence in God and especially a greater reverence for the teachings of Christianity. Of course, England was spared an invasion, and nobody in her immediate circle of family and friends was killed, maimed, or tortured by the Germans.

By comparison, Wiesel's experience of World War II was dramatically different. His horrific encounters with merciless cruelty and unspeakable horrors left him bereft of an affirmative religious faith and worshipful attitude toward God. While West's experience of intermittent threat during World War II abated her misotheism for a while, the unimaginable scale of evil encountered by Wiesel awakened in him a deep resentment against God.

Wiesel's spiritual darkening occurred during his horrific eleven-months' stay in the concentration camps of Auschwitz-Birkenau, Buna, and Buchenwald. The Holocaust leaves its imprint on all of Wiesel's work, and it gives rise to "the question of questions" that has troubled him and many others—Jews and non-Jews—ever since:

"why the silence of God?" (*Twilight* 197). This question hovers at the core of Wiesel's work and, as often as not, sparks answers that are not only skeptical of divine goodness but actually hostile against God.

One of Wiesel's central maxims is that "the opposite of love is not hate but indifference" (*Six Days* 8). Millions of Jews were terrorized, tortured, and murdered, yet no major intervention happened to stop the genocidal slaughter. Thus, the question, "and what about God in all this?" (*Twilight* 214) of necessity implicates God in the catastrophe. God appeared to be indifferent to widespread torture, the obliteration of entire villages, and the extinction of countless families, including the deaths of a million children. Hence, the renewed urgency of Epicurus's probing questions: If God knows about evil and could stop it but chooses not to do so, doesn't that make him an accomplice of evil? And if God knows about crimes on earth but cannot do anything to stop then, isn't he weak? Either one of these propositions undermines the theistic attributes of God, and Wiesel's work makes repeated interventions into this troubling field of inquiries regarding the justice and the power of God during the Holocaust.

But Wiesel's incessant questioning of God's silence leads him down even more provocative avenues than Epicurean skepticism: What if God is in league with Satan, sadistically enjoying the evil perpetrated on earth? What if God has gone mad? What if the Holocaust is merely an acute symptom of a larger cosmic disorder? Wiesel's experience in the camps left him with an enormous reservoir of anger, which is principally directed against a god who is suspected of being indifferent, weak, mad, or positively cruel. Wiesel's incessant questioning of God aims at determining the true nature of God, but it also betrays the hope that maybe it has all somehow been a big mistake, and God will turn out to be on the side of the angels after all.

In order to establish a given writer's misotheistic tendency, we cannot rely solely on his or her explicit statements of a theological nature or on his or her essays on religious matters. As was the case with Zora Neale Hurston and Rebecca West, the sum total of Wiesel's anti-God rhetoric must be distilled form traces scattered throughout all aspects of his work, including fiction, drama, memoir, and interviews. In addition to taking such a broader view, we need to keep in mind the Jewish context of Wiesel's denunciations of God. Indeed, a tradition of protest theology forms an integral part of the Jewish heritage to which Wiesel traces his spiritual development. As Robert McAfee Brown explains:

> It has a long Jewish history, this quarrel with God—Abraham inter-
> cedes against God for Sodom, Moses intercedes against God for those
> who built the golden calf, Job calls God to account for personal indig-
> nities, Jeremiah lives his life as a perpetual quarrel with God. The
> quarrel bursts the bonds of genteel discourse when outrages against
> God's children go unchecked. (149)

Judaism is based on such an agonistic relationship between worshipper and divinity since "the particular relationship of God to His
Chosen People makes him answerable for their suffering" (Landis 7).
The special covenant between God and the Jewish people as outlined
in Deuteronomy ("God has chosen you to be his treasured people
from all the nations that are on the face of the earth" [14:2]) shifts
some responsibility for the fate of God's flock unto the shoulders of
the deity. The central problem that often seeks expression in Jewish
literature is, therefore, the "paradox of the God who was, on the one
hand, the intimate Father, whose book was a family album, for whom
time was irrelevant and place insignificant, and on the other hand, the
God who was destiny and history—remote, inscrutable, unanswer-
ing; the God who had chosen and the God who ignored" (Landis 7).
The tension between these two faces of God is particularly evident in
the Book of Lamentations, according to which God both punished
Jerusalem and grieved over the suffering of the Jews.

Wiesel dramatized this ambivalence in an orchestral piece, *Ani
Maamin* (1973), a version of the Jewish creed. In one passage, the
cantata depicts God as shedding tears over the destruction of Jerusalem and bewailing the exile of the Jews. This idea relates to Lamentations Rabbah,[1] a midrashic text, in which it is written that "the Holy
One, blessed be He, wept saying 'Woe is me for my house! O Children of mine—where are you? O priests of mine—where are you?'"
(Neusner 149). One wonders if Wiesel adopted this version of the
destruction of Jerusalem in order to emphasize God's compassion for
the misery of the Jews. Michael Berenbaum thinks that this is not the
case. In his view, Wiesel's depiction of the weeping God instead highlights the inconsistency of a deity who harshly punishes his people,
refuses to be moved by appeals for mercy, and then weeps at the suffering he himself had imposed. According to Berenbaum, the patriarchs in *Ani Maamin* "refuse to proclaim the righteousness of the
God who murdered innocent children. The theodicy of Israel is in

shambles. There is no hope. . . . The patriarchs have lived a lie. There is no justice, no God who reveals himself through history" (114). In this view, Wiesel's portrayal of God in *Ani Maamin* serves to emphasize God's culpability: "The image of God that Wiesel suggests is somewhat pathetic and frighteningly amoral. God has to be shocked into a response, and His response comes too late and is limited to empathy" (Berenbaum 117). Because Wiesel "undercuts almost all positive images of God to such an extent that they are of limited use in defending Jewish theodicy" (7), Berenbaum judges Wiesel to be "a heretic, albeit a heretic with profoundly Jewish memories and with a deep love and respect for tradition" (67). Now, Wiesel would probably not consider himself to be a heretic. To him, even a fierce critic of God is still operating within the bounds of Jewish protest theology, as evidenced in this quote: "Judaism is the only religion which allows the creature the right to revolt against its creator and to tell him: 'No!' God does not like those who come to him out of weakness. He seeks interlocutors" (*Conversations* 17). However, it can hardly be doubted that Wiesel's brand of anti-God rhetoric goes beyond conventional forms of God-wrestling and crosses quite clearly into the territory of blasphemy.

His early novel *The Accident* (1962, later retitled as *Day*) is a case in point. The story is a fictional reworking of Wiesel's own life: like Wiesel himself, the protagonist in *The Accident* is a Holocaust survivor who, after emigrating to the U.S., is seriously injured after being struck by a taxicab in New York City. In this autobiographical novel, Wiesel's alter ego blasphemes by saying that "God needs man. Condemned to eternal solitude, he made man only to use him as a toy, to amuse himself" (64). According to Berenbaum, this is in fact a rather subversive "twisting" of Kabbalistic thought: "In Lurrianic Kabbalism, God was considered dependent upon humanity in order to become one again. Human salvation and God's liberation were integrally related" (28). And Berenbaum goes on to say that in the passage from *The Accident* quoted above, "God is now depicted as dependent upon humanity solely for entertainment and diversion. . . . In [*The Accident*] Wiesel exposes a world in which God is at best absent in the struggle between life and death. At worst, God may even be an ally of the forces of death" (29). Similarly, in *Messengers of God* (1976), Wiesel deviates from conventional Jewish interpretations of the Book of Job by condemning rather than praising God's dealing with Job and by criticizing Job's acceptance of the fact that "God giveth and God taketh away" (Job 1:21). In Berenbaum's view, although Wiesel's religiosity is deeply rooted in Jewish scriptures, he transforms the meaning of these scriptures to bend them into accord with his existential vision of the void, where the only redeeming factor is the human spirit, a spirit that rebels against "a God unworthy of the continuing faith of the Jewish people" (Berenbaum 116). The wording is significant here, as Berenbaum speaks of a god unworthy of faith, not of one beyond the reach of worship.

Elie Wiesel's path to this new and troubling awareness of the deity was a particularly precipitous and painful one, as it lay straight through the Holocaust. After being liberated from the concentration camp of Buchenwald by American forces in April 1945, Wiesel vowed not to write about his horrific experiences for ten years. When he finally sat down to put into words what he had gone through during the years of 1944–45, the result was his memoir *Night* (1958). Although this book was written a decade after the events it describes and hence cannot be considered as a contemporaneous factual report, it is undeniable that Wiesel wants us to view his work as an authentic testimony of the Nazi horror and as a chronicle of the spiritual transformation he had undergone during these times. Indeed, the memoir is correct in the basic circumstances of Wiesel's life: Until his deportation to Auschwitz in 1944, young Eliezer had been a devoted student of the Talmud and the Kabbalah, vying with his friend to see who was more devout, spending countless hours in prayer and in pious exercises, aimed, as he put it in *Night*, "to hasten the coming of the Messiah" (16). This affirmative, optimistic religious outlook was shattered forever on the first night in Auschwitz: "Never shall I forget that night, the first night in camp, which has turned my life into one long night, seven times cursed and seven times sealed. Never shall I forget that smoke. Never shall I forget the little faces of the children whose bodies I saw turned into wreaths of smoke beneath a silent blue sky. Never shall I forget those flames which consumed my faith forever" (32). Wiesel's anguished experiences in Auschwitz sapped his faith in a benevolent deity. It turned Wiesel from a devoted worshipper into an angry accuser of God: "I did not deny God's existence, but I doubted His absolute justice" (*Night* 42). After months of witnessing inhuman degradation and barbarity in German concentration camps, Wiesel's faith in God snapped on the eve of Rosh Hashanah in 1944.

Together with thousands of other concentration camp inmates, Wiesel heard an officiant recite the central Jewish blessing: "Praised are you, Lord our God, King of the universe, who has chosen us out of all the nations and bestowed upon us his Torah." At that moment, the familiar words from the Jewish prayer book struck Wiesel as a mockery, and he resolved to rebel against God:

> Why, but why should I bless Him? In every fiber I rebelled. Because He had had thousands of children burned in His pits? Because he kept six crematories working night and day, on Sundays and feast days? Because in His great might He had created Auschwitz, Birkenau, Buna, and so many factories of death? How could I say to Him: "Blessed art Thou, Eternal, Master of the Universe, Who chose us from among the races to be tortured day and night." (64)

Wiesel's anti-devotional insight, rather than tempting him to give up the struggle for survival and become a resigned cynic, filled him with new vigor and determination: "I felt very strong. I was the accuser, God the accused. My eyes were open and I was alone—terribly alone in a world without God and without man. Without love or mercy. I had ceased to be anything but ashes, yet I felt myself to be stronger than the Almighty, to whom my life had been tied for so long" (65). This attitude of rebellion is the result of deep, elemental, metaphysical anger. Wiesel admits that that "all my writing was born out of anger. In order to contain it, I had to write" (*Conversations* 82). Although anger is not the same as hatred, there is a sustained hostility in Wiesel's relationship to his god, both in his biographical writings and in his fictional creations. In an interview, he said: "Although I know I will never defeat God, I still fight Him" (*Conversations* 89). Of course, Wiesel is a milder man than, say, Swinburne or Nietzsche, though his adversarial relationship with God places him on (so to speak) a competitive footing with them. But compared to these absolute misotheists, who want to destroy God, Wiesel comes across as a true example of agonistic misotheism, trying to engage God and hoping to glean answers about the sad riddle of existence.

Wiesel is at bottom a mystic who wants nothing more than to enter into direct conversation with God, to reach him with his accusations of betrayal, and to be able to communicate his disapproval to God. His writing is, moreover, a developing eschatological vision, a transcendent view of the last things in order to explain the fragility of life, the brutality of human destiny, and the indifference, or carelessness, of God. The Holocaust plays a key role in this quest for ultimate understanding: "[Auschwitz] has had a tremendous effect on the recognition of limits and the absence of limits in regard to persons, be they good or evil. All of this is Kabbalah. The Kabbalah talks about limitlessness, and here we have something without limits. With horror we find out that there is not only something limitless when it comes to good, but also regarding evil" (*Conversations* 152–53). This mystical turn of Wiesel's mind, aimed at penetrating the mystery of God's silence in the face of unlimited evil, is evidenced in many of his characters, who are also mystics, such as Akiba Drumer in *Night*, Razziel in *Judges*, and Moshe the Madman in *The Oath*.

The line separating mysticism and madness is not always clear-cut, and Wiesel engages this uncertainty by inventing characters like Moshe in *The Gates of the Forest*, whose mystical transports take on the aspect of madness. For Wiesel, madness often has a metaphysical significance:

> rationalism failed philosophically. . . . It also failed theologically, and it failed humanly. So what else remains? Madness. If there is one word that can include all the other words about the Holocaust that word is madness—madness from the victim's point of view, madness from the executioner's point of view, madness from God's point of view, from man's point of view. The winds of madness were blowing. Creation itself was contaminated with madness. (*Conversations* 50–51)

This notion of a mad cosmos created by a mad god is fairly heretical, and the entry point to a religious view that is essentially misotheistic. In the following, I will discuss one novel and one play by Wiesel in order to explore a cluster of themes that relates to man's hostility against God.

The Gates of the Forest (1966) is set during World War II and centers, as do many of Wiesel's books, on the fate of the persecuted Jews. The protagonist, Gregor, is hiding from a Hungarian anti-Semitic posse in the mountains of Transylvania. Wiesel captures the disorienting, out-of-kilter madness of Gregor's world by introducing strange ironies such as calling the opening section "Spring," although instead of a time of renewal and rebirth, it is a time of death and alienation. As the story begins, Gregor is joined by another Jewish refugee who refuses to give his name and whom Gregor names

Gavriel—literally translated as "Man of God." This stranger may indeed be a manifestation of God, but he is also a madman. As Ted Estes has pointed out, "Gavriel corresponds to God, who refuses to name Himself, is the mysterious one who both hides and shows Himself" (70). However, the ironies multiply, when Gavriel, the putative Messiah, confides to Gregor that

> I no longer believe in the coming of the Messiah. The Messiah came, and nothing changed, he lost the path and laid down his arms without fighting; he surrendered himself and voluntarily relinquished his freedom. No, Gregor, there can be no more hope. The Messiah came, and the executioner goes right on executing. The Messiah came and the world is a vast slaughterhouse, as it was before. (47)

These words, coming from Gavriel, the "Man of God," are thus endowed with a special gravity. The painful nihilism of this passage, together with its devastatingly anti-Christian message, is clearly meant to provoke. What emerges is a patently absurd worldview. In keeping with such an existentialist tone, the last and the first communication Gregor receives from Gavriel is a boundless, mocking, absurd laughter. Four years earlier, in his novel *The Accident*, Wiesel had spelled out the cosmic implication of such laughter as follows: "That's what philosophers and poets have refused to admit: in the beginning there was neither the Word, nor Love, but laughter, the roaring, eternal laughter whose echoes are more deceitful than the mirages of the desert" (64). Thus, Gavriel's ringing laughter is not just a defense against the madness of the Holocaust, it is also an echo of the divine laughter that mystics of his sort can't help hear ringing in their ears.

In *The Gates of the Forest*, the whole universe seems to be infected with an absurdity that gives rise to unending cosmic laughter:

> Imagine a life-and-death struggle between two angels, the angel of love and the angel of wrath, the angel of promise and the angel of evil. Imagine that they both attain their ends, each one victorious. Imagine the laugh that would rise above their corpses as if to say, your death has given me birth. (3)

The eschatological vision drawn up here is an ideogram of cosmic senselessness. What could be more meaningless than that the forces of good and evil join in deadly combat only to mutually kill each other, like the brothers of Antigone? Such a vision has no room for a redeeming messiah, for divine order, for Providence—it is another sort of final solution: no more hatred, no more love, no more death, no more life. Such a world, rid of angels, gods, and demons, is beyond conventional notions of good and evil—it is truly a world of existentialist absurdity.

Wiesel had personally known Camus, Sartre, Malraux, and Mauriac, and he admits to having been strongly influenced by their thinking. Interestingly, he also explains that their brand of existentialism actually resonated with his own Hasidic worldview:

> Born in the eighteenth century in Eastern Europe, Hasidism gave hope to hopeless Jews while emphasizing the notion that the way to God was through one's fellow-man. Hasidism then was an existential experience. . . . My characters are Hasidim who are unwittingly influenced by existentialism; or the other way around, existentialists, young people, often not knowing what they are, who are influenced by Hasidism. (*Conversations* 73–74)

Wiesel identified Gregor in *The Gates of the Forest* as a typically "existentialist Hasid" (*Conversations* 74), which means that he is both a mystic and an existentialist, that is, a man who has entered into communion with God *and* someone who has found God to be indifferent to the point of callousness. Gregor is a Jacob who wrestles with his own internal demon of misgivings about God; and although these misgivings take the form of an actual character, Gavriel, he may be nothing more than a projection of Gregor's imagination. Ironically, though, the angel Gregor wrestles with does not strengthen his faith in God; on the contrary, Gavriel undermines faith by laughing hilariously at both bliss and terror: "Gregor shuddered and his legs became weak. Behind every tree and within every shred of cloud someone was laughing. It was not the laughter of one man but of a hundred, of seven times seven hundreds" (7). This cosmic laughter appears to be the only appropriate response to the absence of God during the Holocaust, if only because it eludes God's control. Gavriel says that laughter is "God's mistake. When God made man in order to bend him to his wishes he carelessly gave him the gift of laughter. Little did he know that later that earthworm would use it as a weapon of vengeance" (21). Gavriel's existential laughter, then, is more than a coping strategy, serving to keep insanity at bay: it is a declaration of defiance and hostility ("vengeance") against God.

Wiesel is careful not to characterize this falling off from piety, this rebellion against God, as a perverse act to be condemned by righteous believers. In the same novel, we are told in didactic tones: "Never despise, never spit at a man who has broken with the faith of his fathers. . . . To a man who is freeing himself from God you owe particular respect, because more than others he is accomplishing his destiny" (*Gates* 24). This is a powerful thought, and it has rather large implications: if one man's "destiny" can be found in the rejection of God ("freeing himself from God"), then it may well be that the entire human race is meant to break free from the Almighty. Gavriel, who is speaking these heretical thoughts, represents the part of Gregor which wants to break with God. One reviewer of the novel took note that the physical description of Gregor fits Elie Wiesel to a T (Fiske 43). It seems clear that Gavriel, who is the embodiment of a more existentialist, blasphemous side of Gregor, also stands for these qualities in Wiesel. This is the paradoxical nature of Wiesel's misotheism: on the one hand he regularly goes to the synagogue and says that "the Talmud has sustained me until now" (*Conversations* 19); on the other hand, he is angry at God and attacks him with hostile rhetoric in book after book.

This agon, or conflict, is part of Wiesel's basic religious fabric: "Although I know I will never defeat God," he says, "I still fight Him" (*Conversations* 89). In *The Gates of the Forest*, an imaginary dialogue between the prophet Elijah and Gavriel, Gregor's alter ego, contains this observation by Elijah: "You think you're cursing Him, but all you do is open yourself to Him; you think you're crying out your hatred and rebellion, but all you're doing is telling Him how much you need His support and forgiveness" (33). This is a counterintuitive way of thinking about man's relationship to God, and perhaps more congenial to Judaism than to Christianity. The matter is clarified in the novel as follows: "Gavriel used to say that the difference between Christians and Jews was that for the Christians everything that comes from God is good and everything evil bears the mark of man; the Jews, however, press their search further and more blasphemously, crediting God with evil as well as absolution" (*Gates* 94). I am arguing, however, that such a "pressing further" in order to discover God's implication in evil is not limited to Jews. In fact, misotheistic Christians have arrived at the same conclusion, except that they tend to hide their blasphemy more carefully than writers working in the Jewish tradition.

It is not difficult to locate this kind of "pressing on" in *The Gates of the Forest*, where it takes on the form of an increasingly hostile relationship between the main character and God. Looking back over his life and considering the horrific fate of his people, Gregor engages a rabbi in a heated religious dispute. Although the rabbi at first appears to be a stalwart defender of his faith and his god, in a stunning reversal, his belief in the righteous order of things eventually crumbles under Gregor's misotheistic onslaught: "Do you want me to stop praying and start shouting?' . . . 'Yes,' whispered Gregor. Then the mask shattered. The Rebbe made a gesture of revolt; he threw back his head and spoke in a grave, hoarse, voice. . . . 'Oh God, you have set yourself on the side of the torturer, you are guilty; you are the ruler of the universe, but you are guilty'" (198). At this juncture, the rabbi does not revoke his faith in God, despite his declaration of God's guilt; like Wiesel himself, he accepts that new, dark vision of God and continues to wrestle with him.

In the final passage of *The Gates of the Forest*, it becomes clear that Gregor *is* indeed a stand-in for Wiesel himself. For one thing, "Gregor preached anger" (196) which echoes Wiesel's admission that "all my writing is born out of anger" (*Conversations* 82). More importantly, Gregor recalls a scene from a concentration camp that is the very scene Wiesel had himself witnessed:

> In a concentration camp, one evening after work, a rabbi called together three of his colleagues and convoked a special court. Standing with his head held high before them, he spoke as follows: "I intend to convict God of murder, for he is destroying his people and the Law he gave them from Mount Sinai. I have irrefutable proof in my hands. Judge without fear or sorrow or prejudice. Whatever you have to lose has long since been taken away." The trial proceeded in due legal form, with witnesses for both sides with pleas and deliberations. The unanimous verdict: "Guilty." (*Gates* 197)

One could say that this has become a leading motif in Wiesel's life and work: God, the ultimate judge, finds himself put on trial and condemned by humans. In this sense, Wiesel turns Matthew 7:1 ("For in the same way you judge others, you will be judged") and the Midrash ("And in those days the judges themselves were judged") against God himself. This trial-of-God theme crops up repeatedly in Wiesel's work, both in explicit form, as in *The Gates of the Forest,* or in a more indirect and symbolic fashion, as in *The Judges* (2002). The latter novel features a group of travelers who are stranded in a small American town, only to be locked into a room and faced by a somber man who sits in judgment over them. Throughout *The Judges,* this malign, capricious, God-like judge is himself being judged by the accused, and in the end the judge is slain by his own deformed, demonic servant, although on close inspection one suspects the cause of death to be assisted suicide rather than murder.

As indicated above, the trial-of-God motif harks back to a scene Wiesel had witnessed himself at Auschwitz: "I hinted in some of my books at a scene I had witnessed in the camp: God being judged by three rabbis. One day I decided that since I was the one who had witnessed it, I had to do justice to the theme" (*Conversations* 79). The result of this effort is a three-act play titled *The Trial of God* (1979). This is in fact the most explicit and eloquent attack against God in all of Wiesel's work. It is also one of the most radical documents of misotheism to have been published in recent memory. Wiesel characterizes the play as a comedy, largely because he situates it in the tradition of the *Purimschpiel,* "a play customarily performed on Purim, the annual day of fools, children, and beggars" (*Conversations* 79), but this seems to me a rather clever kind of decoy. The emphasis on Purim and on its association with carnival and foolishness serves to legitimize what is in essence a hard-boiled exercise in misotheism. The play represents the inversion of worship, the negation of piety, and the farce of a religious morality play.

In order to highlight the fictionality of his provocative play, Wiesel removed the action from the Holocaust in Central Europe to Shamgorod, a small town in Russia during the mid-seventeenth century. From this geographical and temporal distance, Wiesel conjures up a scene that has universal implications for Jews and other monotheists anywhere and at any time. It is an ambitious play that probes once again that question of questions: "And God in all this?" (25). Why did God abandon his chosen people? Why did God allow the pogroms of history, culminating in the Holocaust, to run their course without stepping in to avert the horror and the mayhem? Berish, an innkeeper in Shamgorod, knows the answer to those probing questions:

Because God is merciless. . . . He will not prevent me from letting my
anger explode. . . . To mention God's mercy in Shamgorod is an insult.
Speak of His cruelty instead. (42–43)

Berish has come to the point of irreconcilable misotheism through
hard-won experience. Until the fateful day when a crowd of villagers
interrupted his daughter's wedding and slaughtered everybody except
for him and his daughter, he had been a pious Jew. But what happened
to him during that pogrom turned him away from God forever: the
raging mob tied him to a table and forced him to watch his daughter
being gang-raped by drunk, brutish, anti-Semitic neighbors. Berish
knows well that this tragedy, this horror, is not unique, that it is not
limited to his own small circle. The cancer of anti-Semitism has
steadily eaten away at the body of the Jewish people, as documented
in the numerous stories of similar pogroms. In fact, it turns out that
each of the three customers in Berish's inn, Jewish minstrels who
were planning to perform a Purim spiel, are also survivors of pogroms.

It doesn't take much imagination to see in Berish once again an
alter ego of the author. Like Wiesel, Berish had his faith shaken forever by anti-Semitic violence. Berish says, "I have the impression
that since that night I am no longer the same person. That night, life
stopped flowing" (44). In his memoir *Night*, Wiesel says similarly:
"Never shall I forget that night, the first night in camp, which has
turned my life into one long night" (32). Berish's statement "I am
boiling with anger!"—anger directed at God—echoes Wiesel's similar statements. And so, Berish proposes to hold a trial in his inn, with
God the defendant and himself as the prosecutor. The mock court
further consists of the three minstrel players as judges (with Mendel
presiding), of the waitress Maria as the audience, and of Berish's
daughter, driven mad by the trauma of rape, as key witness.

Berish's accusation against God is summed up as follows: "I—Berish, Jewish innkeeper at Shamgorod—accuse Him of hostility, cruelty,
and indifference. Either He dislikes His chosen people or He doesn't
care about them—period! . . . In both cases He is . . . He is . . . guilty!"
(125). Wiesel avoids the impression that Berish is stark mad in his
blasphemous attacks against the Almighty. On the contrary, although
tormented by his horrific experience, Berish remains lucid, affectionate toward his violated daughter and, most of all, courageous. As prosecutor against God, Berish can expect serious retribution, yet he does

not mitigate his rage against the divinity: "You have the courage to do my kind of *Purimschpiel*?" he taunts the three minstrel players, "Tell me! And go to the end of things—and utter words no one has ever uttered before? And ask questions no one has ever dared ask before? And give answers no one has ever had the courage to articulate before? And to accuse the *real* accused? Do you have that kind of courage? Tell me!" (56). It is well that he asks these questions because the task he is aiming to accomplish is indeed of epic proportion. To prosecute and condemn God is not just the trial of the century, it is the trial of all time.

Of course, a proper trial requires not only a prosecutor, a judge, and a witness, but also a defense attorney. A significant portion of the play is dedicated to finding somebody in attendance to take up the task of defending God. Ironically, all present find excuses for avoiding that duty. This is the closest the play comes to being a comedy. Mendel, the presiding judge, asks in desperation: "Is there no one in the whole universe who would take the case of the Almighty God?" (109). As it turns out, there is such a figure. Just, when the possibility of a mock mistrial looms, a mysterious stranger appears from out of nowhere. Sam, as the stranger calls himself, is eager to play the role of God's defender. And he does so with remarkable skill. Sam, who identifies himself as "God's emissary" (158), is a glib and skillful defense attorney. When Berish refuses to convert to Christianity to save his life, arguing that "my sons and my fathers perished without betraying their faith; I can do no less" (154), Sam takes advantage of this opening to deflate Berish's case against God:

> First of all, I wish to pay tribute to the loyalty and courage of my distinguished colleague and opponent. The fact that he refused to give up his faith does him—and us—honor. As for his stubborn attitude with regard to the Almighty, of course I cannot but disagree. I understand him, but I disapprove. God is just, and His ways are just. . . . Faith in God must be as boundless as God Himself. If it exists at the expense of man, too bad. God is eternal, man is not. (157)

Such pious statements, despite sounding somewhat hollow and formulaic, do not fail to impress the presiding judge at the mock trial. Mendel says, "I envy you your love of God: I wish I had one measure of it. Your piety: I wish it were mine. Your faith: mine is less profound, less intact than yours" (158). Still, Berish's fervent dissent commands the stage powerfully. His lament, his attack, his protest against God rings truer than the defense's glib excuses: "I lived as a Jew, and it is as a Jew that I shall die—and it is as a Jew that, with my last breath, I shall shout my protest to God" (156). With yet another pogrom starting to materialize outside his inn, Berish knows that he will either die with a prayer or with a curse on his lips. He chooses the latter: "Because the end is near, I'll tell Him that He's more guilty than ever!" (156). With the attackers sharpening their knives outside, time to bring the trial to conclusion is running out, but Berish will at least die knowing that his argument was on the winning side: "In truth," declares the presiding judge, "if I had to pronounce a verdict right now, it would be, I think, influenced by Berish the innkeeper . . . But we are not going to have enough time for our deliberations. . . . The trial will continue without us" (158). At this point it is impossible not to conclude that God is interrupting the trial in order to avoid a guilty verdict. In other words, the impending pogrom reveals God's complicity with the attackers.

But it gets worse yet. Throughout the final act, the identity of the defense attorney has remained a mystery, and all those present attempt to solve it. The longer the trial lasts, the more curious the other characters grow about who the stranger playing God's attorney is. Only in the very last moment before the curtain falls is the identity of God's defender revealed: Sam is none other than Satan himself! Satan has the last word, mocking his horrified onlookers:

> So—you took me for a saint, a Just? Me? How could you be so blind? How could you be so stupid? If you only knew, if you only knew . . . (*Satan is laughing. He lifts his arm as if to give a signal. At that precise moment the last candle goes out, and the door opens, accompanied by deafening and murderous roars.*) (161)

Because God has failed to stop previous pogroms, and the pogrom is starting just in time to interrupt the trial before it could reach the guilty verdict, and since God's defense attorney is Satan himself, the collusion of God with evil seems all but confirmed. Satan's haunting final words "If only you knew" are likely to confirm the unholy partnership between God and the devil. Tellingly, another one of Wiesel's mock-trial stories, *The Judges*, contains this sentence: "Isn't all human life a game in which the Lord himself makes the rules, in consultation with Satan?" (101). However, while in *The Trial of God*, the righteous Berish serves as the accuser of God, the character in *Judges* who says that God lays down the rules of existence "in consultation with Satan" is himself a demonic figure. This is a subtle but significant shift.

Indeed, it is fair to say that Wiesel's antagonistic religiosity, his blaspheming attacks against God, and his doubts about divine treachery and malevolence gradually weakened as he grew older. This development can be traced in *Elie Wiesel: Conversations*, the collection of interviews from which I have amply quoted in this chapter. The earlier to middle interviews, ranging from 1961 to 1978, reveal an enormous reservoir of anger at God's indifference, betrayal, and cruelty. Wiesel's misotheistic tendency is particularly evident in a compelling interview with John Friedman conducted for *The Paris Review* in 1978. However, by the time he had completed *The Trial of God* (1979), it seems that his anger and rebellion had been spent. What else was there to say? Afterward, we see only an occasional flickering of blasphemy, a shadow of a passing doubt, a hint of misotheism. After 1990, it even appears that Wiesel is taking back some of his earlier statements of open defiance against God. In his memoir *All Rivers Run to the Sea* (1996), he dedicates a whole chapter to "The Suffering of God"—a startling shift of emphasis.

Whereas the suffering of mankind, and in particular the suffering of the Jews, had previously dominated Wiesel's sharp and eloquent rebellion against God, now God suddenly becomes the center of attention, and his presumed suffering trumps even the suffering of mankind: "Surely we have no right to complain, since God, too, knows suffering. . . . He alone has discretion in the thousands of ways of joining His suffering to ours. . . . We know that God suffers, because He tells us so" (104). This is a very long way from the rebellion at Auschwitz, when Wiesel deliberately breaks the fast on Yom Kippur to spite God: "I no longer accepted God's silence. As I swallowed my bowl of soup, I saw in the gesture an act of rebellion and protest against Him" (*Night* 66). In *Night* the emphasis is on God's shocking silence in the face of genocide. Fifty years after the Holocaust, the accent falls differently: "Isn't He the Father of us all? It is in this capacity that He shatters our shell and moves us. How can we fail to pity a father who witnesses the massacre of his children by his other children? Is there a suffering more devastating, a remorse more bitter?" (105). The dramatic shift from raging at the careless deity to pitying God for his suffering is not easy to understand.

Indeed, from the early 1990s onward, one can hardly speak of Wiesel as a misotheist any longer. All that is left of his previous revolt against God is a gentle questioning. This comes as a surprise. How can one forgive God for his silence during the Holocaust? There is a statement in *The Gates of the Forest* that makes any such acceptance unthinkable. When asked by Gregor "After what has happened to us [during the Holocaust], how can you believe in God?" the Rebbe answers, "How can you *not* believe in God after what has happened?" (194). The shocking implication of this question is clear: God *is* responsible for Auschwitz, it could not have happened without him. Thus, during the rebellious stage of Wiesel's work, Michael Berenbaum's diagnosis of Wiesel as a heretic seems to be completely justified.

However, commentators such as the American theologian Robert McAfee Brown and literary critic Carole Lambert have tried to wrest an affirmative religious meaning from Wiesel's negative pronouncements about God. Brown did so by placing Wiesel's misotheism in the context of the "agony of the believer": "For Wiesel, it is God's existence rather than God's nonexistence that is the problem. The dilemma is created by belief, not disbelief. His agony over the question of God is the agony of the believer" (141–42). This position is, of course, perfectly reconcilable with misotheism. But then Brown offers an interesting speculation: "God is not so kind to Elie Wiesel as to be deniable, and unless God is powerful and malevolent (a possibility and a nightmare), God appears weak and victimized by a world that has slipped out of divine control. If the latter, God can be pitied. But if God is really in control, what has happened in God's universe is monstrous" (142). Wiesel's more recent pronouncements that emphasize God's weakness and suffering fall under the second part of Brown's statement: God is the victim. However, it is clear that the middle phase of Wiesel's life and work is just as clearly dictated by the other God invoked here by Brown—the malevolent, monstrous god of nightmare. This is the god of the misotheist, and it is a god that, although commanding belief, is not worthy of worship. It is the god whose deafness and silence to evil encourages murder and mayhem, the god who is in league with Satan.

Carole Lambert, by contrast, finds redemptive religious qualities in Wiesel's depiction of human friendship—a leitmotif that weaves through all of his works. Lambert speaks about "the necessity of friends to help restore the broken relationship between the angry, bitter Shoah survivor and God (5). Her argument is that "Wiesel's novels redeem, if not the elusive God, then His most hoped for qualities. If He can no longer be counted on in times of crisis, then friends, in Whom He abides, can" (9). Lambert qualifies this further by saying "whether or not God can be proven to exist, the survivor finds himself and his task in life through ethically helping others" (9). This is a sensitive reading, and it would be unkind to dismiss it out of hand. However, one cannot help but see it as a least-common-denominator effort to save the theistic claims about God's benevolence. If friendship has to do the work of God, isn't that a sign that God has abdicated as a transcendent supreme force in the universe? Of course, one can turn this argument around by saying that God is present in each and every friend, working with and through him or her, but this humanization of God still suggests a fragmentation and diminution of the divine. Also, it doesn't bode well for God's reputation to delegate all the heavy lifting of creating a better world to puny man. At such a point, belief becomes paper-thin because friendship does not need any religious basis to thrive. It can exist on a purely secular plane, horizontal rather than vertical. The same cannot be said about the other theistic claims about God, such as his creation of the cosmos, his victory over Satan, his providential knowledge about the fate of the world, all of which are premised on the supernatural dimension of the deity, depending on a vertical or hierarchical scale of being and creative influence. If human friendship is the best argument we have in support of a benevolent God, then we must be living in the last ages of religion.

In the final analysis, I believe that Wiesel's legacy will be shaped more by his heretical misotheism than by his pity for God. This is not to diminish the moral and ethical standing of Wiesel in any way. While the bulk of his work outlines his ambivalent conception of a hostile god of terror or indifference, that does not make him an anti-humanist or a person of questionable moral fiber. On the contrary, he became a misotheist precisely because he was so deeply humane, compassionate, sensible, and scarred by tragedy. The title of Brown's book *Elie Wiesel: Messenger to All Humanity* is well chosen: Wiesel speaks to human dilemmas, and he is a champion of humanitarian causes, as evidenced, among other things, in his being awarded the

Nobel Peace Prize in 1986, and in his and his wife, Marion's, establishment of the Elie Wiesel Foundation for Humanity.[2]

As a humanitarian and philanthropist, he rejects hatred: "Hatred is always irrational; it is blind and blinding" (*Conversations* 161), but it is the hatred of *people* that he thinks of: "You can hate only a human being" ("Talking" 272). Since God is not a person (in the common sense of the word), to have feelings of hostility toward him is structurally different from hating a human being or a group. This difference, I argue, is the difference between morally corrosive hatred for one's fellow humans and the nobler impulses associated with the courage of disbelief. Misotheism is an expression of anger against the cosmic preponderance of evil, an outcry against the inhumanity of God's creation, and a call to ignore the will of God. It is also an invitation do man's work, do it well, and do it with love. This humanistic impulse is born out of a profound disappointment with the divine order and from a deep mistrust in God's morality.

But this is not an easy road. As Wiesel affirms again and again, "The tragedy of the believer is much greater than the tragedy of the nonbeliever" (*Conversations* 183). The general tone of this assertion is a fitting way to end this chapter. Certainly, there is something in the nature of theism, in the very fabric of the concept of divinity—quite independent of any specific religious framework—that gives rise to the inverse worship or hatred of God. As long as one conceives of God as an all-powerful and all-knowing being, requiring submission, and as long as the problem of evil does not go away, there will be people who conceive of God as tyrannical and malevolent.

What sets Judaism apart, however, is the liberty with which Jews express their doubts, their quarrels, and their rebellion against God. It would be hard to imagine a full-length play written by a monotheist other than a Jew in which God gets all but convicted for crimes against humanity, and in which God's defense attorney turns out to be the devil. Surely, Salman Rushdie would not be tempted to try a similar feat with Allah, having tasted the wrath of Islamic clerics and becoming the object of a fatwa, all because of a lesser act of blasphemy in *Satanic Verses*. But, as Wiesel remembers his old Hasidic master as saying, "only the Jew knows that he may oppose God as long as he does so in defense of His creation" (*Today* 6). And if one takes the creation to mean first and foremost humanity, this statement implies that it is all right to condemn God in order to honor mankind. This is precisely what Elie Wiesel has done in book after book since losing his piety when faced with the crematoriums at Auschwitz. In the words of Michael Berenbaum, "Wiesel loves the human spirit that resists God and sees it as most necessary in the contemporary situation" (87). It is in this sense that Wiesel speaks for many of the misotheists treated in this study: they are artists and thinkers who are unorthodox, blasphemous, and irreverent; and yet they are also deeply humane and moral, concerned with the well-being of man in the here and now rather than in the afterlife.

Having said this, why don't these enemies of God simply adopt atheism? Some of them may well think "that if God is nothing but silence and inaction, then there is no God" (Berenbaum 114). However, misotheists do not usually take that step. People of Wiesel's constitution may be inherently incapable of shedding religious belief altogether, as if they were indelibly predetermined to seek for manifestation of holiness. When confronted with the problem of evil, people with a misotheistic outlook tend to turn their backs on conventional theodicies, or justifications of the ways of God; instead, they would rather modify the image of God to allow for abusiveness as a divine attribute. This is precisely what David Blumenthal, author of *Facing the Abusing God: A Theology of Protest* has done: "God, as portrayed in our holy sources and as experienced by humans throughout the ages, acts, from time to time, in a manner that is so unjust that it can only be characterized by the term 'abusive.' In this mode, God allows the innocent to suffer greatly" (247). To the believer, such a view is hard to accept, and Blumenthal is aware of this: "Some of what I say is heretical" (239). But he is also clear that heresy is the only position left for him as a Jew after World War II: "To have faith in a post-holocaust, abuse-sensitive world is, first, to know—to recognize and to admit—that God is an abusing God, but not always" (248). To the nonbeliever such statements verge on the ridiculous, especially the careful and repeated qualification "*God is abusive, but not always*" (247). Atheists surely cannot fathom what would compel anybody to continue worshipping a god that is declared to be abusive, no matter how frequently or infrequently. How can one go on worshipping such a god without falling into a debilitating state of self-victimization and masochism? The answer is, of course, that one can protest, and that is why Wiesel gave such warm praise to Blumenthal's volume. Being unable to shed belief in God, protest theology seems the only position left. Blumenthal sums the predicament up as follows:

> I accept also the rule that one cannot reject God. This is a rule inherent in the interpretive process, for to interpret is to stand between God and the people, to mediate, to negotiate; not to deny God. In addition, my own personal religious experience forces itself upon me. I suppose that, if I had no awareness at all of the holy and personal presence of God, I would be free to deny God. But, having experienced that Presence, I cannot deny that it exists, nor can I deny that it engages me and that I engage it. The analogy is to psychology: one can be angry with, accuse, repress, or even curse one's father or mother; but one cannot deny her or his existence. (238)

The analogy is, of course, a fallacy, since the existence of God cannot be proven by the same means as the existence of one's parents. But it shows once again what the misotheist is doing: safeguarding his mental health in the face of his constitutional inability to *dis*believe in God. This is the perennial struggle of the agonistic misotheist, who knows that he cannot impress God with his diatribes, and who knows that he cannot change the course of events and lessen the amount of evil done on earth by shaking his fist at God. But he knows, too, that in order to continue functioning as a sane human being, he has to go on shouting his protest against God and to curse God as long as his sense of moral outrage continues, which, in essence, means as long as his memory and his historical awareness remain intact.

For the agonistic misotheist, the problem of evil has become so urgent as to invalidate the standard theodicies available to him. The only way that such a misotheist can maintain his morality, dignity, and sanity is by making war on the abusing god. It is in this light, as I stated in the introduction, that misotheism is less concerned with divinity than it is with man. This is the impulse that propels Elie Wiesel into misotheism; it is similar to the impulse that causes Pierre-Joseph Proudhon to denounce God in the pursuit of political liberation; and it is what prompts Rebecca West to seek the divine in artistic and humanistic endeavors. They all experienced crises and calamities that deepened their sympathy for man while undermining their admiration of God.

Although it is true that misotheism often arises as a response to a sense of cosmic injustice, it is equally true that any given calamity does not necessarily trigger a misotheistic response in every individual. Only a special correlation between the experience of trauma, a strong sense of righteousness, an inclination toward religious nonconformism, and a rebellious constitution, combined with an indestructible belief in divinity, will precipitate this rare form of dissent called misotheism. In that sense, both internal dispositions and external events contribute to the emergence of misotheism, in a fashion that is not predictable. But, no matter whether the path is first into and then out of misotheism, as in Wiesel's case, or, to the contrary, whether it leads away from misotheism and then back into it, as in the case of West, the God-defying individuals we have treated so far (from Swinburne to Wiesel) are committed to the spirit of human progress and the principle of justice. In the next chapter, however, we shall deal with the darker mainsprings of the misotheistic impulse. Indeed, the work of Peter Shaffer confronts us with a more disturbing and morbid variant of man's hostility toward God.

Absolute Misotheism II

Perverse Worshippers, Divine Avatars, and Peter Shaffer's Attacks Against God

You are the Enemy! I name Thee now—Nemico Eterno! And this I swear:
To my last breath I shall block You on earth, as far as I am able! . . . What
use, after all, is man, if not to teach God His lessons?

—Peter Shaffer, *Amadeus* (1984)

To turn now to the work of Peter Shaffer means to move away from the altruism and humanistic righteousness that marked the anti-God rhetoric of such agonistic misotheists as Zora Neale Hurston, Rebecca West, and Elie Wiesel. These thinkers are prompted by pity and outrage regarding the suffering of mankind, and in consequence they shake their fist at God, lament the existence of cosmic imperfection, and complain bitterly about divine culpability in human misery. This is a deeply paradoxical stance, to be sure. Here are humanists who, out of love for humanity, are willing to express resentment and antipathy, bordering on hatred, against the supposedly universal fountain of love and goodness—God. It almost looks out of character that decent human beings, who otherwise are champions of peace, tolerance, and progress, would express such strong negative sentiments with regard to divinity.

My argument that misotheists are not in the same category as misogynists and misanthropes is based on the fact that they are channeling their negative emotions unto a being that (as far as we know) cannot properly be affected by them. Their misotheism is, therefore, primarily an outlet for the pressure of existential frustration, a way of preserving their dignity by protesting against the supposed root of intractable problems on earth. In the case of a Jewish misotheist such as Elie Wiesel, the struggle against God arises from a sense of personal betrayal due to the special covenant between God and his chosen people, as well as from the enormity of suffering that Jews have been subjected to during millennia of persecution, especially during the Holocaust. Whether they are Christian or Jewish, agonistic misotheists are incapable of mustering a sincere love for God. In their conflict with God, they not only assert the right to protest, but they claim the moral high ground over God. But no matter how militant their misotheistic rhetoric sounds, they "only" berate, condemn, and curse God. They are never seen trampling on divine effigies or attempting to obliterate the divine in any of its manifestations.

By contrast, absolute God-haters are in fact trying to slay the divine avatar or destroy God's symbolical representations. As we have seen, Algernon Charles Swinburne, a forerunner of Nietzschean death-of-God rhetoric, advocates the elimination of the Christian god, so that in his stead the pagan divinities of love and fertility could be reinstated. He imagined it to be a sort of reverse scenario of Christianity's conquest over the Roman gods. Moreover, Swinburne imagined this changing of the divine guards to be a rather cheerful affair, fired by visions of newfound sensual vigor and Nietzschean vitality. This is the more upbeat aspect of absolute misotheism, as the God-hater confidently celebrates the demise of the Judeo-Christian deity while holding out alternatives for spiritual worship in the form of new gods.

When we turn our attention to the work of Peter Shaffer, we encounter a different strand of absolute misotheism. Instead of being fired by Swinburnian notions of classical humanism and heroic paganism, the misotheists in Shaffer's work convey a different range of sentiments, including aggressive, antiheroic, and pathological tendencies. Also, unlike the divine antagonist that is the object of other misotheists' resentment, the objects of Shaffer's misotheists are usually "false gods," that is, avatars of the divine in earthly form. Be it the supremely gifted artist (*Amadeus*), the apotheosized animal (*Equus*), or the earthly representative of the sun (Atahuallpa in *The Royal Hunt of the Sun*), each of these figures is the corporeal image of a transcendent deity. By venting their rage against these divine manifestations, Shaffer's protagonists come as close as any mortal ever will to doing actual physical harm to a god.

In Shaffer's treatment of the misotheistic impulse, worship and deicide become inextricably linked. In fact, excessive worship is only the first stage of a development leading to the desire to slay the divine, as Shaffer's protagonists simultaneously crave identification with the deity while also resenting the higher power. Thus, Shaffer goes to the logical end of a speculative train of thought that other writers have taken only for part of the way: Shaffer brings the divine down to the secular, human, even the animal level. It is by destroying such an earthly manifestation of the deity that the crazed worshipper hopes to snatch a portion of God's essence for himself or to set himself up, self-anointed, as a successor divinity. This ambivalence characterizes the morbid character of Shaffer's absolute misotheists.

Where did Shaffer obtain this ambivalent conception of worship? He doesn't strongly identify with Judaism, despite his upbringing by orthodox Jewish parents. In an interview he said, "I was born Jewish—though how a child can be born into any religion I don't see. You can only be born the child of your parents—not a Jew or a Christian. That's imposed upon you. It's a strange and sad thing that you have to spend so much time unlearning the damaging things you were taught—in all good faith on the part of your parents—as a child" (quoted in Gelb 4). Apparently, in contrast to Elie Wiesel's life-long relation to Hasidic traditions, Shaffer actively strove to overcome whatever religious instruction he had received from his parents. Shaffer's resistance to his parents' religion notwithstanding, it is possible to see traces of Jewish "protest theology" in Shaffer's dramatization of his God-hating worshippers. In David Blumenthal's book *Facing the Abusing God*, the believer's ambivalence is shown to be a reflection of God's own ambivalence: "We will affirm the reality of God's presence, God's power, and even God's love. . . . And we will accuse God of acting unjustly, as fully and as directly as we can, as our greatest poets and sages have done. We cannot forgive God and concentrate on God's goodness" (267). Such an explicitly ambivalent depiction of God is more likely to be the product of Jewish than of

Christian minds. Interestingly, while Wiesel emphasizes the dark side of God more than Shaffer does, he develops characters who gain their heroic stature and dignity precisely from their quarrel with God. By contrast, Shaffer focuses less on God than on his characters' deeply conflicted attitude to their god, ending in misotheistic violence and madness.

Indeed, madness plays as prominent role in Shaffer's work as it does in Wiesel's. But in the latter's case, madness amounts to something saner than sanity. It is a kind of transcendental lucidity born of an absurdist worldview, which in turn results from the anguished experience of mass victimization and genocide during World War II. Shaffer, who is Jewish but did not suffer in the Holocaust, employs a different framework of madness in his work. True, his warriors against God are also possessed of eccentricity that sometimes borders on transcendence, but their madness is ultimately more clinical and less existential. This really puts a different spin on Shaffer's brand of misotheism, compared to the heroic humanism of the four previously discussed authors. When Shaffer's characters battle God, they are demonstrably mad in a pathological sense. Alan Strang in *Equus* (1973) is strange (deranged, really) to the degree of requiring therapy by a professional psychoanalyst. Salieri in *Amadeus* (1979) goes mad in the sense of being committed to a Vienna madhouse. And Pizarro in *The Royal Hunt of the Sun* (1964) is rapidly declining into senility.

Because of the predominantly negative connotations of madness in Shaffer's work, his misotheists are typically outcasts. Salieri is the mediocre composer whose fanatical attempt to eliminate his rival, Mozart, drives him into maniacal seclusion. Strang is an unstable sociopath who blinds six horses with a hoof pick believing them to be embodiments of the god Equus. Pizarro is a crusty cynic whose megalomania drives him to kill his royal Inca hostage for the remote chance of partaking in the victim's resurrection. Shaffer's misotheists are therefore clearly misguided or deranged. Of course, this does not mean that Shaffer himself shares his characters' tendencies. He merely sets himself off from the other misotheists treated in this study by demonstrating a more detached interest in man's enmity to God, as if he were fascinated by the phenomenon and then created characters who push this concept to the extreme. This does not imply that Shaffer wants us to condemn his misotheists in any uncomplicated, self-righteous, conventional way. Not only does he force us to confront the condition of man's enmity toward God, but in his plays there is a sense that the madness of his misotheists has a bearing on the act of worship in general. Looking in greater detail at three of Shaffer's plays, *Equus*, *Amadeus*, and *The Royal Hunt of the Sun*, I will discuss Shaffer's attitude toward his own fictional misotheists and address the question whether, in light of these plays, any form of worship is not merely a more or less controlled form of madness.

Equus centers on the subversive idea of an animistic deity who stands in for the conventional godhead of Christianity. The mental imbalance in the play's protagonist, Alan Strang, is exacerbated by the religious conflict that pervades his home. While his mother is deeply pious, exposing the boy to intense Bible reading sessions, the father is an atheist who, at one point, removes a graphic display of Christ's crucifixion from the wall in Alan's room. Since the boy deeply misses his beloved Christ image, the father gives him instead a poster displaying the head of a white horse. Alan hangs the image in the same place where Christ's picture used to be, and in an act of transference he begins to worship the image of the horse instead of that of Christ. Allusions to the White Horse of Revelation are more than obvious, and Alan himself makes the connection by quoting Rev. 19:11–12: "'He that sat upon him was called Faithful and True. His eyes were as flames of fire, and he had a name written that no man knew but himself'" (40). But there is more to this horse imagery than its biblical source. As Barbara Lounsberry has pointed out, the substituted picture corresponds to "the related Greek image of the horse as God" (82). To be more precise, the Greek god of horses, Poseidon, is a notoriously capricious deity and the cause of earthquakes, storms, and other such devastations. In this view, the replacement of Christ with the avatar of Poseidon implies the exchange of a benevolent deity with the god of strife and destruction.

Following his adoption of the horse as a new god, Alan develops his own "scripture" as he mutters quasi-biblical gibberish to himself: "And Prance begat Prankus! And Prankus begat Flankus . . . Flankus begat Spankus. And Spankus begat Spunkus the Great, who lived three score years. . . . Behold—I give you Equus, my only begotten son" (49–50). In Alan's fevered mind, which Shaffer may consider to be the mind of the worshipper in general, the repetitive principle of Biblical genealogy and other bits of scriptural discourse are transformed into pagan chants, culminating in the act of self-flagellation.

This gives an indication of the direction in which Alan's religious sensibility is developing. Again, he combines a de facto Christian theme—that of Christ's passion—with the sexual connotations of Dionysian frenzy. Not content with worshipping the image of his horse god and flagellating himself in front of it, he seeks out the presence of real horses to mingle personally with the incarnation of divinity. In his secret dealings with the horses at a local stable, Alan imagines himself, like a centaur, to become one with the horse as he rides his favorite steed, Nugget. Not only is he completely naked during his stealthy nighttime rides across the fields, but he is bringing himself to an orgasm on horseback, thereby emphasizing not only the archaic sexual origins of religious practices, but also foregrounding the Dionysian quality of his religious experience. Throughout this phase of the play, Alan's religiousness oscillates between Christian and pagan iconographies, suggesting a deep functional kinship between the two religious systems.

It is by crossing the threshold from worshipping a deity to assuming divine properties himself that Alan attracts the attention of his psychoanalyst, Martin Dysart. The psychoanalyst, himself a Grecophile, is struck by the Dionysian fervor of Alan's private worship. Under hypnosis, Alan describes to his therapist what he did during stealthy outings with his favorite horse, while riding around on "his place of Ha Ha" (61). This strange expression ("place [or field] of Ha Ha") is a reference to the Book of Job, as Alan's mother reveals when questioned by the therapist about her son's behavior:

> DORA: [Horses are] in the Bible, of course. "He saith among the trumpets, Ha, ha."
> DYSART: Ha, ha?
> DORA: The Book of Job. Such a noble passage. *You* know—[Quoting] "Hast thou given the horse strength?"
> ALAN [*RESPONDING*]: "Hast thou clothed his neck with thunder?"
> DORA: The glory of his nostrils is terrible!" (22)

This passage refers to chapter 39 of the Book of Job, where Yahweh answers Job out of the whirlwind, enumerating all the unlimited powers that he has, and conveying to Job the futility of questioning his omniscience and omnipotence. Given this background, the strangely named "field of Ha Ha" reveals itself as the place where Alan places himself on equal footing with God by riding his steed like a god, all the while arousing himself sexually, crying "HA-HA! HA-HA! HA-HA! HA-HA! HA! . . . HA! . . . HAAAAA!" It is a scene worthy of a Bacchanal, except that its context is Biblical. Dysart is smitten by the aspect of such bold self-aggrandizement and potent vitality, as he confesses to his friend: "I'm jealous, Hester. Jealous of Alan Strang" (82). After Hester protests the absurdity of such a feeling, Dysart exclaims: "What worship has *he* ever known? Real worship!" (82).

But it soon becomes apparent that Alan's "real" worship has an obsessive and ultimately violent quality. Seduced by Jill in the stable next to the horses, Alan finds that he is rendered impotent by the equine presence next door. The Christian ban on premarital sex becomes a maddening distraction from going through with his sexual initiation. In Alan's schizoid mind, a chorus of disapproving voices is shouting: "The Lord, thy God is a Jealous God. He sees you. He sees you forever and ever, Alan. He sees you! . . . *He sees you!* (105). In this instance, the horse is no longer the instrument of Alan's deification, his "Godslave," but now it has become his master and antagonist.

Bouchard has argued that this scenario "is the epitome of Freud's archeology. In a sense, Alan enacts the primal conflict postulated in *Totem and Taboo*. Equus—a conflation of father and god—grants Alan autonomy, for which reverence is due, but forbids Alan autonomy with an older girl, for which Equus must be killed" (198). This is perceptive, as Freud considered the figure of God to be a father-surrogate symbolizing the son's ambivalent relationship to the father: on the one hand the son wants to slay the patriarch to accede to his power, on the other hand he longs to be just like the father and worships him. Freud claimed that the deicidal impulse manifests itself strongly in "the son's efforts to put himself in the place of the father god" (*Totem* 152), although there are mechanisms to conceal this motive since "the notion of man becoming a god or of god dying strikes us today as shockingly presumptuous" (149). Surely, Alan's posturing as Christ on the White Horse of Revelation, combined with his intense resentment against his own father, goes to show that he is acting out the Freudian wish to overcome the father while setting himself up as God. In this view, Alan's attack against the horses, whose all-seeing eyes are the dominant attribute of Yahweh, is an attempt to destroy the über-father.

In the end, God is only defeated in the deranged mind of Alan. Both the audience and Dysart know that Yahweh did not come to harm through Alan's act of mutilation. But by striking at the imaginary avatar of all-seeing Yahweh, Alan not only rid himself of the symbol of "though shalt not," but he also destroyed the source of his pagan vitality. Thus, *Equus* is not solely concerned with Christianity *or* with paganism. Rather, it is about the explosive interplay between the two religious systems. It is as though Shaffer suggested that neither the mono- nor the polytheistic frameworks offer valid answers to Alan's fervent religious impulse. On the one hand, Alan's discourse is saturated with motifs drawn from the Bible, while on the other hand he is acting out a Dionysian pagan ritual. If Alan is merely a heightened, more extreme form of the generalized worshipper, then Shaffer's point seems to be that worship itself is the problem, undermining morality, unhinging mental stability, and twisting a healthy sex life.

This sets my reading apart from critics who have located the principal issue of *Equus* in a preference of polytheistic rituals over the institutionalized forms of Christian worship: "[Shaffer] discounts conventional religions . . . as detrimental because they lock men into predetermined, structured worships and lives without regard to the reality of self: the multiplicity of self, which demands a multiplicity of gods" (Gianakaris 110). Gianakaris further suggests that "new answers arise from passionate, primitive worshippers (Atahuallpa, Alan Strang)" (111). I see it differently. It is not that Dysart (or, as we shall see later, Pizarro), cannot overcome an attachment to conventional religious habits, but rather that genuine religious worship is simply shown as impossible to sustain. For Shaffer, to worship any deity inevitably leads to the desire to destroy the object of worship. There is a Freudian sense of deep rivalry between the worshipper and his deity, to such a degree that iconoclasm is inevitable. In this, Shaffer addresses an even more fundamental subject than the preference of one religious system over another.

While *Equus* centers on a Promethean character, Alan Strang, lashing out against God, *Amadeus* features a Faustian protagonist, the composer Salieri, whose relationship with God has soured because of what the composer imagines as God's breach of contract. In keeping with Shaffer's presentation of God-haters in other plays, Salieri turns out to be a less than sympathetic misotheist, raising the question of where the moral and religious center of *Amadeus* is to be located. Is Salieri justified in his revolt against God? What is the moral character of God? Is there a didactic message pertaining to God and worship in general? I shall pursue these questions in the following analysis of the American edition of the play *Amadeus*.

The initial cause that starts Antonio Salieri, a well-respected Italian composer at the court of Joseph II, emperor of Hapsburg-Austria, on the road to misotheism is a perceived injustice and breach of promise on the part of God. Convinced that "music is God's art" (11), Salieri had struck a bargain with the Almighty: if he is gifted with superior musical abilities as a composer, he would in return use his gifts to celebrate God and lead an exemplary, virtuous life:

> I knelt before the God of Bargains, and I prayed through the moldering plaster with all my soul. "Signore, let me be a composer! Grant me sufficient fame to enjoy it. In return, I will live with virtue. I will strive to better the lot of my fellows. And I will honor You with much music all the days of my life!' As I said *Amen*, I saw His eyes flare . . ." *Bene*. Go forth, Antonio. Serve Me and mankind, and you will be blessed!"

Salieri is fully convinced of the validity of this covenant: "Clearly my bargain had been accepted" (12) he says after a combination of fortuitous circumstances had led him to become employed by the court of Austria, a lucky chance that he interprets as evidence that he was doing the will of God.

But Salieri's satisfaction with the rapid progress of his musical career and his self-indulgent certainty that he is the favorite of God comes undone when news reaches him that a boy prodigy by the name of Wolfgang Amadeus Mozart had become the talk of musical Europe. Salieri is disturbed to learn that this boy had composed his first symphony at the age of five and his first opera at the age of twelve. Doubts about Salieri being God's anointed composer become acute when Salieri realizes that Mozart's compositions are superior to his own work. But to add insult to injury, he soon discovers that this genius is an ill-behaved, obnoxious, snotty young man. The ensuing jealousy destroys the religious edifice of Salieri's worldview and his sense of God-given musical vocation: "Dimly the music sounded from the salon above. Dimly the stars shone on the empty street. I was suddenly frightened. It seemed to me that I had heard the voice of God—and that it issued from a creature whose own voice I had also heard—and it was the voice of an obscene child!" (29). After this shock, Salieri implores his god, "Let your voice enter me! Let me conduct you!" (30). But all his pleas are in vain. It dawns on Salieri that his own music is hopelessly mediocre compared to the incomparable genius of Mozart. Salieri's ultimate unraveling comes when he manages to apprehend some sheets of music on which Mozart had scribbled his latest composition: "I was staring through the cages of those meticulous strokes at—an Absolute Beauty!" (72). This ultimate disappointment, this final admission of Mozart's superiority, sets in motion a violent renunciation of faith.

From this point on, Salieri turns into an implacable enemy of God, blaspheming and mocking him:

> *Grazie Signore!* You gave me the desire to serve You—which most men do not have—then saw to it the service was shameful in the ears of the server. *Grazie!* You gave me the desire to praise You—which most men do not feel—then made me mute. *Grazie tanti!* You put into me perception of the Incomparable—which most men never know—then ensured that I would know myself forever mediocre.
> (73–74)

As a Catholic, Salieri has been trained to discern the will of God in acts of divine grace, but he is now fully convinced that God wants to mock him because he gave him insufficient musical abilities while endowing him with a refined enough musical sensibility to appreciate his own inferiority to Mozart. This arrangement would strike a proud man as a rather sadistic joke on God's part. And he will not be made the butt of this joke without fighting back: "So be it! From this time we are enemies, You and I! . . . They say God is not mocked. I tell You, Man is not mocked!. . . . You are the Enemy! I name Thee now— *Nemico Eterno!* And this I swear: To my last breath I shall block You on earth, as far as I am able" (75). And he goes on to promise the audience, "I'll tell you about the war I fought with God through His preferred Creature—Mozart, named *Amadeus*. In the waging of which, of course, the Creature had to be destroyed" (75). Salieri here emphasizes the Latin meaning of Mozart's middle name, "beloved of God" (Ama-deus), and he dedicates his life to scheming against Mozart, so that he would not get employment, that he would be harassed by his erstwhile friends, the Masons, and that he would have no respite in his illness, which would eventually claim Mozart's life at the age of thirty-five. All this is, of course, purely fictional, and the historical Salieri most likely harbored none of these sinister designs against Mozart. In fact, the whole notion of Salieri's leaden mediocrity is mostly Shaffer's own fabrication, as some of Salieri's musical compositions have endured and are still being performed today. But Shaffer exaggerated the musical disparity between Mozart and Salieri in order to develop his theme of one man's solitary revolt against God, based on the perceived injustice of God and the breach of a solemn covenant.

On the surface of it, Salieri comes across as a wholly deluded, crazed, self-important and pathetic man. So, does his case against God and God's instrument, Mozart, have any merit at all? Martin Bidney thinks so. He suggests that Salieri is a modern-day Job who "experience[s] the Jobean dilemma as manifested in the realm of artistic creativity" (184). I am not sure the analogy holds, though, because the fate of Job was so much more horrendous and violent, compared to the kind of adversity that Salieri complains about, notably the "horror" of being mediocre. Moreover, Job never makes a bargain with God and then accuses God for breach of contract. Of course, Salieri's behavior is indicative of a limited understanding of Christian principles and a blinding self-importance. The whole idea of making a deal with God is theologically unsound to begin with. According to St. Augustine's view of Providence, the conferral of divine grace is unpredictable and entirely out of the human subject's control; and according to Protestant notions of predestination, no contract needs to be made because each individual's fate has already been decided prior to his birth. In this sense, Shaffer's Salieri operates wholly outside of such Christian teachings. Here is a mortal who places God in human terms and applies self-made logic to his relationship with God, inferring that if God is just he would act in such and such a way. It is, on the face of it, an absurd proposition. Rather than comparing him to Job, I see parallels to Faust, although the latter, of course, made a pact with the devil; but judged from Salieri's diabolical reaction after finding himself to be the betrayed party, one may well conclude that he thinks his God is really a devil.

But no matter how theologically sound or unsound Salieri's attitude is, Shaffer puts the emphasis again squarely the aspect of worship. Indeed, Salieri's worshipful reverence for Mozart's musical gift is genuine. Peter Shaffer himself sees artistic inspiration in a quasi-religious light: "Shakespeare is my god," he said in an interview, "and I worship him" ("Conversation" 35). Barbara Lounsberry has identified the philosophical origin of such artist-worship in a Neoplatonic strain of thought that links the beautiful with the divine: "Radiance and splendor . . . exude from Mozart's music in *Amadeus*, particularly in the scene from *The Magic Flute*. For Plotinus and for Shaffer such radiance is a divine principle" (86). Judged from this Neoplatonic point of view, the divine spirit has indeed entered the supremely gifted musician Wolfgang Amadeus Mozart. So, when Salieri admits to his own shame that "Mozart [is] the flute and God the relentless player!" (132), he voices a transcendental philosophical position that borders on mysticism. But the vessel of the mystical revelation is provocatively devoid of any aura of solemnity, as though God has misplaced his gift in the wrong individual. This perceived incompatibility of vessel and content is what "nearly seems to justify the Salierian fear of a universe of arbitrary whimsy, in which the undeserving are rewarded" (Bidney 188). Thus, the central issue of this play is once again the devotee's highly conflicted relationship with the object of his worship, followed by the worshipper's intention to kill the incarnated God or destroy the vessel of divine inspiration. In this conflict, there is no social dimension, no collective aspect, and no cosmic vision, as the drama of misotheism is reduced to a personal vendetta.

Salieri's quarrel with Yahweh is a purely personal matter, born of ambition, pride, and self-love. This greatly weakens the nobility of his conflict with God. Rather than wrestling with a god of supernatural stature, he is wrestling with his own demons. When Shaffer has Salieri cry out to God, "I tell You NO!" (74), this "no" is born of pride and narcissism. It is very different from the stance of Elie Wiesel, who tells us that "Judaism . . . allows the creature the right to revolt against its creator and tell him: 'No!'" (*Conversations* 17). For Wiesel, this revolt against God comes from the depth of a collective reckoning, when the fate of the Jewish people or the human condition at large is at odds with the idea of a wise, beneficent, and benevolent god. Wiesel insists that "we may protest against God, provided we do so on behalf of the community" (quoted in Abrahamson 386). His attacks against God always have this collective dimension behind them. And, despite his critiques of God, Wiesel remained a dedicated humanist and never stopped hoping that God might turn out to be on the side of righteousness and justice, despite all the signs to the contrary.

Salieri is cut from an entirely different cloth. He is demonstrably mean, deluded, and spiteful. His conflict with God is only initially of a liberating, heroic nature and then quickly descends to the level of peevishness. The audience of *Amadeus* is encouraged to view Salieri's misotheism as an aberration based on the character's delusional visions of self-importance, a stance that directly hastens the corruption of his moral and ethical standards. By considering Mozart as God's flute, Salieri is concentrating his fight on the physical existence of one man: "My quarrel now wasn't with Mozart—it was *through* him! Through him to God, who loved him so" (80). The problem with that stance is that Salieri would not stop at any baseness, ranging from asking Mozart's wife to perform sexual services for him (in exchange of employment for Mozart), to hastening Mozart's death through overwork and the prevention of adequate medical treatment. Ironically, when Salieri does succeed with his plots and Mozart is pushed back into obscurity as a result of his machinations, Salieri cannot enjoy the fruits of his scheming, and his subsequent rise to be the preeminent composer at the Austrian court is not satisfying: "If I had expected fury from God, none came. *None!* . . . Instead—incredibly—in '84 and '85 I came to be regarded as infinitely the superior composer. And this despite the fact that these were the two years in which Mozart wrote his best keyboard concerti and his string quartets" (84). Rather than being able to enjoy his victory, Salieri is being haunted by Mozart for the rest of his life. In one of his final "conversations" with God, Salieri asks one more time for a little sign of divine favor, but God answers haughtily '"No, no, no: I don't need you, Salieri. I have Mozart! Better for you to be silent!' *Hahahaha-haha!*" (111). Of course, the audience of the play is not asked to believe that God truly speaks to (or through) Salieri; rather, what we hear is a voice conjured up by Salieri himself. And so, Salieri's crazed scheming against Mozart, the "Messenger of God!" (136) looks more like a case of schizophrenia. If Salieri's pact with God is based on a neurotic interaction within himself, then God's victory is nothing more than a different manifestation of that splitting of Salieri's self.

It has been suggested that Salieri is the play's "tragic hero" and that Shaffer succeeded in manipulating "the audience to side with

Salieri in his consciously plotted undermining of Mozart's career and in his hastening of Mozart's death" (Londré 116). I don't agree with this view. To a certain degree we do sympathize with Salieri's plight. After all, his inferiority complex vis-à-vis Mozart is real and so is Mozart's condescension to him. However, there can be no question about where the moral center of this play lies. Mozart does not deserve to be the victim of Salieri's vengeance, and surely the playwright himself is sympathetic with the tragic genius. Although Salieri has some charisma and is certainly a capable villain, when he comes out "declaring evil to be [his] goal and all-out war on the cosmos" (Hinden 152), he is too diabolical to elicit our genuine sympathy. Salieri represents an extreme fringe of man's rebellion against the divine, one in which the misotheist is not denouncing a transcendent object of veneration but is rather fighting demons of his own making.

The Royal Hunt of the Sun (1964) takes up the theme of worship again and develops it in the direction of self-apotheosis. But much of the play is a critique of the church and its function in the colonization of Peru. In other words, Shaffer's first major work follows partly a more conventional line by critiquing the bottomless hypocrisy of colonialism's "civilizing mission" and by chastising the religious rationale used to bolster that mission. Critics agree that "as a reflection of his distaste for bands [religiously motivated militant groups], neither Shaffer nor his characters are satisfied by contemporary religions" (Stacy 329). In his "Introduction" to *The Royal Hunt of the Sun*, Shaffer states that he is distressed by the way "man constantly trivializes the immensity of his experience: the way, for example, he canalizes the greatness of his spiritual awareness into the second-rate formula of a Church—any Church" (v). Tellingly, the stage direction at the opening scene calls for a display of "four black crucifixes sharpened to resemble swords" (1). There follows an elaboration of the familiar proposition that the church facilitates imperial conquest, and that the flag follows the cross: "You are the huntsmen of God," conquistador Francisco Pizarro exhorts his men, "the weapons you draw are sacred! Oh, God, invest us with all the courage of Thy unflinching Son. Show us our way to beat the savage out of this dark forests on to the broad plain of Thy Grace" (8). But lest the audience think that this exhortation is an expression of Pizarro's genuine religious zeal, they are disabused when he lets down his guard soon afterward in a furious anticlerical outburst: "Dungballs to all churches that are or ever could be! How I hate you" (71).

But *The Royal Hunt of the Sun* is not primarily an anti-imperial or anticlerical work. Instead, the play returns to Shaffer's core theme, the problem of worship. Toward the end of the play, Pizarro forms a friendship with his royal hostage, Atahuallpa, emperor of the Incas, a circumstance that is not supported by historical fact but surely a significant development in the play's context. Together, Pizarro and Atahuallpa discuss matters of honor, statesmanship, and, of course, religion. Despite his ongoing humiliation at the hands of the Spaniards, Atahuallpa insists that he is God and that, consequently, he is immortal. This claim of eternal life fascinates the conquistador. Pizarro may have power and prestige, and he may possess more gold than he knows what to do with, but he has also death waiting for him in the wings. This sets up the usual conflict in a Shaffer play wherein a human figure comes into intense rivalry with a godlike being. In a climactic theological disputation, Atahuallpa informs Pizarro that "they cannot kill me. . . . Man who dies cannot kill a God who lives forever" (74). This pronouncement so fascinates Pizarro that he half believes in it, perversely wanting it to be true. Consequently, he won-ders if perhaps another resurrection, that of Atahuallpa, might be in the offing: "But Christ's to be the only one, is that it? What if it's possible, here in a land beyond all maps and scholars, guarded by mountains up to the sky, that there were true Gods on earth, creators of true peace?" (75). After being reminded that he is speaking blas-phemy, Pizarro continues his train of thought about the sun god:

> What else is a God but what we know we can't do without? The flowers that worship it, the sunflowers in their soil, are us after night, after cold and lightless days, turning our faces to it, adoring. The sun is the only God I know. We eat you to walk. We drink you to sing. Our reins loosen under you and we laugh. Even I laugh, here! (75–76)

Note how the motif of Holy Communion is twisted here to apply to sun worship. There is a whole series of analogies between Atahuallpa and Christ, beginning with Atahuallpa's age (thirty-three—the age at which, tradition has it, Christ was crucified) and ending with the Spanish soldiers throwing dice to share out Atahuallpa's possessions. Like Alan Strang, Pizarro is at this point ready to exchange the Christ of his youth with the new object of worship, in this case an Inca god.

Bursting the confines of his bitter and joyless Catholic upbringing, Pizarro wants to embrace a new god that promises a more genuine engagement with the forces of the earth and the body, and hence a more affirmative relationship with life—a project with distinctly primitivist overtones.

Hearing Pizarro's heretical pronouncements, his companions ass- ume that he has gone mad, a notion Pizarro seems to confirm when he goes from worshiping the sun god to lashing out against the new- found godhead. Pizarro suspects that Atahuallpa hates him, that he has been playing games with him, and that he conspired against him. So, he rises up in monstrous anger against the new god: "Oh, yes, you cunning bastard! Look, Martin—behold, my God. I've got the Sun on a string! I can make it rise . . . or set!" (76). A few minutes earlier, Pizarro had tied himself by rope to Atahuallpa in order to be able to better protect the king from the Spanish hordes who are eager to execute the supreme Inca. Now, Pizarro yanks Atahuallpa around on his leash to demonstrate just how superior he is to the god, even lux- uriating in the thought of killing the sun god himself: "I'll make you set forever!" he screams in a frenzy that echoes the deicidal frenzy of Strang and Salieri.

At this point it becomes clear that what Pizarro is really trying to accomplish is to assume Atahuallpa's immortality by killing the god. By this logic, of course, he can only succeed in his quest if Atahuallpa really *is* a god. Hence the abject and boundless disappointment when it emerges that, after his execution, Atahuallpa is confirmed to be dead and no resurrection takes place. Pizarro is furious: "Cheat! You've cheated me! Cheat . . ." (79). Measured by his ambition, Pizarro has now lost everything: not only has he failed to absorb into himself the powers of a godhead because Atahuallpa is a mere mortal, but he has gambled his entire reputation on this experiment because he had given his word of honor that he would not let the Inca king be executed. Pizarro had promised to set the Inca king free if a large storage room were filled to the ceiling with gold artifacts, a condition that was met.

Weeping with frustration, Pizarro gives a final summation of his rebellion: "I lived between two hates: I die between two darks: blind eyes and a blind sky" (79). The two hates are the state and the church, governing structures that always chafed against his freebooting spirit; the blind eyes refer to dead Atahuallpa, and the blind sky refers to absent Yahweh. Faced with such nihilism, and out of his existential disappointment, Pizarro works out a new philosophy, and it is, rather incongruously, a philosophy of life and humanism:

> The sky sees nothing, but you saw. Is there comfort there? The sky knows no feeling, but we know them, that's sure. Martin's hope, and de Soto's honour, and your trust—your trust which hunted me: we alone make these. That's some marvel, yes some marvel. To sit in a great cold silence, and sing out sweet with just our own warm breath: that's some marvel, surely. (79–80)

In this soliloquy, Pizarro concludes in existentialist fashion that all true marvels are man-made, that the cold universe is made hospitable only by man's contribution, and that, ultimately, "God's just a name on your nail" (80); this last quote refers to an earlier scene where Atahuallpa was amazed that the Spaniards could write the word "God" on his fingernail. Putting God on a fingernail—that is the reverse of religious awe. Language, logos, is here used as man's weapon against God, not as God's attribute. Indeed, Pizarro grows more voluble the more he loses his sense of religious piety. He realizes, if only dimly, what power language gives him over the gods: it allows him to make them big or make them small, to imprison them in language or to celebrate them in verse. Language is indeed the misotheist's greatest trump, his source of power over the gods and his claim to ultimate autonomy.

Not surprisingly for a work by Peter Shaffer, the humanistic glimmer of hope in Pizarro's soliloquy is short-lived. As in the other plays discussed above, defying the gods is not a prelude to a secular resurrection or any kind of spiritual healing process. Pizarro's heroic denunciation of God is ultimately pointless. Atahuallpa is dead, Pizarro is declining into madness, and Peru is destined to misery. After witnessing Pizarro's God-defying exultation of man-made miracles, Old Martin somberly sums up the tale of decline that followed after this scene: "So fell Peru. We gave her greed, hunger, and the Cross: three gifts for the civilized life. The family groups that sang on the terraces are gone. In their place slaves shuffle underground and they don't sing there. Peru is a silent country frozen in avarice. So fell Spain, gorged with gold; distended; now dying" (80). The Cross is surely implicated in Peru's misery, as missionary zeal often furnished the justification for Spanish imperial conquests of the Americas.

Ultimately, though, Spain's rapacity did not pay off, as it shrank back to its original size as an Iberian nation long before the decline of other European empires. All in all, the play ends on a pessimistic, defeatist note, with Pizarro unable to set a new course, spiritually and morally, and the Incas doomed to a slow and painful extinction. This is very different from the perspective of Elie Wiesel, whose God-defying rebels served as beacons of hope and representatives of man's dignity in the face of a potentially absurd human condition and a possibly malignant god.

By contrast, Shaffer's take on misotheism dwells strongly on the rebel's deicidal impulse, thereby invoking both Nietzsche's will to power and Camus's metaphysical rebellion. Indeed, his plays bear out Camus's observation that "The rebel who at first denies God, finally aspires to replace Him" (73). According to Camus, the rebel against God "must dominate in his turn. His insurrection against his condition becomes an unlimited campaign against the heavens for the purpose of bringing back a captive king who will first be dethroned and finally condemned to death" (25). As though following Camus's script, Shaffer's Pizarro rebels against the human condition, takes a god captive, talks to him as an equal, and condemns him to death in hopes of acquiring his divine powers. Not surprisingly, Shaffer had read Camus and even explicitly acknowledged the influence of the essay on his work, stating, *"The Rebel* is a terrific book" ("Interview" 64). This is further evidence that Shaffer deliberately worked to dramatize the spiritual, psychological, and philosophical ramifications of metaphysical rebellion, or misotheism. But there is no hope for the coming of a new god after the death of the old one in *The Royal Hunt of the Sun*. What remains are "greed, hunger, and the Cross," as Pizarro crumples up after realizing that Atahuallpa had been mortal after all.

This is a bleak vision and one that undercuts the possibility of existential heroism. Shaffer's plays are full of such antiheroes. The Salieris, Strangs, and Pizarros of the world are lone warriors engaged in a self-destructive game of wanting to be gods and yet having no vision and no impulse beyond hacking at that which they perceive to be the object of their worship. In this assessment, I am in agreement with Gene Plunka's observation that "Shaffer's protagonists are not to be confused with existential heroes who might rebel or revolt to initiate change. His main characters gain a new sense of understanding from their alter egos, but they never act on this newly acquired knowledge" (28). Shaffer's protagonists are absolute misotheists in the most narrow sense: lacking a larger vision and alternative, their primary goal is to destroy the divine. By contrast, Proudhon's alternative to the gods was his vision of an anarchist community based on the principle of mutual aid; Swinburne also envisioned an alternative to Christ and Yahweh, seeking salvation in the pagan gods; Rebecca West saw both human decency and great works of art as alternatives to the shortcomings of God's creation; and Elie Wiesel's redeeming value was the dignity of man in protest against God. Shaffer's misotheists, by comparison, are wholly negative. What emerges from this take on Shaffer's plays is that the whole notion of metaphysical rebellion, of attacks against God, and of hostility toward the divine, would be rather undignified if misotheism only existed in Shaffer's version.

This is not a condemnation of Shaffer. He outlines a fascinating problem—the problem of worship as a contradiction in itself, with the worshipper becoming God's rival, desiring to defeat the deity. Part of this paradox reverts to Shaffer's own contradictory views on worship. He speaks personally through his character Dysart in *Equus*, who affirms that "without worship you shrink, it's as brutal as that" (82). Although a lifelong critic of organized religion and the church, Shaffer refers to a "constant debate" in his life between "the fact that I have never actually been able to buy anything of official religion— and the inescapable fact that to me a life without a sense of the divine is perfectly meaningless" (quoted in Connell 7). At the same time that Shaffer pursues a sense of the divine, he feels that the divine itself is inherently ambivalent. Barbara Lounsberry sums up this predicament: "Beauty and destruction are thus inseparable in Shaffer, just as are worship and destruction. In Shaffer's metaphysics and aesthetics, both creation and destruction are part of God's 'hand.' Humanity, created in the image of the Great Creator/Destroyer, simply reflects His nature" (88). This view, incidentally, is borne out in the Old Testament: "Is it not from the mouth of the Most High that both calamities and good things come?" (Lamentations 3:38). In *Amadeus*, Salieri is convinced that this amounts to fickleness in God. By bestowing the highest concentration of musical genius in an immature, obnoxious boy, God only demonstrates his inconsistency. In *Equus* the horse god is both the conduit of transcendent epiphanies and the imprisoning, punishing purveyor of repressive moral codes. In *The Royal Hunt of the Sun*, Atahuallpa is both a "noble savage" whose dignity is based on his status as the sun god and a power-hungry schemer whose reign is based on fratricide (he defeated his half brother in a civil war). When the psychologist Dysart waxes philosophical over the concept of "the Normal," portraying it as the new god of modern life, he once again takes up the motif of radical ambivalence: "The Normal is the good smile in a child's eyes—all right. It is also the dead stare in a million adults. It both sustains and kills—like a God" (65). This comment sums up Shaffer's attitude toward divinity—it sustains and kills. Therefore, the worshipper who bows down before such a divinity will tend to imitate this contradictory characteristic—adoring and yet hating the divine. This is as much as saying that the tendency to sustain the image of God through worship while desiring to kill him through iconoclastic rage is part and parcel of the religious impulse. If God himself is ambivalent, then worshipping such a deity leads to disorder, confusion, and neurosis.

But the main problem with Shaffer's misotheists is not even that they worship an intractably ambivalent God, but rather that they feel compelled to put on the powers of their God even as they resent his attributes. As a result, Shaffer's misotheists are trapped in a manic pursuit of contradictory impulses. By contrast, the agonistic and political misotheists treated elsewhere in this book are not tempted to acquire divine powers. Instead, they hone the virtues of compassion, endurance, courage, and humanism in *contrast* to the figure of the deity. In a sense, then, by giving us such a bleak version of absolute misotheism, one that is devoid of moral, spiritual, or humanistic virtues, Shaffer helps us to see more clearly the constructive and deeply humane potentials available in other strands of misotheism. As Philip Pullman's trilogy *His Dark Materials* will demonstrate in the next chapter, the desire to defeat God can lead to outcomes that are more affirmative and progressive than is the case with any of Shaffer's troubled misotheists.

Absolute Misotheism III

Anticlericalism, Deicide, and Philip Pullman's Liberal Crusade Against God

It's clear that I haven't been able to escape the presence of this abominable invention Yahweh. He's dead, but he won't lie down.

—Philip Pullman[1]

A FTER EXPLORING THE DARKER MOTIVES OF SHAFFER'S DERANGED misotheists, we will now enter an altogether more affirmative, sunnier realm of absolute misotheism. In the hands of Philip Pullman, absolute misotheism loses much of the sinister appeal that it had in Shaffer's works. *His Dark Materials* (1996–2000), Pullman's immensely popular fantasy trilogy, is reminiscent of the humanistic optimism that fired Shelley's and Swinburne's crusades against Yahweh. And just like many predecessor misotheists, Pullman draws inspiration from the romantic audacity of William Blake, although Milton also plays a role. In fact, the title of the trilogy, *His Dark Materials*, is taken from a line in Book Two of *Paradise Lost*, relating to Satan's voyage out of hell and into Eden. Some of Milton's influence is actually channeled through William Blake, as evidenced in his taking to heart Blake's often-quoted words that "the reason Milton wrote in fetters when he wrote of Gods and Angels, and at liberty when of Devils & Hell, is because he was a true Poet and of the Devil's party without knowing it" (quoted in Erdman 35). This view of human creativity as a rebellious, earthy, even "demonic" enterprise (in the nonpejorative sense) has clearly inspired Pullman; his hero, Lord Asriel, comes across as a kinder, gentler Lucifer, who also pioneers travel between the worlds, and whose aim it is, too, to knock God off his throne. But not only is Pullman of the "Devil's party" *and knowing it*, he does not bother to conceal this circumstance. *His Dark Materials* is as unapologetic and open an instance of absolute misotheism as can be found.

At first sight, though, the story seems to aim its criticism primarily at the church. In this aspect, Pullman follows the precedent set by Blake, who not only wrote that "The Modern Church Crucifies Christ with the Head Downward" (quoted in Erdman 564), but who consistently portrayed priests and ecclesiastics as killjoys and ravenlike agents of morbid perversity. Pullman is also an anticlerical, though of a more universal persuasion, as he revealed in an interview: "when you look at organised religion of whatever sort—whether it's Christianity in all its variants, or whether it's Islam or some forms of extreme Hinduism—wherever you see organised religion and priesthoods and power, you see cruelty and tyranny and repression. It's almost a universal law" ("Dark Agenda"). In *His Dark Materials*, this anticlerical impetus is directed against the evil machinations of a powerful ecclesiastical organization called the Magisterium. At the beginning of the trilogy, the leaders of the Magisterium are conspiring to abduct children from the streets of Oxford and to whisk them to a secret location in the far north. There, as it turns out, a branch of the Church involved in speculative research is conducting experiments on these children in order to separate them from their "daemons" (an animal companion representing one's soul or characteristic essence). This daemon is linked to a person by an invisible, quasi-magnetic attraction, and the Church is developing methods to sever that connection, ostensibly to free children of original sin. Indeed, it appears that a mysterious substance called "Dust," which is associated with both sexual and intellectual maturity, only settles on adolescents but not children. Removing the daemon stops the maturation process and, therefore, repels the affinity of Dust to collect on people. The same operation, however, also leaves children emotionally stunted and subject to slow consumption. This seems too high price to pay for preventing children to acquire original sin, but the procedure has the blessing of the Church. Much depends on solving the riddle of "Dust," and the power to be gained thereby would be comparable in our world if Vatican scientists were the only ones who had discovered the secrets of splitting the atom. This hunger for power and this obsession to purge humanity from sin drives the dystopian machinations of the Church in Pullman's story.

The captive children, who eventually manage to escape from the clutches of the Church, find powerful allies in a tribe of benevolent "witches," who at one point debate the prehistory of the conflict that they have been drawn into:

> For there is a war coming. I don't know who will join with us, but I know whom we must fight. It is the Magisterium, the Church. For all its history . . . it's tried to suppress and control every natural impulse. And when it can't control them, it cuts them out. . . . They cut their sexual organs, yes, both boys and girls; they cut them with knives so that they shan't feel. That is what the Church does, and every church is the same: control, destroy, obliterate every good feeling. So if a war comes, and the Church is on one side of it, we must be on the other, no matter what strange allies we find ourselves bound to. (*Subtle Knife* 50)

By thus condemning the antisexual bias of the "Church," the witches not only make indirect reference to Catholic celibacy, but they also undermine St. Augustine's teachings about original sin, which have for ages tainted the sexual life with the odium of shame and defilement. By depicting the witches as the supernatural helpers of Lyra Bellacqua, the story's precocious heroine, the witches' pronouncements are invested with a moral authority that reveals them to be aligned with Pullman's own beliefs. Indeed, even readers who are unaware that Pullman is a critic of religion and God will sense that the characters' voicing of such anti-ecclesiastical views comes with authorial approval.

The same could be said of Blake's antiecclesiastical opinions as expressed in his poetry. But Blake went beyond the mere critique of church and clergy and attacked God himself, whom he dubbed Nobodaddy, a tyrant and the "Father of Jealousy." Such views are echoed in Philip Pullman's story, which ranges from antiecclesiasticism to misotheism. Take Lord Asriel, for instance, of whom we learn that "a spasm of disgust cross[es] his face when they talk of the sacraments, and atonement, and redemption, and suchlike" (*Subtle* 45). This rejection of Church doctrine is accompanied by a declaration of war against God. Lord Asriel "is aiming a rebellion against the highest power of all. He's gone a-searching for the dwelling place of the Authority Himself, and he's a-going to destroy Him" (*Subtle* 46). Asriel does not seek ecclesiastical reform, nor does he merely want to dismantle the established Church. What he has in mind is a crusade to destroy "the God of the Church, the one they call the Authority" (*Subtle* 45).

In Blakean fashion, the heroes of Pullman's story act on the belief that God is not a champion of mankind but rather its enemy, since his laws are designed to curtail human sensuality, freedom, and creativity. And so, Pullman develops his story to show that "agents of the Authority are sacrificing children to their cruel God," and that "the rebel angels fell because they didn't have anything like the knife," which is "the one weapon in all the universe that could defeat the tyrant. The Authority. God" (*Subtle* 319–20). This, of course, amounts to a frontal attack against the central tenets of theism. Indeed, besides overturning God's attribute of omnibenevolence (because he acts cruelly), Pullman further demolishes the other major theistic attributes, notably, God's supposed omnipresence, his omniscience, omnipotence, and eternal, uncreated nature. Within the context of the story, all of these attributes are shown to be false, thereby dealing a major blow to the Christian creed.

Pullman's direct attack against the Almighty comes into focus in the trilogy's last installment, titled *The Amber Spyglass*, when God's awesome power is revealed as being no more than a legend grown up around political jockeying in heaven. Although God had succeeded by main force in turning the realm of the dead into "a prison camp" (*Amber* 33), God's power in Pullman's trilogy is neither unconditional nor absolute. In *The Amber Spyglass*, the insurgent angels Baruch and Balthamos reveal that

> The Authority, God, the Creator, the Lord, Yahweh . . . was never the creator. He was an angel like ourselves—the first angel, true, the most powerful, but he was formed of Dust as we are. . . . He told those who came after him that he had created them, but it was a lie. One of those who came later was wiser than he was, and she found out the truth, so he banished her. We serve her still. And the Authority still reigns in the Kingdom, and Metatron is his Regent. (*Amber* 31–32)

By countering God's claim to have created the universe ex nihilo (while himself being uncreated), this passage establishes God as a fraud and a liar. Moreover, his moral integrity is called into question by his association with Metatron, the sexually repressed, brutal, and power-hungry regent handpicked for his duty by God.

Pullman not only desecrates God by placing him in the company of such a criminal protégé, but he also emphasizes God's gradual descent into senility. One character relates that God is "at some inconceivable age, decrepit and demented, unable to think or act or speak and unable to die, a rotten hulk? And if that is his condition, wouldn't it be the most merciful thing, the truest proof of our love for God, to seek him out and give him the gift of death?" (*Amber* 328). This "gift" is indeed granted God shortly afterward. By chance, the two protagonists Will and Lyra stumble upon his "crystal litter" (a sort of divine preservation machine) which has gone missing during a botched attempt to transfer God to a safe location. When the two children try to liberate God from this absurd contraption, they witness a puzzling spectacle: "Demented and powerless, the aged being could only weep and mumble in fear and pain and misery, and he shrank away from what seemed like yet another threat" (*Amber* 410). So frail is this decrepit former "Authority" that once "in the open air there was nothing to stop the wind from damaging him, and to their dismay his form began to loosen and dissolve. Only a few moments later he had vanished completely, and their last impression was of those eyes, blinking in wonder, and a sigh of the most profound and exhausted relief" (*Amber* 411).

Such a disoriented, feeble God has obviously no claim to omnipotence or omniscience. And, thus, the question arises whether this weak god is even opposable, or if his harmlessness means that his opponents are wasting their time in attacking him. I think what Pullman wants to convey is the heretical idea that God is mortal and therefore subject to aging, regardless of his former power and splendor. Even an old, tottering tyrant is still a former *tyrant*, and as such he is not only morally accountable for former crimes, but he may in addition still be acting as the gray eminence in the background, holding the reins of power in his hand. Thus, the God of Pullman's fiction, about whom Metatron informs us "his heart was fixed against [human beings], and he made me prophesy their doom" (*Amber* 399), deserves no pity. On the contrary, his tottering condition in the end further dramatizes his transformation from an object of worship to an image of contempt. With this subversion of the Christian view of divinity, Pullman is part of a radical vein in British letters that delights in taking swings at God by mixing scorn with ridicule. In addition to following Blake, Pullman also echoes William Empson, who had opined that "the Christian God the Father, the God of Tertullian, Augustine and Aquinas, is the wickedest thing yet invented by the black heart of man" (251). To Pullman, it is enlightened man's moral imperative to protest against and undermine such a God.

Paradoxically, though, most readers saw right past Pullman's assault against the Church and God in the years directly following the three novels' initial publication. Despite virtually dismantling the Christian teachings about theism, creation, original sin, and divine Providence, Pullman's series garnered much critical acclaim and little concern over the nature of its religious tendencies.[2] How should one account for this complacency vis-à-vis Pullman's radical theological subversion? It appears that this aspect of *His Dark Materials* largely escaped notice because people even today lack a misotheistic "receptor," with the result that a message of God-hatred often fails to register. Indeed, the absence of both a proper term for this antagonistic faith and a generally acknowledged concept of God-hatred made it easier for Pullman's series to escape notice as a blasphemous work of fiction.

Also, Pullman did not immediately reveal all his cards, but rather gradually developed his theme of hostility toward the Almighty from one installment of the trilogy to the next. Hence the full scale of his religious subversion only emerged with the third and concluding volume of the trilogy, *The Amber Spyglass* (2000). Alan Jacobs may be the first to condemn the heretical underpinnings of the work. In an article titled "The Devil's Party" (October 2000), he takes Pullman to task because "the theological freight of his books . . . turns out to be a distinct *anti*-theology" (40), something Jacobs considers to be "a reductive and contemptuous ideology" (40). Jacobs is particularly piqued by Pullman's "*truly* anti-theological point that whether God lives or dies is not in the long run a very significant matter" (42). Jacobs's negative response, however, remained by and large a minority view, as mostly congratulatory reviews kept appearing in the *Times Literary Supplement*, the *Boston Globe*, the *New York Times*, etc. But in October 2001, another religiously inspired critique of

Pullman's literary undertaking appeared. Cynthia Grenier, of the Catholic monthly *Crisis Magazine*, lamented that "few Christians or Jews seem even to notice, much less care about, the all-out attack on their faith just underneath the skillful narration and imaginative fantasy that the critics have praised in *His Dark Materials*." According to Grenier, the view "that Pullman's trilogy is a 'critique of organized religion' is an understatement." She is right: Pullman's work is also an attack against God.

The issue came to a head when *The Amber Spyglass* received the prestigious Whitbread Book of the Year award in 2001. Now conservative Christians on both sides of the Atlantic began to stir. In *The Mail on Sunday* of January 27, 2002, Peter Hitchens published a polemic attack against Pullman's work under the title: "This is the most dangerous author in Britain." Hitchens maintained that "[Pullman] is the anti-Lewis, the one the atheists would have been praying for, if atheists prayed." It did not take long before Peter Hitchens's leftist brother, Christopher, joined in the fray. His review for *Vanity Fair* of October 2002, titled "Oxford's Rebel Angel," is wholly enthusiastic about Pullman's work, not despite Pullman's attacks against Christianity but precisely because of them. Christopher Hitchens writes approvingly that "Pullman's daring heresy is to rewrite the Fall as if it were an emancipation, and as if Eve had done us all a huge favor by snatching at the forbidden fruit. Our freedom and happiness depend on that 'first disobedience'" (178). According to Christopher Hitchens, Pullman's departure from the pious standards set by C. S. Lewis, Lewis Carroll, and J. R. R. Tolkien is a liberating rather than a deplorable act of innovation. As this controversy shows, the question of misotheism becomes a litmus test of political ideology: the progressive, leftist humanist sees nothing wrong with challenging God's dignity and authority, whereas the conservative, Tory commentator, Peter Hitchens, warns darkly that liberals like Pullman undermine the social order and threaten established moral values.

It is clear from Christopher Hitchens's favorable review that he shares more than a superficial similarity of opinion with the writer of "that fabulous trilogy" (178). But there is also a significant difference between Hitchens, an enemy of religion, and Pullman, a misotheist. Although Hitchens's advocacy "of Promethean revolt and the pleasures of skeptical inquiry" (*Letters* 66) would sit very well with the writer of *His Dark Materials*, Pullman approaches the matter from a different angle. Indeed, he expends a significant amount of imaginative and intellectual resources to write God into existence, so that his protagonists can then struggle against him. In Pullman's imaginary world, the Almighty exists, as do hosts of angels and other celestial beings. Neither Hitchens nor Dawkins, nor Bill Maher, for that matter, would trouble themselves with a project that, under close scrutiny, would reveal itself to be an implicit acknowledgment of God, albeit a God that is very different from the biblical, theistic deity. True atheists would not care to dramatize the fight against an anthropomorphic God, no matter how fanciful the story line is. Such a project would constitute too great a concession to religion. But that is precisely what Pullman is doing. Thus, the charge leveled against him by the American Catholic League, that "the trilogy, *His Dark Materials*, was written to promote atheism and denigrate Christianity" (Donahue) misses the mark. Yes, Pullman does denigrate Christianity, if by that we understand biblical teachings and the doctrine of theism. But just like Algernon Charles Swinburne, of whom Welby says that despite his attacks against Christianity, he was "a profoundly religious poet" (114), so Pullman, too, plays with religious ideas. Rather than being a poster boy for atheism or radical nonbelief, he is a misotheist who selectively attacks the conventional representation of God without denying a spiritual dimension to existence or indeed an alternative deity.

With the release of the movie *The Golden Compass* in December 2007, attention to Pullman's trilogy redoubled, and a flurry of lengthy commentaries have since appeared. The year 2007 alone saw the publication of three book-length studies about the religious and spiritual aspects of the trilogy. The strangest fruit of this recent crop of commentaries is certainly the somewhat misleadingly titled *Shedding Light on His Dark Materials: Exploring Hidden Spiritual Themes in Philip Pullman's Popular Series* (2007). This book, sold in mass-market outlets like Wal-Mart, is not so much an interpretive venture than an exercise in overwriting. Obviously disturbed by the popular success of the trilogy, which sold more than 15 million copies worldwide by 2007,[3] the coauthors Kurt Brunner and Jim Ware transparently try to neutralize Pullman's religious (or antireligious) message by blatantly contradicting his ideas. The procedure they follow is quite simple: state one of Pullman's anti-biblical premises, discuss its implications, and then flatly deny its truth. For instance, the authors sum up Pullman's misotheistic stance: "From his perspective . . . God is the *real* culprit, the ultimate sponsor of chains, oppression, and injustice, the worst of all usurping tyrants" (97). Then they shed the following "light" on this view: "God is a loving Father, not a cruel tyrant" (49). In other words: Pullman says A, we say B, case closed.

This procedure often bears ludicrous fruits, as when the authors deal with one of Pullman's most celebrated inventions: the daemons (that is, animal companions who portray a vital aspect of a person's character). After Lyra finds Tony, one of the victims of "intercision" (the aforementioned procedure by which the connection between a child and his daemon is severed), the boy is presented to the reader as a human being robbed of his soul, a zombie who "was like someone without a face" (*Golden Compass* 214). Here is the "light" that Brunner and Ware shed on the scene where the brutal effects of the Church's "intercision" manifest themselves: "Inward wholeness comes through relationship with Christ alone" (29). This method is obviously not getting us very far in the way of probing the deeper mainsprings and ramifications of Pullman's religious critique, and I will therefore pass on to more productive encounters.

An earlier effort of Christian apologia in the face of Pullman's misotheism is Tony Watkins's similarly titled book *Dark Matter: Shedding Light on Philip Pullman's Trilogy His Dark Materials* (2004). Watkins is associated with the Damaris Trust, which describes itself on the book's dust jacked as "an organization that helps people relate contemporary culture and Christian faith." Watkins's book is somewhat more restrained in its criticism of Pullman, but it still bristles with a disapproving air of righteous condemnation. While Watkins clearly respects Pullman's narrative skills and lauds "the dazzling breadth of Pullman's story and its complexity" (17), he regrets "the less satisfying elements" of the trilogy, notably the radical "reversal that underpins the whole of *His Dark Materials* [because] Philip Pullman portrays the Magisterium and God as unremittingly bad" (126). Although less brazen than Brunner and Ware, Watkins still employs the method of countering Pullman's religious ideas by essentially proclaiming their untruth. According to Watkins, Pullman's story clashes "with God's utterly pure and holy nature" (128), and he laments that "Pullman has misrepresented God" (129). Watkins goes on to say that Pullman falsely reinterpreted the story of the Fall as "the moment at which we cast off God's shackles and grew up

202 | *Six Case Studies in Literary Misotheism*

so that we could stand on our own two feet" (126). In an ever tight-
ening circle of condemnation, Watkins states that in "Pullman's attack
on the kingdom of heaven, then, he misrepresents history and mis-
reads the Bible to create a caricature of Christianity, inverting all the
categories in the process. He makes God out to be a cruel and vindictive impostor who is part of the universe, not its transcendent Creator" (179). For Watkins, this amounts to a fallacy: "the picture of both
God and the church that Pullman paints in *His Dark Materials* is a
straw man" (178). In this view, to look at God as a source of evil may
be therapeutic but it has nothing to do with God's true character.
Because of its centrality to the question of misotheism, Watkins's
straw man argument deserves a closer look.

Indeed, someone could argue that misotheists put up God as a
straw man for perceived problems and sufferings that have nothing
to do with God. When people rise up in revolt against God, they often
do so because of natural catastrophes (such as tsunamis, earthquakes,
hurricanes), because of political injustices and systems of exploitation
(colonialism, sexism, racism), and after personal misfortunes
(divorces, deaths, illnesses). Thus, it is possible to say that misotheists
attack God merely as a stand-in for sufferings that baffle human
comprehension or outrage our sense of justice. However, the argument that misotheists blame God for calamities that have nothing to
do with him does not quite hold up under scrutiny. As for natural
catastrophes, it is not unreasonable to hold God accountable for
effects of his own creation. Indeed, pious people often reflexively see
in an earthquake or hurricane an "act of God" (this is, indeed, the
legal language used on insurance documents to refer to unforeseeable
natural disasters). But if an earthquake is an act of God, then it is also
a responsibility of God, and hence God is not only a straw man.

But what about the relationship between God and man-made
causes of suffering? Let us consider the misotheistic feminist, for
whom God is the ultimate patriarch, overseeing a sexist universal
order; or the misotheistic socialist, according to whom God is the ultimate boss, enslaving humanity; or the misotheistic antiracist, who
paints God as a white supremacist, denying nonwhite races opportu-
nities granted to white people. It would be quite easy to argue that in
these cases, God is indeed propped up as a mere straw man, were it
not that these kinds of oppressions have traditionally been justified
precisely in the name of God. The Bible furnishes ample material for

arguments that God made woman inferior to man; Christianity has been invoked as a palliative (Marx called it "opium") to instill patience into those exploited by the economic system; and Biblical justifications of slavery are legion. All of this, one can argue, has the potential to implicate God in the situation.

Pullman directly addressed this issue in an interview, saying, "those people who claim that they do know that there is a God have found this claim of theirs the most wonderful excuse for behaving extremely badly. So belief in a God does not seem to me to result automatically in behaving very well" ("Dark Agenda"). What is merely implied in this statement is the view that when God is invoked by people behaving badly, then some of that badness reflects back on God. And we end up with the argument that God, if he is all-knowing and omnipresent, has to take some of the responsibility for people doing evil in his name. It is the same argument voiced so vehemently by the character Berish in Elie Wiesel's *The Trial of God*: "Men and women are being beaten, tortured and killed. True, they are victims of men. But the killers kill in God's name. Not all? True, but let one killer kill for God's glory, and God is guilty. Every person who suffers or causes suffering, every woman who is raped, every child who is tormented implicates Him" (54). By this logic, condemning people who do evil in the name of God is only a first step along the way to misotheism, and it will in due course lead to condemning God outright. Surely, by Berish's logic, God is more than a straw man. He is a puppeteer.

But there is an even more fundamental problem associated with the straw man argument. If we grant the straw man theory voiced by Watkins, then we must also accept the obverse of this theory: just as the ills of humanity may be pinned on God by way of projection, so the good qualities attributed to God—notably mercy, pity, and love—may also be attributed to God without him actually deserving them. The straw man theory, in other words, works both ways: pious people can invoke this defense to denigrate the misotheistic anger against God; and the misotheist can invoke it to counter the worshipper's sincere admiration of God. The question of God's character hinges on the question of God's revelation to human beings. And that, ultimately, is a question that in itself does not have a neutral, verifiable answer independent of a religious belief or theological creed.

The whole problem of making assertive statements about God's character is revealed in Watkins's statement that "Christians are not claiming a monopoly on morality and values. But they believe that morality only functions because it has an objective basis in the character of God, *whether or not* anybody believes in him" (162). This is a shaky argument in more ways than one. When Watkins says that God is the basis of morality, regardless of whether or not people believe in him, he violates the rules of logic. Since God's existence cannot be subjected to empirical proof—being contingent upon belief—Watkins's affirmation of an "objective basis" of God's character is voided. Most people will agree that a tree falls in the forest whether or not somebody is there to witness it. The tree's falling can be empirically verified after the fact. But the same principle does not apply to divinity. It is not true that even if nobody believes in God, then God still exists. If nobody believes in divinity then God *may or may not* be there. This is precisely Pullman's position, as stated in an interview: "I've got no evidence whatsoever for believing in a God. But I know that all the things I do know are very small compared with the tings that I don't know. So maybe there is a God out there. All I know is that if there is, he hasn't shown himself on earth" ("Dark Agenda"). As opposed to Watkins's argument, Pullman has the benefit of logic on his side. Of course, Christians may take issue with this position, insisting that God has "shown himself on earth" through Jesus. Again, even if the existence of Jesus can be empirically proven, whether or not he was divine is a matter of belief. Most Unitarians, for that matter, reject this belief.

But there is a further problem with Watkins's formulation regarding the objective basis of God's moral character. First, he admits that nonbelievers can have good values and morals, just like Christians. Then in the next sentence he takes half of that admission back, insisting that morality is based in God, even the morality of nonbelievers. The first sentence, admitting morality's independence from religious belief, contradicts the second part of the statement, linking morality explicitly to the centerpiece of religious belief—God. It is at this point that two reference systems clash—a rational, skeptical one in the case of Pullman, and a revelatory, religious one in the case of Watkins— making it difficult to establish common ground between these two fundamentally different worldviews.

So, while Watkins is trying to undermine the logic of Pullman's religious views, what he is actually doing is undoing his own. Besides this blunder, we need to ask further: What exactly *is* God's character as invoked by Watkins? If we go to the Bible for an answer, then we will find support for the existence of both a benevolent and a malignant character. Surely, Jude's God, and the God of Psalms is an all-good and praiseworthy deity. But there are other passages that reveal a vindictive, manipulative, and violent God, such as when God is shown to advocate cruelty and extermination against the Canaanites (Deuteronomy 7), or where he hardens the heart of the Pharaoh (Exodus), and then brutally punishes him and his people for being hard-hearted against the Israelites, and so on. It is such passages that inspired people such as Thomas Paine, Mark Twain, and William Empson to paint a rather sinister image of Yahweh. Thus, as far as the character of God is concerned, the last word has not been spoken. And as long as the debate continues, there will be skeptics and misotheists who cast doubt on God's benevolence. The objective of both Watkins and Brunner and Ware is to influence readers already enthralled by Pullman's trilogy by flatly contradicting the story's misotheistic, antiecclesiastical message. Considering Pullman's fiction as a form of propaganda, they meet it with open counterpropaganda. The success of this strategy remains to be seen.

Lois H. Gresh takes a much more objective approach to Pullman's controversial lore. In *Exploring Philip Pullman's* His Dark Materials (2007), Gresh pays close attention to scientific, technological, and mythological aspects of Pullman's story rather than to his religious outlook. In fact, she exempts herself from the whole controversy by stating that while she "focuses on traditionally religious ideas, it's not my intention, as author, to support specific religious ideas over others. It's not my position to suggest that angels, Gods, or heaven exist—or that they don't: I leave such contemplations to my readers" (44). What Lois does, instead of taking sides in the religious controversy over *His Dark Materials*, is simply to demonstrate a dense web of connections and influences between the story and a range of scientific theories, mythological precedents, and theological principles. In doing so, she still conveys a good deal of religious explications, revealing just how many spiritual aspects Pullman has integrated into his story. For example, she contends that Pullman's notion of "Dust" draws on the tradition of *"monistic idealism.* In this view, we have a universal or cosmic consciousness, which seems to be more in line with the philosophies of *His Dark Materials*. An example of monistic idealism might be Buddhism, in which Nirmanakaya is the material realm and Samghokaya is the mind and spirit realm. . . . Other examples of a cosmic consciousness might be the atman of the Hindus and the Christian Holy Spirit" (37). Other spiritual implications emerge in Gresh's analysis as well. With regard to the Semitic concept of the underworld, Gresh writes that "Sheol was dark, misty, and depressing, but it wasn't what we think of as hell. Rather, Sheol was more like the world of the dead in *His Dark Materials*" (135). These connections are illustrations of Pullman's abiding interest in spiritual matters, and they attest to his grounding in manifold religious traditions, no matter how fiercely opposed he is to aspects of the Christian doctrine.

While Pullman is averse to the supreme, anthropomorphic god as depicted in the monotheistic religions, he is not against divinity per se. Several critics have noted the divine attributes of "Dust" in Pullman's trilogy. Anne-Marie Bird specifically argued that "Dust" "reflect[s] a Spinozan monistic doctrine that there exist one and only one substance . . . 'Dust' is the *logos* or 'Total Being,' the ultimate cause" (Bird 191). This notion is taken further in one of the most interesting among the recent book-length studies of Pullman's trilogy: *Killing the Imposter God: Philip Pullman's Spiritual Imagination in* His Dark Materials (2007). The coauthors Donna Freitas and Jason E. King, both religious scholars, present the provocative argument that Pullman is essentially a religious writer—though he may not be aware of that himself. In what should certainly be a shocking revelation to all those who lament Pullman's atheism, Freitas and King argue, "Pullman's work echoes the concerns of liberation theologians—people whose primary concern is that the divine be an empowering, life-changing energy for humanity and the earth, so much so that this trilogy can be read as a religious classic" (xiv). They do not deny the misotheistic impulse behind Pullman's work, acknowledging the fact that in his work "God is the villain" (8). But they interpret Pullman's presentation of an evil god as perfectly compatible with an essentially theological outlook: "we present Pullman's work as embodying a sophisticated theology and so make the atheist Philip Pullman a theologian in spite of himself" (xxiv).

Thus, these critics differentiate between Pullman the public persona, who self-identifies as an atheist (or an agnostic, depending on what interview one reads) and Pullman the imaginative writer, who apparently does not have complete control over the religious and spiritual implications of his own fictional creations: "we find some of the most eloquent testimony against Pullman-the-atheist in Pullman-the-writer" (xxi). In making this argument, Freitas and King home in close to the very core of the misotheistic project. First of all, they acknowledge that Pullman does, indeed, perform a symbolical deicide: "the trilogy acts as a kind of obituary for God" (xix–xx), but their argument hinges on the claim that Pullman does not aim at killing the concept of divinity altogether. Instead, he only selectively eliminates a particular version of God: "He has killed off only one understanding of God—*God-as-tyrant*—and an oddly antiquated and unimaginative one at that. Pullman has done away with the malicious, lying, controlling, manipulating being in charge of his universe in order to put an end to unjust cruelty and domination" (19). In place of this tyrannical god, the authors say, Pullman places a more palatable conception of divinity: "Even as Pullman is killing off his medieval imposter God, he raises up for his readers a divinity fit for our age—one compatible at once with science, popular spirituality, and contemporary theology" (xxi). This crucial move, however, is underpinned by a nonconformist understanding of divinity, one that is essentially Feuerbachian and, hence, prone to attacks as being atheistic in itself. As I demonstrated in Part One, Ludwig Feuerbach posited the rationalist thesis that God is merely the projection of man's idealized self-image, not a transcendent entity independent of humanity.

If Pullman deposes the tyrannical God image and replaces it with a more benevolent "divinity fit for our age," then presumably there will be other deities over the course of time that will be worshiped in the future. Such an emphasis on the historical contingency, the social constructedness, and the plurality of God carries within it the negation of theism. The god that Freitas and King write about is neither omniscient nor omnipotent or eternal. Their god, like Feuerbach's, is a human construction, liable to be modified by sociocultural changes and liable, also, to be killed and resurrected in a different guise by humans. It is, in the last consequence, a radically man-made, secular god. Thus, by arguing that Pullman only kills a particular kind of god followed by the resurrection of a different one, King and Freitas demolish the central theorem of monotheism.

This is only one of the problems with *Killing the Imposter God*. There are other problems, of terminology and of historical scope. As for terminology, the authors use the imprecise denominator "protest atheism" to name the enmity against God: "Protest atheism is a category in the study of religion used to name a person or tradition that explicitly rejects a particular notion of God—the Trinitarian God of Christianity, for example, or a Jewish God who allows the Holocaust to occur" (19). This is imprecise on two counts: Unitarians, who reject the doctrine of the Trinity and worship only one singular deity, are not, therefore, protest atheists. And Elie Wiesel's play *The Trial of God*, which is cited as another example of protest atheism, is not a work of unbelief, whether protesting or not. No variety of atheism is really compatible with misotheism. "Protest atheism" is therefore as imprecise and misleading a denominator as Freeman Dyson's term "passionate atheism." What one should be saying instead is that Pullman is a representative of misotheism. In fact, that's what Pullman himself should say, so as to avoid prevaricating and hedging statements about whether he is more of an atheist or an agnostic.

This discussion raises another fundamental question, namely, what the relationship is between the ideology apparent in a work of fiction, and the convictions of its author. Pullman himself claims that *His Dark Materials* is not a theological tract or polemic of any sort, but simply a fictional work of the imagination. A good yarn, nothing more. Asked about his character's provocative statement that "the Christian religion is a very powerful and convincing mistake" (*Amber* 441), Pullman answers, "Mary is a character in a book. Mary's not me. It's a story, not a treatise, not a sermon or a work of philosophy. I'm telling a story, I'm showing various characters whom I've invented saying things and doing things and acting out beliefs which they have, and not necessarily which I have. The tendency of the whole thing might be this or it might be that, but what I'm doing is telling a story, not preaching a sermon" ("Dark Agenda"). Of course, one wouldn't really expect any other answer from an author. Writers notoriously feign surprise when confronted with interpretations of their works. But we shouldn't let Pullman get away that easily. As I have been arguing throughout this book, fiction is precisely the preferred forum for voicing misotheistic ideas. Oftentimes, writers who are reluctant to state their opposition to God in their nonfiction will put traces of it into their fiction. In the case of Philip Pullman, there is much more than a trace of misotheism in his fiction. Moreover, Pullman has made so many explicit statements about his beliefs and values that it is quite easy to see a strong consensus between the climate of opinion in his novels and his own ideology.

Although I find much of value in Freitas and King's book, I am not persuaded by their conclusion that "although Pullman seems to fit the heading of 'protest atheist,' he diverges from this category in one crucial way. Protest atheists do not reject one god in order to offer up another in its place" (20). As I have demonstrated in this book, the people whom Freitas and King call "protest atheists," and whom I call "misotheists," do indeed often offer an alternative or "new god" to step into the void left by the elimination of the unjust, hurtful god. Freitas and King themselves point to Nietzsche, originator of the "new god" idea: "A god dies in *Thus Spoke Zarathustra*. But in that same text the seeds of a 'new god' are sown—an alternative vision of the divine that makes room for becoming, imagination, creativity, and all those other things that Nietzsche valued" (18). One can add to Nietzsche and Pullman a whole string of other misotheists, who offered their own version of a new god. Rebecca West may well have had Nietzsche in mind when she titled her misotheistic essay "The New God." Blake invented a whole legion of deities that were relevant to him and his age, including Orc (revolution), Los (prophecy), and Ahania (intellectual desire), and his work can be seen as a sustained attempt to overturn the Christian Trinity in favor of a divine pantheon that answers the needs of his time. In Swinburne, the "old," Christian god is eliminated to make room, again, for the vitality of the ancient pagan deities. In Proudhon, it is the anarchic spirit of mutual aid and self-regulated social harmony that steps into the void left behind by the deposed god of Christianity. And the list goes on. And with this historical context in mind, Pullman's procedure does indeed look less unique.

But what, then, is the new concept of divinity that Pullman wants to erect in place of Yahweh? Freitas and King argue that "Pullman is not an atheist. He is instead a *panentheist*. *Pan* means 'all' and *theos* means 'God,' so, while *pantheism* literally means 'all is God,' *panentheism* means 'all *in* God' and reflects the notion that God retains a kind of transcendent quality" (30–31). In other words, while pantheism posits that the world and all of its inhabitants literally are God, panentheism proposes a transcendent divine essence that pervades all of creation. Of course, this spiritual principle is a far cry from any mainstream Christian doctrine. Panentheism is properly speaking antitheistic in that it is not based on a personal creator God. So, after "rescuing" Pullman from the category of "atheist," Freitas and King simply put him into another heretical category. Still, on the face of it, they have a point. There is a spiritual dimension in Pullman's work, and it goes beyond even the mysterious all-pervasive essence of Dust to imply a female kind of deity.

Indeed, a hint of feminist theology wafts through *His Dark Materials*. Notably, there is the character of Xaphania, who invokes the Gnostic figure of Sophia. Toward the end of the trilogy, Xaphania makes her appearance as an entirely benevolent, graceful, and wise angelic presence worthy of religious reverence. Moreover, Pullman's heroine, Lyra, is a female prophetess, his witches are powerful and dignified characters, and the ending of the story affirms the spirituality of the body—all this might well lead one to conclude that Pullman has a feminist theological agenda. Feminist theologians such as Mary Daly and Rosemary Ruether advocate the overthrow of masculine gods, and they acknowledge a form of spiritual transcendence that recognizes the value of female experience. Indeed, when Xaphania identifies "grace" (*Amber* 491) as the source of Lyra's prophetic powers, we hear echoes of the other meaning of grace, namely feminine elegance. On the other hand, Xaphania reminds Lyra that even after the loss of her graceful prophetic talents (coinciding with the onset of sexual maturity), she could regain the same state of bliss "after a lifetime of thought and effort" (491). This seems to suggest a feminine understanding of grace as fusing both sexuality and wisdom, something that is promoted as more wholesome and affirmative than the arbitrary operations of Providence that were worked out in the masculine theology of St. Augustine and Martin Luther.

There's an unmistakable didacticism involved in such revisions of religious thought. In his Carnegie Medal acceptance speech, Pullman emphasized that "all stories teach, whether the storyteller intends them to do so or not. They teach the world we create. They teach the morality we live by. They teach it much more effectively than moral precepts and instructions" ("Carnegie"). This didactic impulse is premised on a set of affirmative, progressive, liberal ideas. Pullman's message is indeed symptomatic of a liberal, humanistic ideology. What he places in the void created by his misotheistic iconoclasm are values that define modern liberal societies: gender equality (Lyra becomes the savior), tolerance of sexual orientation (there are homosexual angels), affirmation of sex (the salvation at the end of the book is keyed into sexual consummation), celebration of the life force (the daemons are a symbol of animal vitality), tolerance toward other races and ethnicities (the book's multicultural agenda is reinforced by its elaboration of multiple worlds), and anti-imperialism (one of the story's collective heroes, the *mulefas*, resist their foreign invaders), to name only some of the virtues endorsed in Pullman's trilogy.

The prevalence of such values makes for a different reading experience compared to the darker and more morbid ideas embedded in Shaffer's misotheistic tales. Shaffer's absolute misotheists invariably self-destruct or slowly lose their rational faculties. By trying to absorb the power of divinity into themselves, they cut themselves off from any didactic relevance for others. Pullman's fictional scenario is entirely different. His characters' fight against the Church and God serves the purpose of a broadly defined liberationist project that promotes justice, freedom, and tolerance for others. And this brings us back to the band of original misotheists, the anarchists, who believed that challenges to God's authority were directly related to challenging absolute state power and institutionalized injustice. Given this background, it is quite obvious that the feudal and monarchical eras lacked the social and cognitive preconditions for a development of misotheism. This is the implication of Camus's statement that "metaphysical rebellion, in the real sense of the term, does not appear in the history of ideas until the end of the eighteenth century—when modern times begin to the accompaniment of the crash of falling ramparts" (26). Among the biggest ramparts that fell in that fateful century were the walls of absolutism. And with those walls beginning to crumble, the other rampart, surrounding God's throne, also started to wobble. It took the rationalist climate of the Enlightenment, together with emergent ideas about democracy and republicanism, to render possible the thought of "metaphysical rebellion," or misotheism, in the first place. In this light, misotheism appears as one of the more radical symptoms of liberty, emancipation, and humanism. Pullman is merely adding some provocative facets to this liberationist creed by creating a band of children who act morally without bowing to scripture and who participate in the struggle to bring about a vibrant post-God world in what he boldly calls "the Republic of Heaven" (*Amber* 518).

This radical kind of liberalism was not so well received in the birthplace of modern democracy. When the movie *The Golden Compass* was released in December 2007, the box office returns in the United States were disappointing.[4] The reason for this shortfall was blamed in part on the fact that the movie studio, New Line Cinema, had made a bet by toning down the heretical and anti-Christian aspects of Pullman's story to appeal to the audience in the movie's most important market, the U.S. However, while this strategy did not placate parts of the religious establishment (with groups like the Catholic League organizing a boycott of the movie), taming Pullman's critique of organized religion and the deity infuriated the author's more radical constituency, thereby hurting movie sales on the religious as well as the anti-religious side of the spectrum. As of November 2009, plans for sequels to *The Golden Compass* have been put on hold, and there is no indication that the franchise will be revived.

One wonders if a similar fate would ever befall any of Shaffer's productions. It seems to me that depicting misotheism as a sane, sincere, rational, and humanistic undertaking is less acceptable than depicting it as a murderous aberration. Pullman's trilogy did not initially generate much adverse criticism partly because some of its premises—for example, that God is an old doddering liar and that the Church is a structure of oppression—were almost too bold to register properly. But when the concept was transferred from the written page to the big screen with its mass appeal, a religious backlash followed, as a part of the American public turned away from a (toned down) version of a story that shows anti-God themes in a positive light. In the case of Peter Shaffer, the tortured cast of his misotheistic characters served as a protective shield against the possible charge of religious subversion or the corruption of young minds. It is unlikely that a blockbuster version of *Equus* would ever get pious groups up in arms against it, despite its deicidal theme.

Pullman's version of a humane, liberal misotheism may well be deemed far more "dangerous" than Shaffer's stories involving demonstrably deranged misotheists. What Pullman is trying to do is to correct once and for all the view that enmity against God has anything to do with perversity. With the exception of Shaffer, every author treated in this study made that claim, more or less implicitly. But it is Pullman who shows most clearly that enemies of God are not only *not* depraved, but that they see themselves as the harbingers of true liberty and the creators of a "Republic of Heaven." This is a long way from Albert Camus's ambivalence about metaphysical rebellion. Indeed, Pullman's optimistic misotheism contrasts starkly with Camus's fear that the metaphysical rebel will eventually turn into another tyrant, usurping God's throne and clearing the path for a resurgence of nihilism.

But Pullman's alignment of liberalism (in its true sense of the word) with misotheism has some precedents: Shelley was equally a champion of Promethean revolt and a sympathizer of disadvantaged classes. And in Swinburne there is the "devotional note heard again and again in his appeals to the principle of liberty" (Welby 114). Rebecca West, too, repeatedly proclaims her "hope in the feeling of sacredness that I intuitively perceive in all efforts to extend the sphere of personal liberty" ("My Religion" 38). Let us remember, then, that all of these thinkers were enemies of God to one degree or another; but they were also advocates of freedom and human flourishing. Pullman's far greater mass appeal exceeds the potential of any of his predecessors to spread similar ideas about the connection between misotheism and liberty. It is because of this power to bring such a radical moral and political proposition to millions of people that Pullman has opened up a new chapter in the history of misotheism.

Conclusion

Such a wasteful God cannot be totally benevolent. History itself is
God's indictment.

—John Roth

THIS BOOK HAS CHARTED THE TERRITORY OF A RELIGIOUS PHENOMENON
that is seldom discussed and even less often identified properly.
Part of the perplexing nature of misotheism has to do with the fact
that opponents of God, especially of the agonistic variety, are not, as
a rule, enemies of religion. They still operate within religious frameworks, thereby bearing out Erin Carlston's view that "blasphemy is,
as it were, a way of being reconciled with a God who cannot be forgiven" (121). Among the various strands of God-hatred, only the political misotheists approach a more categorical rejection of religion,
based on their conviction that as the head of the religious hierarchy,
God has corrupted the whole system from the top downward. But
even they are still anchored in a religious sensibility, if a somewhat
tenuous one.

While this study has explored anti-God sentiments in the works
of prominent thinkers and writers, it can be assumed that there are
many more unknown misotheists who remain silent about their disaffection with God. A recent book by Julia Duin titled *Quitting*

Church: Why the Faithful Are Fleeing and What to Do about It (2008) investigates the frustration that drives people away from the church and perhaps even away from God or religion altogether. Duin comments with a degree of surprise that she "ran across something impossible to measure in a survey: many people I encountered were disappointed and perplexed in some way with God" (22). The people Duin refers to face a number of options, and misotheism is only one of them. Some of those disappointed with God will doubtlessly renounce religious belief altogether. For instance, in Jon Krakauer's *Into the Wild* (1996), one man is so deeply wounded by his young friend's seemingly senseless death in Alaska that he said, "when I learned what happened, I renounced the Lord. I withdrew my church membership and became an atheist. I decided I couldn't believe in a God who would let something that terrible happen to a boy like Alex" (60). Faced with a similar predicament, another person might have said, "I raised my fist against God and vowed eternal enmity." However, being a full-blown misotheist is a difficult position to maintain. In *Quitting Church*, Duin says that many who were "disappointed and perplexed" with God had

> been Christians for more than a decade, and some had experienced serious suffering. The more honest ones admitted something was not working in their Christian faith. They were not connecting with God as to the reasons for their sorrows; in fact, God seemed to be confounding their prayers. Their churches were useless in giving meaningful counsel, and if these people brought up their concerns in Bible study, their doubts and anger toward God were frowned on by others in the group. They were like wounded soldiers returning from Iraq and Afghanistan to a country that barely knew they were at war. (22)

It is quite true that the psychologically, emotionally, and physically wounded are most likely to turn away from God. Although Duin suggests that these perplexed and disappointed individuals should make every effort to rejoin the fold of the faithful, it is by no means certain that more effective forms of ministering would help to douse the fires of misotheism or block the path toward atheism. In some cases, intense religious coaching might only accelerate the flight away from church and belief. However, the project of pious commentators such as Julia Duin is to rescue persons about to exit the realm of conventional religious belief. In their view, to doubt God in the way the Apostle Thomas doubted Jesus's resurrection till he was shown physical evidence may be acceptable, but to reject God or even hate him is wrong and unacceptable.

But, as I have demonstrated in this study, it would be reductive and unfair to condemn God's opponents as unworthy and in league with the devil. Instead, the majority of the blasphemers treated in this book are decent citizens and committed humanists. Among them are master story-tellers, great thinkers, and dedicated humanitarians who also happen to maintain an adversarial relationship with God. Having said this, it is certainly true that many roads lead to misotheism. I hope to have shed a revealing as well as sympathetic light on the spiritual struggles, the personal vicissitudes, the historical traumas, and the social and political aims that have prompted individual misotheists to rise in rebellion against God.

It can, of course, be argued that socially and politically motivated misotheists only use God as a scapegoat for their secular protests and angers. The question to be asked, then, is whether the feminist misotheist really attacks God for having created patriarchal privilege and for condoning the oppression of women. Or is she instead attacking the social conditions and ideological frameworks of oppression that happen to be compatible with Judeo-Christian values, falsely pinning the problems on God? The same type of question could be asked with regard to racism, class conflict, and a host of other issues: What, if anything, has God to do with these problems and the anger that they elicit?

I have provided answers to these questions in the foregoing chapter on Philip Pullman, based on a general position of rational skepticism. However, answers to this question will ultimately depend on whom one asks. If we put this question to an atheist, the answer would probably be that the misotheist is only attacking a chimera, since God does not exist; therefore, the misotheist's real targets are (or should be) the various conditions of injustice and betrayal that exist on earth, as well as the people who perpetrate them in the name of God. For atheists, the question is never about God's actual culpability in the genocides, wars, famines, oppressions, and epidemics that plague our planet. Since God does not exist, no such entity can be held responsible for these evils.

The situation is different with the misotheist. To him, the incompatibility of widespread evil with the image of a benevolent God is a real problem, not merely a case of hairsplitting theological arguments. Misotheists are genuine accusers of God, and they will hold him accountable for random evil and undeserved suffering. Thus, atheists and misotheists come to the question of God's role in human suffering from opposed directions: the unbeliever would say that the misotheist makes an invalid claim based on a fiction. To the misotheist himself, precisely because he is a believer, God is not a scapegoat but an accomplice or an instigator of evil.

There is, of course the third position, namely that of the pious believer. It is he who will say that the misotheist is using God as a scapegoat. The believer will argue that God is there but cannot be blamed for human suffering, and anyone who tries to blame God sets him up as a straw man. But, as I have shown in the chapter on Philip Pullman, this argument is based on an apologetic premise that is rooted in unverifiable claims about God's character. Indeed, believers in God's absolute benevolence may well be invoking the obverse of the straw man argument, what could be called the "giving-God-the-benefit-of-the-doubt" argument. According to this line of thinking, if a little child dies through some misfortune, this does not meant that God is indifferent, callous, or powerless; instead it is alleged that "things happen for a reason" and that what seems a blatantly meaningless tragedy to human eyes may be perfectly meaningful in the eyes of God. There may be some purpose, inscrutable, beyond our ken. It is, in short, the message given in the Book of Job where the believer is told that, compared to God, man has such a narrow understanding of the workings of the cosmos, and he is so puny and insignificant, that he simply cannot measure up in terms of comprehending the deeper meaning of events on earth. However, this approach raises the question of what then, precisely, distinguishes the impulse to *acquit* God from responsibility for the tragedies on earth from the impulse to *accuse* God for these very same tragedies? Both arguments are based on conjectures about the nature of God, not on empirical observations of God. But there is one major difference between the apologist and the accuser of God: while the pious number in the hundreds of millions, and while they have thousands of years of religious tradition behind them, those who charge God with criminal neglect or evil intent are a small minority, and they have become more or less vocal only in the last two hundred years.

How small the number of misotheists is cannot easily be ascertained. According to a recent American Religious Identification Survey (ARIS 2009), roughly 2.3 percent of Americans (about seven million) declare themselves to be atheists, whereas 10 percent indicate that they are agnostic about the question of God's existence (Kosmin and Keysar 8). It is difficult to speculate what tiny proportion of the population would admit to being inclined toward misotheism. In most cases, self-censorship and the threat of public disapproval have prevented opponents of God from revealing their views. The lack of a broad consensus about how even to name the phenomenon of God-hatred has further hampered the public awareness about this attitude.

This terminological impasse has also affected the work of theologians. It is remarkable that even protest theologians who are willing to admit God's culpability in human suffering do not explicitly name man's hostility to God. David Blumenthal, author of *Facing the Abusing God: A Theology of Protest* (1996) is one example of this evasiveness. Although he explores the harsh and unloving aspects of God's character, he refuses to give a name or collective identity to those who dislike such a god. Similarly, John Roth's essay "A Theodicy of Protest" (1982) is groping for a conceptual foothold to capture Elie Wiesel's rebellion against God: "To deny God outright would go too far. But to affirm God's total goodness, to apologize for God, to excuse or exonerate God. . . . these steps go too far as well" (6). Roth's essay is one long indictment of God. He calls his approach "antitheodicy," but it is, like Wiesel's work, indicative of such a deep-seated anger and disappointment with God that it verges on misotheism: "in spite and because of God's sovereignty, this God is everlastingly guilty, and the degrees run from gross negligence to murder" (14).

But here is one distinctive feature that separates antitheodicy from misotheism properly speaking. Despite all his evidence that God is not worshipful, in the final analysis John Roth still apologizes for God. In doing so he risks logical entanglements. Although Roth assures us that "the odds set by God are too high," he maintains that "one can still be for God by being against God" (16). In a last-ditch effort to rescue God from becoming the object of human loathing, he suggests that maybe God will somehow redeem himself in the future: "the issue of whether God is without any justification depends on what God does with the future" (13). Not only is this a weak defense of God on the face of it, but Roth keeps missing the mark rhetorically whenever he attempts to reconcile defending God with accusing him: "the net result of God's choices is that the world is more wild and wasteful than any good reason that we can imagine would require it to be. Thus, to be for such a God requires some sense of being against

God as well" (16). This language of being "for or against" God seems too tame to capture the intense visceral response of believers who are faced with the fact that "the world is more wild and wasteful" than would seem to be consistent with an all-good God who is in control of his creation. The term "misotheism" would help to sharpen Roth's discourse and give a historical scope and conceptual identity to the stance vaguely identified as "being against God." In the end, Roth avoids the question of how a God who is indictable for evil escapes becoming an object of resentment and even hatred. But by putting up a long list of charges against God, Roth maneuvers himself into the position of a devil's advocate, for his premise is that God is worshipful, despite all the evidence to the contrary.

Compared to this beleaguered practitioner of "antitheodicy," the misotheists come across as more honest and convincing critics of God. They refuse to engage in speculative theological acrobatics to acquit God from blame in human misery. And so it emerges that antitheodicy is still a God-centered approach, whereas the misotheistic attitude is resolutely human-centered. While theological writers like Roth focus almost exclusively on solving the mysteries of God's perplexing nature, the misotheist is interested in the *human* ramifications of the problem of evil, and he puts priority on the human response to the seeming randomness of cruelty and pain in God's universe.

Despite the preponderance of a humanistic ethic among misotheists, there is the possibility that the term "misotheism" could be taken as a byword for crankiness, malice, and depravity. However, a crucial difference between misotheists and, say, misogynists exists insofar as the latter unreasonably hate half the human race, an attitude that cannot be justified by rational human beings. More important, there is no evidence that misotheism diminishes a person's potential for love. It would be plainly absurd to suggest that misotheists like Percy Bysshe Shelley, Zora Neale Hurston, Rebecca West, William Empson, or Elie Wiesel are deficient in their ability to experience, express, or receive love from others. In fact, for many misotheists, love is precisely the centerpiece of their moral philosophy. One could go so far as to argue that misotheists are *more* likely to foster love for humanity because they have already channeled and contained whatever capacity of hatred they possessed when they direct their hostility against an intangible antagonist—God. There is nothing (or much less) of the bitterness, destructiveness, and violence in the misotheist that marks the determined racist, misogynist, or religious bigot.

However, as with most basic philosophical and theological concepts, one size doesn't fit all, and it is therefore necessary to make finer distinctions between various types of misotheism. My own taxonomy is designed to capture the three main branches that converge on the common theme of hostility against God. I used the term misotheism in conjunction with the qualifiers "political," "absolute," and "agonistic" to denominate the three main traditions that I have identified within the history of this phenomenon. Of course, even these distinctions could be parsed more minutely. Take political misotheism, for instance: those prompted by that particular motif can act on the basis of socialism, feminism, or racism, taking Yahweh variously to be the supreme boss and enslaver, the supreme patriarch, or the ultimate white supremacist. Hence, there are smaller roads that converge with each of the three main thoroughfares that lead to the hatred of God.

As for agonistic misotheism, we can also perceive subtle differences between the individual practitioners of this stance. Elie Wiesel, for one, came at the problem of God-hatred from the direction of Jewish protest theology, while Rebecca West compensated for her hatred of Yahweh with a corresponding reverence for Christ. West, in particular, is a typical agonistic misotheist, insofar as she was deeply religious and even, at times, considered converting to Catholicism, while at other times she sought spiritual solace in the offices of the Serbian Orthodox Church. And yet she flew into the face of religious piety by attacking the Almighty on account of her conviction that the universe he created was so deeply flawed; in her view, a truly benevolent and wise God would not allow his creation to spin out of control during two world wars, and he would reign in such aberrations as sexism, slavery, and totalitarianism. She could allow for some imperfection in a God-created universe, and she knew about the argument that God had given humanity free will in order to make the distinction between good and evil morally meaningful. But in her view mankind precisely does *not* have genuine free will. Her familiarity with the crimes of fascist and communist dictators demonstrated that they were acting on some evil impulse that was outside the realm of free will. And certainly, to the countless victims of totalitarian oppression the notion of free will seemed cynical, a cruel joke. According to the misotheist, one should hold God responsible for letting evil forces gain the upper hand in the universe, rather than excusing him for responsibility in the predominance of evil by citing human free will. At the same time that she condemned God for being callous, incompetent, or uncaring, she yearned for signs that, maybe, she was wrong after all, and that the universe was established on a better foundation than she thought. However, Rebecca West died at an advanced age without ever having found confirmation for a redemptive view of God.

In the case of Zora Neale Hurston, her father tried to instill his religious zeal into her from early childhood on. However, as her autobiographical writings reveal, the religious fervor in her home had the reverse effect of making her less devout. Like Rebecca West, she came up all her life against the problem of evil, putting herself in the position of Job, but ultimately finding it impossible to believe that God was truly worshipful. I imagine her, figuratively speaking, as going through life with her eyes flung wide open in an accusatory stare, much like the expression she describes in the eyes of the hurricane victims awaiting burial in *Their Eyes Were Watching God*. Hurston is a particularly apt example for the secretive quality of misotheism, because she always carefully coded her expressions of animosity against God, an undertaking that was essentially successful because hardly anybody noticed the presence of this antagonistic faith in her. But no matter how intermittent and secretive it was, upon close inspection Hurston's work reveals elements of Epicureanism, deism, and anarchism that tie her misotheism to the long trajectory of human struggles against God.

In contrast to West and Hurston, Elie Wiesel's theological protesters openly fling angry accusations against God. His heroes are inspired by the noble impulses of charity, generosity, and love, but trying to uphold these values in the face of rampant and random evil drives them to the edge of madness. One could argue that Wiesel is more of a "dystheist" (a believer in an unpredictable, ambivalent "trickster god") because his case against God is based on persistent doubts about the true nature of God's moral character and on the suspicion that God harbors both good and evil tendencies. But the term "dystheist," just like "maltheist," (a believer in an entirely malignant god) makes an assertion about God's nature, and that is inherently problematic. While it is arguably futile and certainly elusive to define God's true nature, it is possible to gain empirical evidence about man's attitude to God. Hence my preference for the term agonistic misotheist in reference to Elie Wiesel. Also, the outright hatred for God expressed by characters such as Berish in *The Trial of God* goes far beyond the milder form of heresy identified as dystheism. In any case, Wiesel's fictional characters appear to take a more radical view on God than Wiesel admits for himself. Thus, once again we can observe a degree of concealment and distancing when it comes to publicly avowing misotheism, although the operation of masking it is less conspicuous in Wiesel than it is in Hurston and West. However, I have found that authors tend to use fictional devices to express their most deeply held beliefs. This would argue that Wiesel identified strongly with his characters' misotheistic views, although he may not admit it openly.

Just as there are differences among practitioners of agonistic misotheism, absolute misotheists also have their share of dissimilarities. Peter Shaffer explores the perversity of fanatical worship as it modulates from obsession with the deity to deicide and self-adulation. Shaffer's work contains the most unflattering psychological profiles of God-haters treated in this book because his misotheists tend to be driven by vengeance and jealousy. Yet, despite the unattractiveness of Peter Shaffer's absolute misotheists, their protest does invoke the need to justify God's character. Take Salieri, for example: if God has created mediocrity as well as genius and the ambition for artistic perfection, then those who have received only a modicum of talent but an outsize ambition should be programmed for despair. The uneven distribution of such characteristics, much like random evil, is easier to bear if one does not assume that there is an all-wise, beneficial power behind it all. And as for Alan Strang's horses and Pizarro's Atahuallpa, a Freudian view of divinity would prompt one to see these "lesser" gods as father figures that the son must overcome before he can achieve an authentic sense of selfhood. Again, it may strike one as a curious order of things that such rivalry between father and son should be part of a divinely ordained plan.

Contrary to artists like West, Wiesel, and Hurston, all of whom struggle perpetually with their antagonistic faith, and contrary to Shaffer, whose misotheists are trying to absorb into them the powers of the gods they are striving to defeat, Swinburne and Pullman happily heap contempt upon God and don't mind writing his obituary. Of course, these two absolute misotheists are not without ideals of their own, and they can even be said to place new gods in the void created by the ones they helped to demolish. Among these new gods are pagan deities of vitality as well as republican ideals in the case of Swinburne, and a "panentheistic" spiritual entity ("Dust"), coupled with secular humanist principles of tolerance, diversity, and emancipation in Pullman's case.

What all six authors have in common is that what they say about God in their fiction is not unlike what they say about him in their nonfiction essays, private jottings, letters, or interviews. This basic congruence between their fiction and nonfiction convinces me that whatever imaginary scenarios involving misotheism we encounter in these writers' literary creations reflects similarly dissenting and blasphemous views in their own outlook. Certainly, fiction allows a given writer more freedom to explore and express ideas of misotheism that otherwise might be considered too risky or unacceptable for straightforward nonfiction. Some truths are better delivered in the form of a dream, or a parable. Moreover, in their literary works, authors grapple most valiantly and interestingly with the reasons for adopting a misotheistic religious stance. These writers invent new scenarios for implementing this view, and they imagine radical outcomes of their characters' rebellion against God. As this book has demonstrated, the hidden history of misotheism is complex and evolving. People are hostile to God for different reasons—political, moral, psychological, historical, sexual, etc. For many individuals, the realization that they are misotheists is a wrenching, agonizing recognition. The more religious they are, the more painful this realization is apt to be.

Often, literature provides a therapeutic means for dealing with these troubling ideas. That is one reason why misotheists will turn to literary expressions to vent their frustration with God. The only surprising thing is that not more readers have actually noticed this, for there is no shortage of condemnations of God in poetry, drama, and fiction. Several books I have recently picked up contain explicit references to misotheism, including Alain de Botton's *The Art of Travel* (2002), which casually quotes Baudelaire's line "Money? I hate it as you hate God" (32), or J. M. Coetzee's novel *Elizabeth Costello* (2003), whose protagonist protests against "an evil universe invented by an evil god" (159), or Aravind Adiga's character Balram in *The White Tiger* (2008), who is *"spitting* at God again and again . . . for having created the world in this particular way" (75). And there is a host of other texts that mention God-hatred either in passing or as an under-lying thematic motif, thus providing a strong rationale for a wider application of the word misotheism.

But despite its obvious lexical usefulness, the word "misotheism" has heretofore failed to gain a foothold in common language use. Most dictionaries do not even list it. From the second edition of the *Oxford English Dictionary* (1989) to the unabridged *Random House Dictionary of the English Language*, and from the *Webster's Third International Dictionary* (1968) even to *The Encyclopedia of Unbelief* (1985), one looks in vain for "misotheism." But the word does have an ety-mology, if only a precarious one. According to Wiktionary.org, the word was included in the 1913 edition of Noah Webster's *Dictionary of the English Language*, where it is attributed to Thomas De Quincey. Indeed, De Quincey used the word exactly once in a discussion of the pagans' impulse to slay their most hateful gods. As I have shown in this study, however, misotheism usually denotes the hatred of a *mono-theistic* deity, notably Yahweh, rather than disgust at particular gods within a polytheistic system. In this sense, then, the term originally coined by De Quincey has taken on a somewhat different meaning.

Despite its absence from dictionaries, the term misotheism now seems poised to enter the vocabulary. When I "googled" the word in 2001, not a single use of it came back. (Of course, Google only started in 1998 and had not yet scanned the text of everything ever published in the world as it seems to have done since then.) However, in Novem-ber 2007, a new page on "misotheism" went up on Wikipedia. The history tab on this entry shows a significant amount of controversy about what to name the stance of God-hatred, with "maltheism" and "dystheism" vying with misotheism for prominence. The editors (independently of me and unbeknownst to me) finally settled on the term misotheism, explaining the other related terms in the body of the entry. Partly because of the Wikipedia entry, partly because of my own previous work on the subject, and partly due to factors unknown to me, uses of the word "misotheism" have exploded, and in December 2009, the number of returns for a Google search of this term hit 52,000. Going from zero to 52,000 in eight years is a significant development, even considering that the amount of data captured by the search engine in 2001 was much smaller compared to that trawled in 2009. Obviously, the term is beginning to take root, and before we know it, misotheism might become a household word.

It remains to be seen what such a popularization of the concept will do to the literary treatment of man's hostility to God. Possibly, such treatments will become more like Pullman's or James Morrow's, that is, less apologetic, less obscure, and more irreverent.[1] No matter what the precise future of misotheism is going to be, God-hatred will continue to play a role in fiction and memoir as long as there are people who feel that they have been harmed by God, either as individuals or as a community, and as long as there are writers and thinkers among these sufferers who see in literary and artistic expression a valid tool to combat an unjust or indifferent God. Blasphemy has a place only in a religious context. To get rid of blasphemy and to be free from misotheism would require an end to religious belief. And there are no signs that this will happen anytime soon. In the meantime, those hostile to God—supposedly the fountainhead of goodness—will continue to labor under the burden of making their paradoxical stance meaningful, both to themselves and to the larger community.

Notes

Introduction

1. On its website, HarperCollins reports that *"Their Eyes Were Watching God* sells nearly 150,000 copies a year" (www.harpercollinscatalogs .com/harper/515_1676_333037323439.htm, accessed April 25, 2010).

2. I am grateful to Roland Kübler (University of Fribourg) for pointing out that "Yahweh," rather than "Jehova," should be used to refer to the Judeo-Christian God.

3. Blasphemy and blasphemous libel were considered offences against common law in England and Wales since the seventeenth century. But there hadn't been a conviction under this rule since 1922; other laws, such as the 1968 Theatres Act, further undermined its enforcement. The code was considered wholly outdated, not least because it only protected Christians, and was finally abolished by the British Parliament in May 2008.

4. Several of Mark Twain's anti-religious essays were posthumously published, including the severely blasphemous "Reflections on Religion" (1963). These essays are collected in *The Outrageous Mark Twain* (1987), edited by Charles Neider.

5. *Blameless in Abaddon* (1996), part two of Morrow's *Godhead Trilogy*, is a deicidal tour-de-force. On more than 400 pages of speculative fiction, Morrow presents the five major Christian theodicies and then systematically dismantles them. This latter-day re-telling of Job's story is one of the most theologically thorough takes on the trial-of-God theme.

6. "A whole world of ideas needs to be discovered behind 'The supreme evil, God.' May the critics begin." (My translation.)

7. In Part Two, Camus dedicates eighty-one pages to probing the phenomenon of metaphysical rebellion, then moves on to a long discussion of individual and state terrorism in Part Three ("Historical Rebellion"), before expanding on the role of rebellion in the arts (Part Four), and concluding with thoughts about nihilism.

8. The root of the word agonistic, "agon," is Greek, referring to a solemn struggle or contest.

9. Typescript draft of a memoir; McFarlin Special Collections, Tulsa.

10. I owe this idea to Roland Kübler, who has read large parts of the book manuscript with a critical eye.

A Brief History of Misotheism

1. For a subversive re-telling of Job's story, one can turn to James Morrow's misotheistic novel *Blameless in Abaddon* (1996). The novel's contemporary protagonist, Martin Candle, prosecutes God for criminal neglect and cosmic malfeasance in the World Court at The Hague and almost wins his case. Upon God's narrow victory, Candle goes out, slays the comatose God by severing his life-support, and shortly afterward succumbs to metastatic prostate cancer.

2. According to Freud, the boy's libidinal desire for his mother and his jealous rivalry with his father is finally laid to rest when, due to intense castration anxiety, the boy agrees to play by the father's rules, which, in turn, activates the superego. Rather than getting rid of the father, the son is finally reconciled with him.

3. The most extreme manifestation of this danger today is Islamic sharia law, under which the sentence for being "mohareb" (an enemy of God) is execution. In 2010, Iran executed several people whom it charged with being "enemies of God."

Absolute Misotheism I

1. Neither Jerome McGann and Charles L. Sligh's selection of Swinburne's poetry, *Major Poems and Selected Prose*, nor three other randomly selected collections of Swinburne's poetry contains "Hymn of Man."

2. The parallelism with Nietzsche goes only so far, though. While Nietzsche was an unapologetic elitist, Swinburne, who was born into the aristocracy, became a fervent republican.

Agonistic Misotheism II

1. See my *Rebecca West: Heroism, Rebellion, and the Female Epic*, p. 28.

2. Manuscript draft of "Survivors in Mexico," McFarlin Special Collections, Tulsa.

3. Typescript draft; McFarlin Special Collections, Tulsa.

4. This abbreviated summary of the Manichaean creation myth is based on Mircea Eliade's *A History of Religious Ideas, Volume II: From Gautama Buddha to the Triumph of Christianity*.

5. Letter dated 1950 to Margaret and Evelyn Hutchinson. Beinecke Rare Book and Manuscript Library, Yale University.

6. Letter to the Hutchinsons, 1950, my emphasis.

7. Letter to the Hutchinsons, 1950.

8. Letter dated June 22, 1952, to Margaret and Evelyn Hutchinson. Beinecke Rare Book and Manuscript Library, Yale University.

9. Ever since she visited Yugoslavia in the late 1930s, West idolized the Serbs as the bona fide representatives of spiritual vitality, cultural authenticity, and valor.

10. Private letter to the author, February 1, 2006.

11. Private letter to the author, February 1, 2006.

Agonistic Misotheism III

1. I owe this insight to Eric Ziolkowski, head of the Department of Religious Studies at Lafayette College, who read an earlier draft of this chapter.

2. The characterization of Wiesel as a leading humanist can be challenged today by critics of his stance on the Israeli-Palestinian conflict, notably his misguidedly idealistic statement that "Jerusalem is above politics" ("For Jerusalem"). But such political missteps cannot void Wiesel's remarkable accomplishments as a commentator on the human condition, a chronicler of the Holocaust, and a philanthropist.

Absolute Misotheism III

1. From a personal correspondence with the author.

2. See my "'And he's agoing to destroy Him': Religious Subversion in Philip Pullman's Trilogy *His Dark Materials*." In *His Dark Materials Illuminated: Critical Essays on Philip Pullman's Trilogy*.

3. This sales figure was reported in an article by Laura Miller, "The 'Golden' Rule," in the *Los Angeles Times*, December 2, 2007.

4. The picture is considered a flop in the U.S., having brought in less than $70 million on a budget of $180 million. The movie's foreign sales, however, were extremely strong, topping $300 million.

Conclusion

1. There is much hilarity in James Morrow's *Blameless in Abaddon*. In order to prepare his brief against God, the novel's protagonist, Martin Candle, goes on a fact-finding mission inside the brain of God's huge, comatose body. There he holds conversations with the archetypal "ideas" of biblical figures like Noah, Lot, and Job, all of whom defy God's benevolence and Providence, while St. Augustine cuts a hapless figure as the lone defender of God.

Works Cited

Abrahamson, Irving, ed. *Against Silence: The Voice and Vision of Elie Wiesel*. Vol. I. New York: Holocaust Library, 1985.

Adiga, Aravind. *The White Tiger*. New York: Free Press, 2008.

Aldrich, Robert, and Garry Wotherspoon, eds. *Who's Who in Gay and Lesbian History: From Antiquity to World War II*. New York: Routledge, 2001.

Anidjar, Gil. *The Jew, the Arab: A History of the Enemy*. Stanford, CA: Stanford University Press, 2003.

Anonymous. Review of Algernon Swinburne's *Atalanta in Calydon* in *London Review*. 6 May, 1865. In *Algernon Swinburne: The Critical Heritage*. Ed. Clyde K. Hyder. New York: Routledge, 1996.

Anonymous. Review of Algernon Swinburne's *Songs Before Sunrise* in *Saturday Review*. 14 January, 1871. In *Algernon Swinburne: The Critical Heritage*. Ed. Clyde K. Hyder. New York: Routledge, 1996.

Armstrong, Isobel. *Victorian Poetry: Poetry, Poetics, Politics*. New York: Routledge, 1993.

Armstrong, Karen. *The Case for God*. New York: Alfred A. Knopf, 2009.

————. *The Great Transformation: The Beginning of Our Religious Traditions*. New York: Knopf, 2006.

Augustine. *The Confessions of St. Augustine, Bishop of Hippo*. Trans. J. G. Pilkington. Edinburgh: Clark, 1876.

Bakunin, Michael. *God and the State*. New York: Dover, 1970.

Barrell, Joseph. *Shelley and the Thought of His Time: A Study in the History of Ideas*. New Haven, CT: Yale University Press, 1947.

Baudelaire, Charles. *Prose Poems and La fanfarlo*. Trans. Rosemary Lloyd. New York: Oxford University Press, 2001.

Berenbaum, Michael. *The Vision of the Void: Theological Reflections on the Works of Elie Wiesel*. Middletown, CT: Wesleyan University Press, 1979.

Besant, Annie, and Charles Bradlaugh. "Why I Do Not Believe in God." Reprinted in *American Atheist* 35:3 (Summer 1997).

Bidney, Martin. "Thinking about God and Mozart: The Salieris of Puškin and Peter Shaffer." *The Slavic and East European Journal* 30:2 (Summer 1986): 183–95.

Blake, William. *"America: A Prophecy" and "Europe: A Prophecy."* New York: Dover, 1983.

———. *Songs of Experience*. Facsimile Reproduction with 26 Plates in Full Color. New York: Dover Publications, 1984.

———. *Songs of Innocence*. Facsimile Reproduction with 31 Plates in Full Color. New York: Dover Publications, 1971.

Bloom, Harold. "Introduction." In *Zora Neale Hurston*. Modern Critical Views. Ed. Harold Bloom. New York: Chelsea House, 1987.

Blumenthal, David R. *Facing the Abusing God: A Theology of Protest*. Louisville, KY: Westminster/John Knox Press, 1993.

Brontë, Emily. *The Complete Poems by Emily Jane Brontë*. Ed. Charles William Hatfield. New York: Columbia University Press, 1941.

Bonikowski, Wyatt. "The Return of the Soldier Brings Death Home." *Modern Fiction Studies* 51:3 (Fall 2005): 513–35.

Bouchard, Larry D. *Tragic Method and Tragic Theology: Evil in Contemporary Drama and Religious Thought*. University Park: Penn State University Press, 1989.

Boyd, Valerie. *Wrapped in Rainbows: The Life of Zora Neale Hurston*. New York: Scribner, 2003.

Buchanan, Robert. Review in *Athenaeum*. Reprinted in *Swinburne: The Critical Heritage*. Ed. Clyde K. Hyder. London: Routledge, 1970.

Camus, Albert. *The Myth of Sisyphus and Other Essays*. New York: Alfred A. Knopf, 1955.

———. *The Rebel: An Essay on Man in Revolt*. Revised new translation by Anthony Bower. New York: Vintage, 1991.

Carlston, Erin. C. "Paul Celan's *Die Niemandsrose*." In *Borders, Exiles, Diasporas*. Ed. Elazar Barkan and Marie-Denise Shelton. Palo Alto, CA: Stanford University Press, 1998.

Christ, Carol P. *She Who Changes: Re-Imagining the Divine in the World*. New York: Palgrave Macmillan, 2003.

Coetzee, J. M. *Elizabeth Costello*. New York: Viking Penguin, 2003.

Cronin, Gloria. "Introduction: Going to the Far Horizon." In *Critical Essays on Zora Neale Hurston*. Ed. Gloria L. Cronin. New York: G. K. Hall, 1998.

Daly, Mary. *Beyond God the Father: Toward a Philosophy of Women's Liberation*. Boston: Beacon Press, 1985.

"A Dark Agenda." Susan Roberts interviews Philip Pullman. November 2002. Accessed online 1 September 2009: www.surefish.co.uk/culture/features/pullman_interview.htm.

Dawkins, Richard. *A Devil's Chaplain: Reflections on Hope, Lies, Science, and Love*. Boston: Houghton Mifflin, 2003.

———. *The God Delusion*. New York: Houghton Mifflin, 2006.

De Quincey, Thomas. *Theological Essays and Other Papers*. Vol. I. Boston: Ticknor and Fields, 1860.

Donahue, Bill. "'The Golden Compass' Sparks Protest." The Catholic League, 9 October 2007. Accessed online 17 December, 2008. www.catholicleague.org/release.php?id=1342

Duin, Julia. *Quitting Church: Why the Faithful Are Fleeing and What to Do about It*. Grand Rapids, MI: Baker Books, 2008.

Dyson, Freeman. "Religion from the Outside." *The New York Review of Books* 53: 11 (June 22, 2006).

Eliot, George. *Silas Marner*. New York: Signet, 1960.

Empson, William. *Milton's God*. London: Chatto and Windus, 1965.

Epicurus. *Epicurus: The Extant Remains*. Ed. Cyril Bailey. Oxford: Clarendon, 1926.

———. *The Epicurus Reader*. Trans. and ed. Brad Inwood and L. P. Gerson. Indianapolis: Hackett Publishing, 1994.

———. *The Philosophy of Epicurus*. Ed. George K. Strodach. Chicago: Northwestern University Press, 1963.

Erdman, David V., ed. *The Complete Poetry and Prose of William Blake*. Newly Revised Edition. New York: Anchor Books, 1965, 1982.

Estes, Ted. L. *Elie Wiesel*. New York: Frederick Ungar, 1980.

Finlan, Stephen. *Problems with Atonement: The Origins of, and Controversy about, the Atonement Doctrine*. Collegeville, MN: Liturgical Press, 2005.

Fish, Stanley. *Surprised by Sin: The Reader in* Paradise Lost. New York: St. Martin's, 1967.

Flint, Robert. *Anti-Theistic Theories*. Edinburgh: Blackwood, 1880.

Franciosi, Robert, ed. *Elie Wiesel: Conversations*. Jackson: University of Mississippi Press, 2002.

Freud, Sigmund. *The Future of an Illusion*. Trans. James Strachey. New York: W. W. Norton, 1961.

———. *Totem and Taboo*. Trans. James Strachey. New York: W. W. Norton, 1950.

Gates, Henry L. "Zora Neale Hurston: 'A Negro Way of Saying.' " Afterword in *Jonah's Gourd Vine*. New York: HarperPerennial, 1990.

Gelb, Barbara. ". . . And Its Author." *New York Times*, 14 November 1965, Sec. 2: 2, 4.

Ghnassia, Virginia Jill Dix. *Metaphysical Rebellion in the Works of Emily Brontë*. New York: St. Martin's Press, 1994.

Gianakaris, C. J. "The Artistic Trajectory of Peter Shaffer." In *Peter Shaffer: A Casebook*. Ed. C. J. Gianakaris. New York: Garland, 1991.

Glendinning, Victoria. *Rebecca West: A Life*. New York: Alfred A. Knopf, 1987.

Goldenberg, Naomi. *Changing of the Gods: Feminism and the End of Traditional Religions*. Boston: Beacon Press, 1979.

Goldman, Emma. "The Philosophy of Atheism." In *Red Emma Speaks*. Ed. Alix Kates Shulman. New York: Schocken, 1982.

———. "What I Believe." In *Red Emma Speaks*. Ed. Alix Kates Shulman. New York: Schocken, 1982.

Grenier, Cynthia. "Philip Pullman's Dark Materials." *Crisis Magazine*. October 2001. Accessed online 14 May 2010: http://www.catholic culture.org/culture/library/view.cfm?recnum=4004

Gresh, Lois H. *Exploring Philip Pullman's* His Dark Materials: *An Unauthorized Adventure Through* The Golden Compass, The Subtle Knife, *and* The Amber Spyglass. New York: St. Martin's Press, 2007.

Hampshire, Stuart. *Spinoza and Spinozism*. Oxford: Oxford University Press, 2005.

Hansberry, Lorraine. *A Raisin in the Sun*. New York: Vintage, 1988.

Harris, Sam. *The End of Faith: Religion, Terror, and the Future of Reason*. New York: W. W. Norton, 2004.

Harrod, Howard. "Christian Ethics *Post Mortem Dei*." In *Radical Theology: Essays in a Continuing Discussion*. Ed. C. W. Christian and Glenn R. Wittig. Philadelphia: Lippincott, 1967.

Haynes, Stephen R. *Noah's Curse: The Biblical Justification of American Slavery*. New York: Oxford University Press, 2002.

Heller, Erich. "The Modern German Mind: The Legacy of Nietzsche." In *Toward a New Christianity: Readings in the Death of God Theology*. Ed. Thomas J. J. Altizer. New York: Harcourt, 1967.

Hemenway, Robert E. *Zora Neale Hurston: A Literary Biography*. Foreword by Alice Walker. Urbana: University of Illinois Press, 1977.

Hinden, Michael. "Where All the Ladders Start': The Autobiographical Impulse in Shaffer's Work." In *Peter Shaffer: A Casebook*. Ed. C. J. Gianakaris. New York: Garland, 1991.

Hine, Darlene C. "Rape and the Inner Lives of Black Women in the Middle West: Preliminary Thoughts on the Culture of Dissemblance." *Signs: Journal of Women in Culture and Society* 14:4 (Summer 1989): 912–20.

Hitchens, Christopher. *God Is Not Great: How Religion Poisons Everything*. New York: Twelve, 2007.

———. *Letters to a Young Contrarian*. Cambridge, MA: Basic Books, 2001.

———. "Oxford's Rebel Angel." *Vanity Fair*, No. 506 (October 2002): 174–80.

Hitchens, Peter. "This is the most dangerous author in Britain." *The Mail on Sunday*, 27 January, 2002. Accessed online 14 May 2010: http://home.wlv.ac.uk/%7Ebu1895/hitchens.htm

Hubbard, Dolan. " ' . . . Ah said Ah'd save de text for you': Recontextualizing the Sermon to Tell (Her)Story in Zora Neale Hurston's *Their Eyes Were Watching God*. In *Critical Essays on Zora Neale Hurston*," 100–114. Ed. Gloria L. Cronin. New York: G. K. Hall, 1998.

Hurston, Zora Neale. *Dust Tracks on a Road*. New York: HarperPerennial, 1996.

———. *Jonah's Gourd Vine*. New York: HarperPerennial, 1990.

———. *Mules and Men*. New York: Harper and Row, 1970.

———. *Their Eyes Were Watching God*. New York: Perennial Classics, 1998.

———. *Zora Neale Hurston: A Life in Letters*. Ed. Carla Kaplan. New York: Doubleday, 2002.

Hyder, Clyde K., ed. *Swinburne: The Critical Heritage*. London: Routledge, 1970.

Jacobs, Alan. "The Devil's Party." *The Weekly Standard* 6:6 (October 23, 2000).

Jameson, Storm. *The Clash*. Boston: Little, Brown, 1922.

Jaspers, Karl. *Nietzsche and Christianity*. Trans. E. B. Ashton. Chicago: Regnery, 1961.

Johnson, James Weldon. *Complete Poems*. Ed. Sondra K. Wilson. New York: Penguin, 2000.

Kaplan, Carla. "Introduction." *Zora Neale Hurston: A Life in Letters*. Ed. Carla Kaplan. New York: Doubleday, 2002.

Kosmin, Barry A., and Ariela Keysar. *American Religious Identification Survey 2008*. Hartford, CT: The Institute for the Study of Secularism in Society and Culture, 2009.

Krakauer, Jon. *Into the Wild*. New York: Anchor Books, 1997.

Kropotkin, Peter. "The Shortcomings of Christianity." In *Kropotkin: Selections from His Writings*. Ed. Herbert Read. London: Freedom Press, 1942.

Lactantius. *On the Anger of God. Hellenistic Philosophy: Introductory Readings.* Trans. Brad Inwood and Lloyd P. Gerson. Indianapolis: Hackett, 1988.

Lambert, Carole J. *Is God Man's Friend? Theodicy and Friendship in Elie Wiesel's Novels.* New York: Peter Lang, 2006.

Landis, Joseph. "Introduction." In *Three Great Jewish Plays.* Trans. Joseph C. Landis. New York: Applause Theatre Publishers, 1966.

Lapham, Lewis H. "The Wrath of the Lamb." In *Harper's,* May 2005: 7–9.

Larrimore, Mark Joseph. *The Problem of Evil: Readings.* Malden, MA: Blackwell, 2001.

Lauer, Quentin. "The Atheism of Karl Marx." In *Marxism and Christianity: A Symposium.* Ed. Herbert Aptheker. New York: Humanities Press, 1968.

Londré, Felicia H. "Straddling a Dual Poetics in *Amadeus*: Salieri as Tragic Hero and Joker." In *Peter Shaffer: A Casebook.* Ed. C. J. Gianakaris. New York: Garland, 1991.

Louis, Margot Kathleen. *Swinburne and His Gods: The Roots and Growth of an Agnostic Poetry.* Montreal: McGill-Queens Press, 1990.

Lounsberry, Barbara. "The Cosmic Embrace: Peter Shaffer's Metaphysics." In *Peter Shaffer: A Casebook.* Ed. C. J. Gianakaris. New York: Garland, 1991.

Lucretius. *On the Nature of The Universe.* Trans. R. E. Latham. Harmondsworth, UK: Penguin, 1951.

Marion, Jean-Luc. *Cartesian Questions: Method and Metaphysics.* Chicago: University of Chicago Press, 1999.

Marx, Karl. *A Reader.* Ed. Jon Elster. New York: Cambridge University Press, 1986.

Maughan, Shannon. "Whose Dark Materials: The culmination of Philip Pullman's *His Dark Materials* trilogy raises theological questions." *Publishers Weekly,* 18 December 2000: 25.

McAfee Brown, Robert. *Elie Wiesel: Messenger to All Humanity.* Notre Dame, IN: University of Notre Dame Press, 1983.

McGrath, Alister. *The Twilight of Atheism: The Rise and Fall of Disbelief in the Modern World.* New York: Doubleday, 2004.

Mill, John Stuart. *Autobiography.* New York: Houghton Mifflin, 1969.

Morrow, James. *Blameless in Abaddon.* New York: Harcourt, Brace, 1996.

Neusner, Jacob. *The Perfect Torah.* Boston: Brill, 2003.

Nietzsche, Friedrich. *The Anti-Christ.* Trans. H. L. Mencken. Tucson: See Sharp Press, 1999.

———. *The Gay Science.* Trans. Walter Kaufmann. New York: Vintage Books, 1974.

————. *Thus Spake Zarathustra: A Book for All and None*. Trans. Thomas Common. New York: Russell & Russell, 1964.

————. *The Twilight of the Idols: Or, How to Philosophize with a Hammer*. Trans. Anthony M. Ludovici. New York: Russelll & Russell, 1964.

Paine, Thomas. *Age of Reason*. Part I. New York: The Freethought Press Association, 1954.

Plant, Deborah G. *Every Tub Must Sit on Its Own Bottom: The Philosophy and Politics of Zora Neale Hurston*. Urbana: University of Illinois Press, 1995.

Plath, Sylvia. "Daddy." In *The Cambridge Book of English Verse, 1939–1975*. Ed. Alan N. Bold. New York: Cambridge University Press, 1976.

Plunka, Gene A. *Peter Shaffer: Roles, Rites, and Rituals in the Theater*. Rutherford, NJ: Fairleigh Dickinson University Press, 1988

Proudhon, Joseph-Pierre. *The Philosophy of Misery*. Whitefish, MT: Kessinger Publishing, n.d.

————. "Concerning the Principle of Art and Its Social Purpose." In *Nineteenth-Century Theories of Art*. Ed. Joshua Charles Taylor. Berkeley: University of California Press, 1987.

Pullman, Philip. *The Amber Spyglass*. New York: Alfred A. Knopf, 2000.

————. *The Golden Compass*. New York: Alfred A. Knopf, 1995.

————. *The Subtle Knife*. New York: Alfred A. Knopf, 1997.

————. "Carnegie Medal Acceptance Speech." Accessed online 14 May 2010: http://www.randomhouse.com/features/pullman/author/carnegie .html.

Reber, Arthur S., and Emily S. Reber. *The Penguin Dictionary of Psychology*. Third edition. New York: Penguin, 2001.

Reclus, Elisée. *Evolution and Revolution*. London: W. Reeves, n.d.

Reiman, Donald H. *Percy Bysshe Shelley*. Boston: Twayne, 1990.

Rist, John. M. *Epicurus: An Introduction*. London: Cambridge University Press, 1972.

Rollyson, Carl. *Rebecca West: A Life*. New York: Scribner, 1996.

Roth, John. "A Theodicy of Protest." In *Encountering Evil: Live Options in Theodicy*. Ed. Stephen T. Davis. Revised edition. Louisville, KY: Westminster/John Knox Press, 2001

Ruether, Rosemary Radford. *Gaia and God: An Ecofeminist Theology of Earth Healing*. New York: HarperCollins, 1992.

Russell, Bertrand. *A History of Western Philosophy*. New York: Simon and Schuster, 1945.

————. *Why I Am Not a Christian: And Other Essays on Religion and Related Subjects*. New York: Simon and Schuster, 1967.

Schweizer, Bernard. *Rebecca West: Heroism, Rebellion, and the Female Epic*. Westport, CT: Greenwood Press, 2002.

Severance, Julia H. "Thomas Paine: A Memorial Address." Pamphlet of the Chicago Society of Anthropology, 28 January, 1906.

Shaffer, Peter. *Amadeus*. New York: Signet, 1980.

———. *Equus*. New York: Samuel French, 1976.

———. *The Royal Hunt of the Sun*. New York: Stein and Day, 1965.

———. "A Conversation with Peter Shaffer (1990)." In *Peter Shaffer: A Casebook*. Ed. C. J. Gianakaris. New York: Garland, 1991.

———. "Interview with Barry Pree." *The Transatlantic Review* 14 (Autumn 1963): 64.

Sheffey, Ruthe T. "Zora Neale Hurston's *Moses, Man of the Mountain*: A Fictionalized Manifesto on the Imperatives of Black Leadership." In *Critical Essays on Zora Neale Hurston*. Ed. Gloria L. Cronin. New York: G. K. Hall, 1998.

Shelley, Mary. "Note by Mrs. Shelley." In *Complete Poetical Works of Percy Bysshe Shelley*. Vol. 3. Charleston, SC: BiblioBazaar, 2006.

Shelley, Percy Bysshe. *Prometheus Unbound*. In *Shelley's Poetry and Prose: Authoritative Texts and Criticism*. Ed. Donald H. Reiman and Sharon B. Powers. New York: W. W. Norton, 1977.

———. *Queen Mab*. In *The Complete Poetry of Percy Bysshe Shelley*. Vol. 2. Ed. Donald H. Reiman and Neil Fraistat. Baltimore: Johns Hopkins University Press, 2004.

———. "Letter to the Examiner." *Notes to the Complete Poetical Works of Percy Bysshe Shelley*. Ed. Mary Shelley. San Diego, CA: ICON Group, 2008.

Snyder, Phillip A. "Zora Neale Hurston's *Dust Tracks*: Autobiography and Artist Novel." In *Critical Essays on Zora Neale Hurston*. Ed. Gloria L. Cronin. New York: G. K. Hall, 1998.

Stacy, James R. "The Sun and the Horse: Peter Shaffer's Search for Worship." *Educational Theatre Journal* 28:3 (October 1976): 325–37.

Stanton, Elizabeth Cady. *The Woman's Bible*. Boston: Northeastern University Press, 1993.

Sternberg, Robert J., and Karin Sternberg. *The Nature of Hate*. New York: Cambridge University Press, 2008.

Stevenson, Lionel. *The Pre-Raphaelite Poets*. Chapel Hill: University of North Carolina Press, 1972.

Stirner, Max. *The Ego and His Own: The Case of the Individual Against Authority*. Trans. Steven T. Byington. Ed. James J. Martin. Mineola, NY: Dover, 2005.

Swinburne, Algernon. *Major Poems and Selected Prose*. Ed. Jerome McGann and Charles L. Sligh. New Haven, CT: Yale University Press, 2004.

———. *Songs Before Sunrise*. Whitefish, MT: Kessinger Publishing, 2004.

———. *William Blake: A Critical Essay*. London: Chatto and Windus, 1906.

Thomson, James. *The City of Dreadful Night and Other Poems*. Portland, ME: Thomas Mosher, 1903.

Turner, James. *Without God, Without Creed: The Origins of Unbelief in America*. Baltimore: Johns Hopkins University Press, 1985.

Twain, Mark. *The Outrageous Mark Twain: Some Lesser-known But Extraordinary Works*. Ed. Charles Neider. New York: Doubleday, 1987.

Vertue, H. St. H. "Lucretius, the Poet of Our Time." *Greece and Rome* 17:50 (June 1948): 49–64.

Vidal, Gore. "Monotheism and Its Discontents." In *United States: Essays 1952–1992*, pp. 1048–54. New York: Random House, 1993.

Wagner, Linda. *Sylvia Plath*. New York: Routledge, 1988.

Weber, Thomas. *Gandhi as Disciple and Mentor*. New York: Cambridge University Press, 2004.

Welby, T. Earle. *A Study of Swinburne*. Port Washington, NY: Kennikat Press, 1968.

West, Rebecca. *Black Lamb and Grey Falcon*. New York: Penguin, 1994.

———. "Can Christian faith survive this war?" Interview with Rebecca West, Dr. H. C. Wilson, and Dr. C. E. M. Joad. *Daily Express*, January 17, 1945.

———. "Charlotte Brontë." In *Rebecca West: A Celebration*. New York: Penguin, 1978.

———. "Goodness Doesn't Just Happen." In *Woman as Artist and Thinker*. Lincoln, NE: iUniverse, 2005.

———. "I Believe." In *Woman as Artist and Thinker*. Lincoln, NE: iUniverse, 2005.

———. "Indissoluble Matrimony." In *The Longman Anthology of British Literature*. Volume B. New York: Longman, 2003.

———. *The Judge*. New York: Carroll & Graf, 1995.

———. *A Letter to a Grandfather*. London: The Hogarth Press, 1933.

———. "My Religion." In *Woman as Artist and Thinker*. Lincoln, NE: iUniverse, 2005.

———. "A Night in the Luxembourg." *The Freewoman*, June 20, 1912.

———. "Parthenope." In *Woman as Artist and Thinker*. Lincoln, NE: iUniverse, 2005.

———. *The Return of the Soldier*. New York: Penguin, 1998.

———. *The Sentinel: An Early Incomplete Novel by Rebecca West*. Ed. Kathryn Laing. Oxford: Legenda, 2002.

———. *Survivors in Mexico*. Ed. Bernard Schweizer. New Haven, CT: Yale University Press, 2003.

Wheatley, Kim. *Shelley and His Readers: Beyond Paranoid Politics.* Columbia: University of Missouri Press, 1999.

Wiesel, Elie. *The Accident*. Geneva: Bibliophile Library, 1962.

———. *All Rivers Run to the Sea*. New York: Alfred A. Knopf, 1996.

———. *Elie Wiesel: Conversations*. See Franciosi, Robert.

———. "For Jerusalem." Accessed online 14 May 2010: http://www .israelnationalnews.com/News/news.aspx/137057

———. *The Gates of the Forest*. New York: Holt, Rinehart and Winston, 1966.

———. *A Jew Today*. New York: Random House, 1978.

———. *The Judges*. New York: Alfred A. Knopf, 2002.

———. *Night*. New York: Bantam, 1982.

———. *The Six Days of Destruction*. Mahwah, NJ: Paulist Press, 1988.

———. "Talking and Writing and Keeping Silent." In *The German Church Struggle and the Holocaust*. Ed. Franklin H. Littell and Hubert G. Locke. Detroit: Wayne State University Press, 1970.

———. *The Trial of God*. New York: Random House, 1979.

———. *Twilight*. New York: Summit Books, 1988.

Williams, Michael Allen. *Rethinking "Gnosticism": An Argument for Dismantling a Dubious Category*. Princeton, NJ: Princeton University Press, 1999.

Williams, Tennessee. *The Night of the Iguana*. New York: New Directions, 1962.

Wilson, A. N. *God's Funeral*. New York: W. W. Norton, 1999.

Winston, Kimberly. "Other Worlds, Suffused With Religion." *Publishers Weekly*, 16 April 2001.

Woolf, Virginia. *The Letters of Virginia Woolf*, 6 vols., 1923–28, Volume 3. Ed. Nigel Nicolson and Joanne Trautmann. New York: Harcourt Brace Jovanovich, 1975.

———. *The Letters of Virginia Woolf*, 6 vols., 1936–41, Volume 6. Ed. Nigel Nicolson and Joanne Trautmann. New York: Harcourt Brace Jovanovich, 1980.

———. *Mrs. Dalloway*. New York: Houghton Mifflin Harcourt, 2002.

Index